Frommer's ®

P O R T A B L E

San Francisco

2nd Edition

**by Erika Lenkert &
Matthew R. Poole**

Macmillan • USA

ABOUT THE AUTHORS

A native San Franciscan, **Erika Lenkert** spends half her time in Los Angeles and the other half traveling to San Francisco and throughout the state. She's currently a contributing writer for *Los Angeles Magazine* and dozens of guides to California. Erika is pleased she actually gets paid to force her opinions onto others—something she'd done pro bono for years. Her next challenge? To convince San Franciscans that LA's actually kind of cool.

Matthew R. Poole, a native Californian, has authored 17 travel guides to California and Hawaii. A graduate of the University of California, Santa Barbara, Poole has managed to combine three of his stronger passions—writing, photography, and traveling—to his advantage. Before becoming a full-time travel writer, Matthew worked as an English tutor in Prague, ski instructor in the Swiss Alps, and a scuba instructor in Maui. He currently lives in San Francisco and can be reached at mrpoole@sirius.com.

MACMILLAN TRAVEL

A Simon & Schuster Macmillan Company
1633 Broadway
New York, NY 10019

Find us online at **www.frommers.com**

ISBN: 0-02-862578-1
ISSN: 1090-5480

Editor: Bob O'Sullivan
Production Editor: Michael Thomas
Page Creation by John Bitter, Eric Brinkman, David Faust, Angel Perez, and Heather Pope
Design by Michele Laseau
Digital Cartography by Ortelius Design

SPECIAL SALES

Bulk purchases (10+ copies) of Frommer's and selected Macmillan travel guides are available to corporations, organizations, mail-order catalogs, institutions, and charities at special discounts, and can be customized to suit individual needs. For more information write to Special Sales, Macmillan General Reference, 1633 Broadway, New York, NY 10019.

Manufactured in the United States of America.

Contents

List of Maps

ACKNOWLEDGMENTS

Matthew and Erika would like to thank Emily Goldman, Donalyn Mason, Tom Walton, and Cyndi Holcombe for their contributions.

AN INVITATION TO THE READER

When we first started writing for Frommer's, we'd call our editors after each of our books was published and excitedly ask, "Any reader mail?" We were just dying to learn whether folks were enjoying our books—or actually reading them for that matter. When we were disappointed that we'd received almost no mail, our editors assured us it was a compliment; most people write only to complain, so we must be doing something right. But the fact is, we want to hear what you think. What did you love? What did you hate? What was over- or underrated? Did you find a hotel, restaurant, bar, attraction—whatever—that we should have included? Tell us your opinion, so we can share the information with your fellow travelers in upcoming editions. That way, perhaps we'll stop accosting and questioning poor, innocent tourists when we see them carrying our guides through the streets of our favorite city. C'mon, drop us a note. Write to:

Frommer's Portable San Francisco
Macmillan Travel
1633 Broadway
New York, NY 10019

AN ADDITIONAL NOTE

Please be advised that travel information is subject to change at any time—and this is especially true of prices. We therefore suggest that you write or call ahead for confirmation when making your travel plans. The authors, editors, and publisher cannot be held responsible for the experiences of readers while traveling. Your safety is important to us, however, so we encourage you to stay alert and be aware of your surroundings. Keep a close eye on cameras, purses, and wallets—all favorite targets of thieves and pickpockets.

WHAT THE SYMBOLS MEAN
✪ Frommer's Favorites

Our favorite places and experiences—outstanding for quality, value, or both.

The following abbreviations are used for credit cards:

AE	American Express	JCB	Japan Credit Bank
CB	Carte Blanche	MC	MasterCard
DC	Diners Club	V	Visa
DISC	Discover		

FIND FROMMER'S ONLINE

Arthur Frommer's Outspoken Encyclopedia of Travel (www.frommers.com) offers more than 6,000 pages of up-to-the-minute travel information—including the latest bargains and candid, personal articles updated daily by Arthur Frommer himself. No other Web site offers such comprehensive and timely coverage of the world of travel.

The San Francisco Experience

*Y*ou are standing on the corner of Powell and Geary streets at San Francisco's famed Union Square, pausing a moment to catch your breath. Bags in hand bear the rewards of a memorable day of shopping. It's about four in the afternoon on a summer Sunday; a stiff, cool breeze from the west mocks the cloudless skies. Above the din and traffic you hear the clang of a bell, and moments later a cable car—precariously overloaded with wide-eyed tourists—approaches from behind, groaning its way up yet another steep hill. A steady stream of chattering pedestrians passes by, few of whom seem to speak English as a first language. Across the way a bellman hails a taxi for an older couple, both men dressed in black. Though the sun is out, glimmering skyscrapers block any hope of a warm ray. "Should've dressed warmer," you reply to a shiver as you head back to your hotel to get ready for dinner. As you round the corner, an old man selling flowers on the street corner smiles and hands you a rose—a fitting end to a thoroughly enjoyable day.

Welcome to San Francisco.

Consistently rated one of the top tourist destinations in the world, San Francisco is awash with multiple dimensions: Its famous, thrilling streets go up, and they go down; its multifarious citizens—along with their native culture, architecture, and cuisine—hail from San Antonio to Singapore; and its politics range from hyper-liberalism to an ever-encroaching wave of conservatism. Even something as mundane as fog takes on a new dimension as it creeps from the ocean and slowly envelops San Francisco in a resplendent blanket of mist.

The result is a wee bit o' heaven for everyone: In a city so multi-faceted, so enamored with itself, it's truly hard not to find what you're looking for. Feel the cool blast of salt air as you stroll across the Golden Gate. Stuff yourself on a Chinatown dim sum. Browse the Haight for incense and crystals. Walk along the beach, pierce your nose, see a play, rent a Harley—the list is endless. Like an eternal world's fair, it's all happening in San Francisco, and everyone's invited.

1 Frommer's Favorite San Francisco Experiences

- **Cafe-Hopping in North Beach.** One of the most pleasurable
  smells of San Francisco is the aroma of roasted coffee beans waft-
  ing down Columbus Avenue. Start the day with a cup of
  Viennese at Caffè Trieste (a haven for true San Francisco characters), followed by a walk in and around Washington Square,
  lunch at Mario's Bohemian Cigar Store (à la focaccia sandwiches),
  book browsing at City Lights, more coffee at Caffè Greco, and
  dinner at L'Osteria del Forno or Moose's. Finish off the day with
  a little flamenco dancing at La Bodega or a nightcap with Enrico
  Caruso on the jukebox at Tosca.
- **A Walk Along the Coastal Trail.** Walk the forested coastal trail
  from the Cliff House to the Golden Gate Bridge, and you'll see
  why San Franciscans put up with living on a fault line. Start at
  the parking lot just above Cliff House and head north. On a clear
  day you'll have incredible views of the Marin Headlands, but even
  on foggy days it's worth the trek to scamper over old bunkers and
  relish the crisp, cool air. Dress warmly.
- **An Adventure to Alcatraz.** Even if you loathe tourist attractions,
  you'll like Alcatraz. The rangers have done a fantastic job of pre-
  serving The Rock—enough to give you the heebie-jeebies just
  looking at it—and they give excellent guided tours (highly recommended). Heck, even the boat ride across the bay is worth the
  price, so don't miss this one.
- **A Stroll Through Chinatown.** Chinatown is a trip. We've been
  through it at least 100 times, and it's never failed to entertain us.
  Skip the crummy camera and luggage stores and head straight for
  the outdoor markets, where a cornucopia of the bizarre, unbeliev-
  able, and just plain weird sits in boxes for you to scrutinize (one
  day we saw an armadillo for sale, and it wasn't meant to be a pet).
  Better yet, take one of Shirley Fong-Torres's Wok Wiz tours of
  Chinatown for the full effect.
- **A Date in the Haight.** Though the flowers of power have wilted,
  the Haight is still, more or less, the Haight: a sort of resting home
  for aging hippies, dazed Dead-heads, skate punks, and an assort-
  ment of rather pathetic young panhandlers. Think of it as visiting a "people" zoo as you walk down the rows of used clothing
  stores and leather shops, trying hard not to stare at that girl (at
  least we *think* it's a girl) with the pierced eyebrows and shaved
  head. End the mystery tour with a plate of mussels at Cha Cha
  Cha, one of San Francisco's top restaurants.

- **A Walk Across the Golden Gate Bridge.** Don your windbreaker and walking shoes and prepare for a wind-blasted, exhilarating walk across San Francisco's most famous landmark. It's simply one of those things you have to do at least once in your life.

- **A Cruise Through the Castro.** The most populated and festive street in the city is not just for gays and lesbians (though the best cruising in town is right here). While there are some great shops and cafes—particularly Café Flore for lunch—it's the people-watching that makes the trip a must. And if you have the time, catch a flick at the beautiful 1930s Spanish colonial movie palace, the Castro Theatre.

- **A Day in Golden Gate Park.** A day at Golden Gate Park is a day well spent. Its arboreal paths stretch from the Haight all the way to Ocean Beach, offering dozens of fun things to do along the way. Top sites are the Conservatory of Flowers, Japanese Tea Garden, Asian Art Museum, and the Steinhart Aquarium. The best time to go is Sunday, when portions of the park are closed to traffic (rent skates or a bike for the full effect). Toward the end of the day, head west to the beach and watch the sunset.

- **A Soul-Stirring Sunday Morning Service at Glide.** Preacher Cecil Williams turns church-going into a spiritual party that leaves you feeling elated, hopeful, and unified with the world. All walks of life attend the service, which focuses not on any particular religion, but on what we have in common as people. It's great fun, with plenty of singing and hand clapping.

- **An Early Morning Cable Car Ride.** Skip the boring California line and take the Powell-Hyde cable car down to Fisherman's Wharf—the ride is worth the wait. When you reach the top of Nob Hill, grab the rail in one hand and hold the camera with the other, because you're about to see a view of the bay that'll make you a believer. Oh, and don't call it a trolley.

- **A Visit to MOMA.** Ever since the new MOMA opened in 1995, it's been the best place to go for a quick dose of culture. Start by touring the museum, then head straight for the gift shop (oftentimes more entertaining than the rotating exhibits). Have a light lunch at Caffè Museo, where the food is a vast improvement from most museums' mush, then finish the trip with a stroll through the Yerba Buena Gardens across from the museum.

2

Planning a Trip to San Francisco

*R*egardless of whether you chart your vacation months in advance or travel on a whim, you'll need to do a little advance planning to make the most of your stay. This chapter will help you with all the logistics.

1 Visitor Information

The San Francisco Convention and Visitors Bureau, 900 Market St. (at Powell Street), Hallidie Plaza, Lower Level, San Francisco, CA 94102 (☎ **415/391-2000;** www.sfvisitor.org), is the best source for any kind of specialized information about the city. Even if you don't have a specific question, you may want to send them $2 for their 100-page magazine, *The San Francisco Book,* which includes a 3-month calendar of events, city history, shopping and dining information, and several good, clear maps, as well as an additional 50-page lodging guide. The bureau only highlights members' establishments, so if they don't have what you're looking for, it doesn't mean it's nonexistent.

You can also get the latest on San Francisco at the following on-line addresses:

- *Bay Guardian,* free weekly's city page: **http://www. sfbayguardian.com**
- Hotel accommodations, reserve on-line: **http://www.hotelres. com/**
- *Q San Francisco,* for gays and lesbians: **http://www. qsanfrancisco.com/**
- *SF Gate,* the city's combined *Chronicle* and *Examiner* newspapers: **http://www.sfgate.com**
- Channel 7, ABC, and KGO's city guide: **http://www. citysearch7.com**

2   When to Go

If you're dreaming of convertibles, Frisbee on the beach, and tank-topped evenings, change your reservations and head to Los Angeles. Contrary to California's sunshine-and-bikini image, San Francisco weather is mild and can often be downright fickle—it's nothing like that of neighboring southern California. While summer is the most popular time to visit, it's also often characterized by damp, foggy days, cold, windy nights, and crowded tourist destinations. A good bet is to visit in spring, or better yet, autumn. Every September, right about the time San Franciscans mourn being gypped (or fogged) out of another summer, something wonderful happens: The thermostat rises, the skies clear, and the locals call in sick to work and head for the beach. It's what residents call "Indian summer." The city is also delightful during winter, when the opera and ballet seasons are in full swing, there are fewer tourists, many hotel prices are lower, and downtown bustles with holiday cheer.

CLIMATE

Northern California weather has been extraordinary recently. In the past 2 years, the Bay Area has experienced one sizzling and one non-existent summer, one winter that ended in late June (and kept Tahoe's ski lifts open until Aug), a series of floods in the surrounding 'burbs (thanks to the infamous El Niño), and a storm whose 80-mile-per-hour winds blew century-old trees right out of the ground. However, San Francisco's temperate, marine climate usually means relatively mild weather year-round. In summer, temperatures rarely top 70°F, and the city's chilling fog rolls in most mornings and evenings. Even when autumn's heat occasionally stretches into the 80s and 90s, you should still dress in layers, or by early evening you'll learn firsthand why sweatshirt sales are a great business at Fisherman's Wharf. In winter, the mercury seldom falls below freezing, and snow is almost unheard of, but that doesn't mean you won't be whimpering if you forget a coat. Still, compared to most of the States' varied weather conditions, San Francisco is consistently pleasant.

It's that beautifully fluffy, chilly, wet, heavy, and sweeping fog that makes the city's weather so precarious. Northern California's summer fog bank is produced by a rare combination of water, wind, and topography. It lies off the coast and is pulled in by rising air currents when the land heats up. Held back by coastal mountains along a 600-mile front, the low clouds seek out any passage they can find. And the access most readily available is the slot where the Pacific Ocean penetrates the continental wall—the Golden Gate.

San Francisco's Average Temperatures (°F) & Rainfall (in.)

	Jan	Feb	Mar	Apr	May	June	July	Aug	Sept	Oct	Nov	Dec
High	56	59	60	61	63	64	64	65	69	68	63	57
Low	46	48	49	49	51	53	53	54	56	55	52	47
Rain	4.5	2.8	2.6	1.5	0.4	0.2	0.1	0.1	0.2	1.1	2.5	3.5

SAN FRANCISCO CALENDAR OF EVENTS

January

- **San Francisco Sports and Boat Show,** Cow Palace. Draws thousands of boat enthusiasts over a 9-day period. Call **Cow Palace Box Office** (☎ **415/469-6065**) for details. Mid-January.

February

✪ **Chinese New Year,** Chinatown. In 1999, the year of the rabbit, public celebrations will again spill onto every street in Chinatown. Festivities begin with the crowning of "Miss Chinatown USA" pageant parade, and climax a week later with a celebratory parade of marching bands, rolling floats, barrages of fireworks, and a block-long dragon writhing in and out of the crowds. New Year is February 16 and the parade is scheduled for February 27; festivities go for several weeks and wrap up with a memorable parade through Chinatown. Arrive early for a good viewing spot on Grant Avenue. Make your hotel reservations early. For information call ☎ **415/982-3000.**

March

- **St. Patrick's Day Parade.** Almost everyone's honorarily Irish at this festive affair starting at 12:30pm at Market and Fifth streets and continuing toward the Ferry Building. But the party doesn't stop there. Head down to the Embarcadero's Harrington's bar after work hours and celebrate with hundreds of the Irish-for-a-day as they gallivant amidst the closed-off streets and numerous pubs. Call ☎ **415/391-2000** for details. The Sunday before March 17.

✪ **San Francisco International Film Festival,** the AMC Kabuki 8 Cinemas, at Fillmore and Post streets and many other locations. Started 40 years ago, this is one of America's oldest film festivals, featuring more than 100 films and videos from more than 30 countries. Tickets are relatively inexpensive, and screenings are very accessible to the general public. Entries include new films by beginning and established directors. For a schedule or information call ☎ **415/931-FILM.** Mid-April to early May.

April

- **Cherry Blossom Festival,** Japantown. Meander through the arts-and-crafts and food booths aligning the blocked-off streets; watch traditional drumming, sumo wrestling, flower arranging, origami, or a parade celebrating the cherry blossom and Japanese culture. Call ☎ **415/563-2313** for information. Mid- to late April.

May

- **Cinco de Mayo Celebration,** Mission District. This is the day the Latino community celebrates the victory of the Mexicans over the French at Puebla in 1862. Mariachi bands, dancers, food, and a parade fill the streets of the Mission. Parade starts at 10am at 24th and Bryant streets and ends at the Civic Center. Sunday before May 5.

- ✪ **Bay to Breakers Foot Race,** Golden Gate Park. Even if you don't participate, you can't avoid this run from downtown to Ocean Beach that stops morning traffic throughout the city. Around 80,000 entrants gather—many dressed in wacky, innovative, and sometimes X-rated costumes—for the approximately 7¹/₂-mile run. If you're feeling lazy, join the throng of spectators who line the route in the form of sidewalk parties, bands, and cheerleaders of all ages to get a good dose of true San Francisco fun. The event is sponsored by the *San Francisco Examiner* (☎ 415/777-7770). Third Sunday of May.

- ✪ **Carnival,** Mission Street between 14th and 24th streets, and Harrison Street between 15th and 21st streets. The San Francisco Mission District's largest annual event, Carnival, is a 2-day series of festivities that culminates with a parade on Mission Street over Memorial Day weekend. One of San Franciscans' favorite events, more than half a million spectators line the route, and the samba musicians and dancers continue to play on 14th Street, near Harrison, at the end of the march. Just show up, or call the **Mission Economic and Cultural Association** (☎ **415/826-1401**) for complete information.

June

- **Union Street Fair,** along Union Street from Fillmore to Gough streets. Stalls sell arts, crafts, food, and drink. You'll also find a lot of great-looking, young, yuppie cocktailers packing every bar and spilling out into the street. Music and entertainment are on a number of stages. Call ☎ **415/346-4446** for more information. First weekend of June.

- **Haight Street Fair.** Featuring alternative crafts, ethnic foods, rock bands, and a healthy number of hippies and young street kids whooping it up and slamming beers in front of the blaring rock 'n' roll stage. The fair usually extends along Haight between Stanyan and Ashbury streets. For details call ☎ **415/661-8025.** In June; call for date.

✪ **North Beach Festival,** Grant Street in North Beach. Nineteen ninety-nine marks the 45th year this party has taken place, and organizers claim its the oldest urban street fair in the country. Close to 80,000 city folk meander Grant Avenue, between Vallejo and Union streets, to eat, drink, and browse the arts-and-crafts booths. But the most enjoyable part of the event is listening to music and people-watching. Call ☎ **415/989-6426** for details. Usually Father's Day weekend.

- **Lesbian and Gay Freedom Day Parade,** Market Street. A prideful event drawing up to half a million participants. The parade's start and finish have been moved around in recent years to accommodate road construction. Regardless of its path, it ends with hundreds of food, art, and information booths and soundstages. Call ☎ **415/864-3733** for information and location. Usually the third or last weekend of June.

✪ **Stern Grove Midsummer Music Festival.** Pack a picnic and head out early to join thousands who come here to lie in the grass and enjoy classical, jazz, and ethnic music and dance in the Grove at 19th Avenue and Sloat Boulevard. These free concerts are held every Sunday at 2pm. Either show up with a lawn chair or blanket. There are food booths if you forget snacks, but you'll be dying to leave if you don't bring warm clothes—the Sunset District can be one of the coldest parts of the city. Call ☎ **415/ 252-6252** for listings. Mid-June through August.

July

- **Jazz and All That Art on Fillmore.** The first weekend in July starts off with a bang when the upscale portion of Fillmore (between Post and Jackson streets) closes off traffic and fills the street with several blocks of arts and crafts, gourmet food, and live jazz. The festivities will be held on July 4 and 5 from 10am to 6pm. Call ☎ **415/346-4446** for further information.

- **Fourth of July Celebration and Fireworks.** This event can be somewhat of a joke, since more often than not, like everyone else, fog comes into the city on this day to join in the festivities. Sometimes it's almost impossible to view the million-dollar fireworks from Pier 39 on the northern waterfront. Still, it's a party and if the skies are clear, it's a damn good show.
- **San Francisco Marathon.** One of the largest marathons in the world. For entry information contact IMG, the event organizer, at ☎ **415/296-7111** or 415/648-9410. Usually the second weekend in July.

August

✪ **À La Carte, A La Park,** usually at Sharon Meadow, Golden Gate Park. You probably won't get to go to all the restaurants you'd like while you're visiting the city, but you can get a good sampling if you attend this annual event. Over 40 of the town's favorite chefs, accompanied by 20 microbreweries and 20 wineries, offer tastings in the midst of San Francisco's favorite park. There's entertainment as well, and proceeds benefit the San Francisco Shakespeare Festival. Admission was $8.50 adults, $7 seniors, and free for children under 12 in 1998. Prices were not determined for 1999 when this book went to press. Call ☎ **415/383-9378** for details. Always Labor Day weekend.

September

✪ **San Francisco Blues Festival,** on the grounds of Fort Mason. The largest outdoor blues music event on the West Coast will be 27 years old in 1999 and will again feature both local and national musicians performing back-to-back during the 3-day extravaganza. You can charge tickets by phone through **BASS Ticketmaster** (☎ **510/762-2277**). For **schedule** information call ☎ **415/826-6837.** Usually in late September.

- **Castro Street Fair.** Celebrates life in the city's most famous gay neighborhood. Call ☎ **415/467-3354** for information. Usually end of September or beginning of October.

October

- **Columbus Day Festivities.** The city's Italian community leads the festivities around Fisherman's Wharf celebrating Columbus's landing in America. The festival includes a parade along Columbus Avenue and sporting events, but for the most part, it's just a great excuse to hang out in North Beach and people-watch. For information call ☎ **415/434-1492.** Sunday before Columbus Day.

- **Reggae in the Park,** usually in Sharon Meadow in Golden Gate Park. Going into its 10th year, this event draws thousands to Golden Gate Park to dance and celebrate the soulful sounds. Big-name reggae and world-beat bands play all weekend long, and ethnic arts-and-crafts and food booths are set up along the stage's periphery. Tickets are around $12 in advance, and a few dollars more on-site. Two-day passes are available at a discounted rate. Free for children under 12. Call ☎ **415/383-9378** for further details. Always the second weekend in October.
- **Halloween.** A huge night in San Francisco. A fantastical parade is organized at Market and Castro, and a mixed gay/straight crowd revels in costumes of extraordinary imagination. While the past few years they've been trying to divert festivities to the Civic Center, the action's still best in the Castro. October 31.
- **San Francisco Jazz Festival.** This festival presents eclectic programming in an array of fabulous jazz venues throughout the city. With close to 2 weeks of nightly entertainment and dozens of performers, the jazz festival is a hot ticket. Past events have featured Herbie Hancock, Dave Brubeck, the Modern Jazz Quartet, Wayne Shorter, and Bill Frisell. For information call ☎ **800/ 627-5277** or 415/398-5655. End of October, beginning of November.

December

- **The *Nutcracker,*** War Memorial Opera House. Performed annually by the **San Francisco Ballet** (☎ **415/776-1999**). Tickets to this Tchaikovsky tradition should be purchased well in advance.

3 Safety

San Francisco, like any large city, has its fair share of crime, but unlike New York and Los Angeles, most folks here don't have first-hand horror stories. There are some areas where you need to exercise extra caution, particularly at night—notably the Tenderloin, the Western Addition, the Mission District, and around the Civic Center. In addition, there are a substantial number of homeless people throughout the city with concentrations in and around Union Square, the Theater District, the Tenderloin, and Haight Street, so don't be alarmed if you're approached for spare change. Basically, just use common sense.

See "Fast Facts: San Francisco," in chapter 3, for city-specific safety tips. For additional crime-prevention information, phone **San Francisco SAFE** (☎ **415/553-1984**).

4 Tips for Travelers with Special Needs

FOR PEOPLE WITH DISABILITIES

Most of San Francisco's major museums and tourist attractions are fitted with wheelchair ramps. In addition, many hotels offer special accommodations and services for wheelchair-bound and other visitors with disabilities. These include extra-large bathrooms and ramps for the wheelchair-bound and telecommunication devices for deaf people. The San Francisco Convention and Visitors Bureau (see section 1, "Visitor Information," above) has the most up-to-date information.

Travelers in wheelchairs can secure special ramped taxis by calling **Yellow Cab** (☎ **415/626-2345**), which charges regular rates for the service. Travelers with disabilities may also obtain a free copy of the *Muni Access Guide,* published by the San Francisco Municipal Railway, Accessible Services Program, Municipal Railway, 949 Presidio Ave., San Francisco, CA 94115 (☎ **415/923-6142**). Call this number Monday to Friday from 8am to 5pm.

FOR GAY MEN & LESBIANS

If you head down to the Castro—an area surrounding Castro Street near Market Street that's predominantly a gay and lesbian community—you'll understand why the city is a mecca for gay and lesbian travelers. Since the 1970s, this unique part of town has remained the colorfully festive gay neighborhood teeming with "outed" city folk who meander the streets shopping, eating, partying, or cruising. If anyone feels like an outsider in this part of town, it's heterosexuals, who, although warmly welcomed in the community, may feel uncomfortable or downright threatened if they happen to harbor any homophobia or aversion to being "cruised." For many San Franciscans, it's just a fun area (especially on Halloween) with some wonderful shops.

It is estimated that gays and lesbians form one-fourth to one-third of the population of San Francisco, so it's no surprise that in recent years clubs and bars catering to them have popped up all around town. Although lesbian interests are concentrated primarily in the East Bay (especially Oakland), a significant community resides in the Mission District, around 16th Street and Valencia.

Several local publications are dedicated to in-depth coverage of news, information, and listings of goings-on around town for gay men and lesbians. The *Bay Area Reporter* has the most comprehensive listings, including a weekly calendar of events, and is distributed

free on Thursdays. It can be found stacked at the corner of 18th and
Castro streets and at 9th and Harrison streets, as well as in bars,
bookshops, and various stores around town. It may also be available
in gay and lesbian bookstores elsewhere in the country.

GUIDES & PUBLICATIONS   Gay men and lesbians might like
to get either of the guides specifically for San Francisco, *Betty and
Pansy's Severe Queer Review of San Francisco* ($10.95) and *The Of-
ficial San Francisco Gay Guide* ($10.95). For accommodations, check
with two international guides: *Odysseus* ($29) and *Inn Places* ($16).
These books and others are available by mail from **Giovanni's
Room,** 1145 Pine St., Philadelphia, PA 19107 (☎ **215/923-2960;**
E-mail: giophilp@netaxs.com) and **A Different Light bookstore,**
489 Castro St., San Francisco, CA 94114 (☎ **415/431-0891;** Web
site: http://www.adlbooks.com). Other locations are in New York
City (☎ **212/989-4850**) and Los Angeles (☎ **310/854-6601**).

Our World, 1104 N. Nova Rd., Suite 251, Daytona Beach, FL
32117 (☎ **904/441-5367**), is a magazine devoted to gay and lesbian travel worldwide. It costs $35 for 10 issues. *Out and About,*
8 W. 19th St., Suite 401, New York, NY 10011 (☎ **800/929-
2268;** Web site: http://www.outandabout.com), has been hailed for
its "straight" reporting about gay travel. It profiles the best gay or
gay-friendly hotels, restaurants, clubs, and other places, with coverage of destinations throughout the world. It costs $49 a year for 10
information-packed issues. *Out and About* aims for the more upscale
gay or lesbian traveler and has been praised by everybody from
Travel and Leisure to the *New York Times.* Both these publications
are also available at most gay and lesbian bookstores.

FOR SENIORS

Seniors regularly receive discounts at museums and attractions and
on public transportation; such discounts, when available, are listed
in this guide, under their appropriate headings. Ask for discounts
everywhere—at hotels, movie theaters, museums, restaurants, and
attractions. You may be surprised how often you'll be offered
reduced rates. When making airline reservations, ask about a seniors'
discount, but find out if there is a cheaper promotional fare before
committing yourself.

The **Senior Citizen Information Line** (☎ **415/626-1033**)
offers advice, referrals, and information on city services. The
Friendship Line for the Elderly (☎ **415/752-3778**) is a sup-
port, referral, and crisis-intervention service.

FOR FAMILIES

San Francisco is full of sightseeing opportunities and special activities geared toward children. See Section 8, "Especially for Kids," in chapter 6, "What to See & Do in San Francisco," for information and ideas for families. *Frommer's San Francisco with Kids* is a comprehensive guide geared specifically toward families; it is available at bookstores.

5 Getting There

BY PLANE

THE MAJOR AIRLINES   San Francisco is serviced by the following major domestic airlines: American Airlines, 433 California St. (☎ **800/433-7300**); Delta Airlines, 433 California St. and 124 Geary St. (☎ **800/221-1212**); Northwest Airlines, 124 Geary St. and 433 California St. (☎ **800/225-2525**); Southwest Airlines, at the airport (☎ **800/I-FLY-SWA**); TWA, 595 Market St., Suite 2240, at the corner of Second Street (☎ **800/221-2000**); United Airlines, 433 California St., 124 Geary, and Embarcadero One (☎ **800/241-6522**); and US Airways, 433 California St. (☎ **800/428-4322**).

THE MAJOR AIRPORTS   Two major airports serve the Bay Area: San Francisco International and Oakland International.

San Francisco International Airport   San Francisco International Airport, located 14 miles south of downtown directly on U.S. 101, is served by almost four dozen major scheduled carriers. Travel time to downtown during commuter rush hours is about 40 minutes; at other times it's about 20 to 25 minutes.

The airport offers a toll-free **hot line** available weekdays from 7:30am to 5pm (PST) for information on ground transportation (☎ **800/736-2008**). During operating hours the line is answered weekdays by a real person who will provide you with a rundown of all your options for getting into the city from the airport. Each of the three main terminals also has a desk where you can get the same information.

A cab from the airport to downtown will cost $28 to $32, plus tip.

SFO Airporter buses (☎ **415/495-8404**) depart from outside the lower-level baggage-claim area to downtown San Francisco every 15 to 30 minutes from 6:15am to midnight (picking up at hotels as early as 5am). They stop at several Union Square–area hotels, including the Grand Hyatt, San Francisco Hilton, San Francisco Marriott, Westin St. Francis, Parc Fifty-Five, Hyatt Regency, and Sheraton Palace. No reservations are needed. The cost is $10 each way, and children under 2 ride for free.

Other private shuttle companies offer door-to-door airport service, in which you share a van with a few other passengers. **SuperShuttle** (☎ **415/558-8500**) will take you anywhere in the city, charging $10 per person to a hotel; $12 to a residence or business, plus $8 for each additional person; and $40 to charter an entire van for up to seven passengers. **Yellow Airport Shuttle** (☎ **415/282-7433**) charges $10 per person. Each shuttle stops every 20 minutes or so and picks up passengers from the marked areas outside the terminals' upper level. Reservations are required for the return trip to the airport only and should be made 1 day before departure. Keep in mind that these shuttles demand they pick you up 2 hours before your flight, 3 hours during holidays.

The San Mateo County Transit system, **SamTrans** (☎ **800/660-4287** within northern California, or 650/508-6200) runs two buses between the airport and the Transbay Terminal at First and Mission streets. The 7B bus costs $1 and makes the trip in about 55 minutes. The 7F bus costs $2 and takes only 35 minutes but permits only one carry-on bag. Both buses run daily, every half hour from about 5:30am to 7pm, then hourly until about midnight.

Oakland International Airport   Located about 5 miles south of downtown Oakland, at the Hagenberger Road exit of Calif. 17 (U.S. 880), **Oakland International Airport** (☎ **510/577-4000**) is used primarily by passengers with East Bay destinations. Some San Franciscans, however, prefer this less-crowded, accessible airport when flying during busy periods.

Again, taxis from the airport to downtown San Francisco are expensive, costing approximately $45, plus tip.

Bayporter Express (☎ **415/467-1800**) is a shuttle service that charges $20 for the first person, $10 each additional to downtown San Francisco (it costs more to outer areas of town). **Easy Way Out** (☎ **510/430-9090**) is another option, which charges $20 per person, $10 each additional rider. Both accept advance reservations. To the right of the airport exit there are usually shuttles that will take you to the city for around $20 per person. Keep in mind that they are independently owned and prices vary.

The cheapest way to downtown San Francisco is to take the shuttle bus from the airport to **BART** (Bay Area Rapid Transit;

☎ **510/464-6000**). The AirBART shuttle bus runs about every 15 minutes Monday to Saturday from 6am to 11:30pm and Sunday from 8:30am to 11:30pm, stopping in front of Terminals 1 and 2 near the ground transportation signs. The cost is $2 for the 10-minute ride to BART's Coliseum terminal. BART fares vary, depending on your destination; the trip to downtown San Francisco costs $2.45 and takes 20 minutes once on-board. The entire excursion should take around 45 minutes.

RENTING A CAR   All the major companies operate in the city and have desks at the airports. Call their toll-free numbers before leaving home, and shop around for the best price. When we last checked, a compact car could be secured for a week for about $190, including all taxes and other charges, but prices change dramatically on a daily basis, as well as depending on which company you rent from.

Most rental firms pad their profits by selling an additional loss/damage waiver (LDW), which can cost an extra $19 or more per day. Before agreeing to this, check with your insurance carrier and credit-card company. Many people don't realize that they're already covered by either one or both. If you're not, the LDW is a wise investment.

A minimum-age requirement—usually 25—is set by most rental agencies. Some also have a maximum-age limit. If you're concerned that these limits may affect you, ask about rental requirements at the time of booking to avoid problems later.

Some of the national car-rental companies operating in San Francisco include: **Alamo** (☎ 800/327-9633), **Avis** (☎ 800/331-1212), **Budget** (☎ 800/527-0700), **Dollar** (☎ 800/800-4000), **Hertz** (☎ 800/654-3131), **National** (☎ 800/227-7368), and **Thrifty** (☎ 800/367-2277).

In addition to the big chains, there are dozens of regional rental places in San Francisco, many of which offer lower rates. These include **A-One Rent-A-Car,** 434 O'Farrell St. (☎ 415/771-3977) and **Bay Area Rentals,** 229 Seventh St. (☎ 415/621-8989).

BY CAR

San Francisco is easily accessed by major highways: Interstate 5, from the north, and U.S. 101, which cuts south-north through the peninsula from San Jose and across the Golden Gate Bridge to points north. If you drive from Los Angeles, you can either take the longer coastal route (437 miles and 11 hr.) or the inland route (389 miles and 8 hr.). From Mendocino, it's 156 miles and 4 hours; from Sacramento it's 88 miles and 1¹/₂ hours; and from Yosemite it's 210 miles and 4 hours.

If you are driving and aren't already a member, then it's worth joining the **American Automobile Association (AAA)** (☎ **800/ 922-8228**), which charges $40 to $60 per year (with an additional one-time joining fee), depending on where you join, and provides roadside and other services to motorists. **Amoco Motor Club** (☎ 800/334-3300) is another recommended choice.

PACKAGES & TOURS

Tours and packages combining transportation, hotel accommodations, meals, and sightseeing are sometimes available to San Francisco. Sometimes it's worth signing onto a tour package just to secure the savings that operators can achieve by buying travel services in bulk. Often you'll pay much less than if you had organized the same trip independently, and you can always opt out of the preplanned activities. To find out what tours and packages are available to you, check the ads in the travel section of your newspaper or visit your travel agent.

Getting to Know San Francisco

*H*alf the fun in becoming familiar with San Francisco is wandering around and haphazardly stumbling upon great shops, restaurants, and viewpoints that even locals may not know exist. But you'll find that although metropolitan, San Francisco is a small town, and you won't feel like a stranger for long. If you get disoriented, just remember that downtown is east, Golden Gate Bridge is north, and even if you do get lost, you probably won't go too far since three sides of the city are surrounded by water. The most difficult challenge you'll have, if traveling by car, is mastering the maze of one-way streets. This chapter offers useful information on how to become better acquainted with the city.

1 Orientation

VISITOR INFORMATION

Once in the city, visit the **San Francisco Visitor Information Center,** on the lower level of Hallidie Plaza, 900 Market St., at Powell Street (☎ **415/391-2000;** fax 415/362-7323), for information, brochures, discount coupons, and advice on restaurants, sights, and events in the city. They can provide answers in German, Japanese, French, Italian, and Spanish, as well as English, of course. To find the office, descend the escalator at the cable-car turnaround.

Dial ☎ **415/391-2001** anytime, day or night, for a recorded message about current cultural, theater, music, sports, and other special events. This information is also available in German, French, Japanese, and Spanish.

Keep in mind that this service supports only members of the Convention and Visitors Bureau and is very tourist-oriented. While there's tons of information here, it's not representative of all the city has to offer. The office is open Monday to Friday from 9am to 5:30pm, on Saturday from 9am to 3pm, and on Sunday from 10am

San Francisco at a Glance

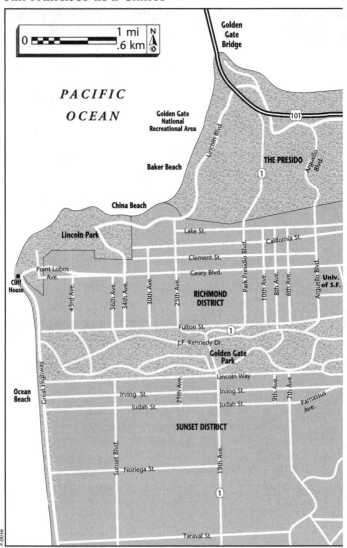

PACIFIC
OCEAN

Golden Gate
Bridge

101

Golden Gate National
Recreational Area

THE PRESIDO

Baker Beach

Lincoln Blvd.

Arguello Blvd.

China Beach

Lincoln Park

Lake St.

California St.

Clement St.

Point Lobos
Ave.

Geary Blvd.

Park Presidio Blvd.

10th Ave.

8th Ave.

6th Ave.

Arguello Blvd.

Cliff
House

43rd Ave.

36th Ave.

34th Ave.

30th Ave.

25th Ave.

RICHMOND
DISTRICT

Univ.
of S.F.

Fulton St.

J.F. Kennedy Dr.

Golden Gate
Park

Lincoln Way

Great Highway

Ocean
Beach

Irving St.

25th Ave.

Irving St.

9th Ave.

7th Ave.

Parnassus
Ave.

Judah St.

Judah St.

SUNSET DISTRICT

Sunset Blvd.

Noriega St.

19th Ave.

Taraval St.

P-0036

18

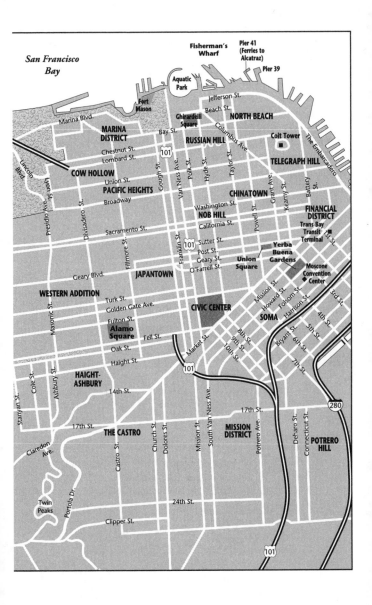

San Francisco Bay

Fisherman's Wharf

Pier 41 (Ferries to Alcatraz)

Pier 39

Aquatic Park

Jefferson St.

Fort Mason

Ghirardelli Square

Beach St.

NORTH BEACH

Marina Blvd.

MARINA DISTRICT

Bay St.

Coit Tower

RUSSIAN HILL

Columbus Ave.

Chestnut St.

Lombard St.

101

TELEGRAPH HILL

COW HOLLOW

Union St.

The Embarcadero

PACIFIC HEIGHTS

Broadway

CHINATOWN

FINANCIAL DISTRICT

Presidio Ave.

Divisadero St.

Gough St.

Van Ness Ave.

Polk St.

Hyde St.

Taylor St.

Grant Ave.

Kearny St.

Battery St.

Washington St.

NOB HILL

Powell St.

Trans-Bay Transit Terminal

1st St.

Lincoln Blvd.

Sacramento St.

Fillmore St.

Franklin St.

101

California St.

Sutter St.

Post St.

Geary St.

O'Farrell St.

Union Square

Yerba Buena Gardens

Moscone Convention Center

Geary Blvd.

JAPANTOWN

WESTERN ADDITION

Masonic St.

Turk St.

Golden Gate Ave.

CIVIC CENTER

Mission St.

Howard St.

Folsom St.

Harrison St.

3rd St.

4th St.

SOMA

Fulton St.

Alamo Square

Fell St.

Oak St.

Market St.

8th St.

9th St.

10th St.

Bryant St.

5th St.

6th St.

7th St.

Haight St.

101

HAIGHT-ASHBURY

Stanyan St.

Cole St.

Ashbury St.

14th St.

280

17th St.

17th St.

THE CASTRO

Castro St.

Church St.

Dolores St.

Mission St.

South Van Ness Ave.

MISSION DISTRICT

Potrero Ave.

Deharo St.

Connecticut St.

POTRERO HILL

Claredon Ave.

Twin Peaks

Portola Dr.

24th St.

Clipper St.

101

19

to 2pm. It's closed on Thanksgiving Day, Christmas Day, and New Year's Day.

Pick up a copy of the *Bay Guardian.* The city's free alternative paper lists all city happenings—their kiosks are located throughout the city and in most coffee shops.

For specialized information on Chinatown's shops and services, and on the city's Chinese community in general, contact the **Chinese Chamber of Commerce,** 730 Sacramento St., San Francisco, CA 94108 (☎ **415/982-3000**), open daily from 9am to 5pm.

CITY LAYOUT

San Francisco occupies the tip of a 32-mile-long peninsula between San Francisco Bay and the Pacific Ocean. Its land area measures about 46 square miles. Twin Peaks, in the geographic center of the city, is more than 900 feet high.

San Francisco may seem confusing at first, but it quickly becomes easy to negotiate. The city's downtown streets are arranged in a simple grid pattern, with the exception of Market Street and Columbus Avenue, which cut across the grid at right angles to each other. Hills appear to distort this pattern, however, and can be disorienting. But as you learn your way around, these same hills will become your landmarks and reference points.

MAIN ARTERIES & STREETS   Market Street is San Francisco's main thoroughfare. Most of the city's buses travel this route on their way to the Financial District from the outer neighborhoods to the west and south. The tall office buildings clustered downtown are at the northeast end of Market; 1 block beyond lie the Embarcadero and the bay.

The Embarcadero curves along San Francisco Bay from south of the Bay Bridge to the northeast perimeter of the city and terminates at Fisherman's Wharf, the famous tourist-oriented pier. Aquatic Park, Fort Mason, and the Golden Gate National Recreation area are located farther on around the bay, occupying the northernmost point of the peninsula.

From the eastern perimeter of Fort Mason, **Van Ness Avenue** runs due south, back to Market Street. The area we have just described forms a rough triangle, with Market Street as its southeastern boundary, the waterfront as its northern boundary, and Van Ness Avenue as its western boundary. Within this triangle lie most of the city's main tourist sights.

NEIGHBORHOODS IN BRIEF

Union Square   Union Square is the commercial hub of the city. Most major hotels and department stores are crammed into the area surrounding the actual square (named for a series of violent pro-union mass demonstrations staged here on the eve of the Civil War), and there is a plethora of upscale boutiques, restaurants, and galleries tucked between the larger buildings.

Nob Hill/Russian Hill   Bounded by Bush, Larkin, Pacific, and Stockton streets, Nob Hill is the genteel, well-heeled district of the city, still occupied by the major power brokers and the neighborhood businesses they frequent. Russian Hill extends from Pacific to Bay and from Polk to Mason. It is marked by steep streets, lush gardens, and high-rises occupied by both the moneyed and the more bohemian.

SoMa   The area is officially demarcated by the Embarcadero, Highway 101, and Market Street, with the greatest concentrations of interest around Yerba Buena Center, along Folsom and Harrison streets between Steuart and 6th, and Brannan and Market. Along the waterfront are an array of restaurants. Farther west, around Folsom between 7th and 11th streets, is where much of the city's nightclubbing occurs.

Financial District   East of Union Square, this area bordered by the Embarcadero, Market, Third, Kearny, and Washington streets is the city's business district, and the stomping grounds for many major corporations. The pointy TransAmerica Pyramid, at Montgomery and Clay streets, is one of the district's most conspicuous architectural features. Ferries to Sausalito and Larkspur still leave from this neighborhood.

Chinatown   The official entrance to Chinatown is marked by a large red-and-green gate on Grant Avenue at Bush Street. Beyond lies a 24-block labyrinth, bordered by Broadway, Bush, Kearny, and Stockton streets, filled with restaurants, markets, temples, and shops—and, of course, a substantial percentage of San Francisco's Chinese residents. This area is jam-packed, so don't even think about driving here.

North Beach   The Italian quarter, which stretches from Montgomery and Jackson to Bay Street, is one of the best places in the city to grab a coffee, pull up a cafe chair, and do some serious people-watching. Nightlife is equally happening; restaurants, bars, and clubs along Columbus and Grant avenues bring folks from all over the Bay Area here to fight for a parking place and romp through the festive neighborhood. Down Columbus toward the Financial District are the remains of the city's beat-generation landmarks. Telegraph Hill looms over the east side of North Beach, topped by Coit Tower, one of San Francisco's best vantage points.

Fisherman's Wharf   North Beach runs into Fisherman's Wharf, which was once the busy heart of the city's great harbor and waterfront industries. Today, it is a tacky-but-interesting tourist area with little if any authentic waterfront life, except for recreational boating and some friendly sea lions.

Marina District   Created on landfill for the Pan Pacific Exposition of 1915, the Marina boasts some of the best views of the Golden Gate. Streets are lined with elegant Mediterranean-style homes and apartments, which are inhabited by the city's well-to-do singles and wealthy families. Here, too, is the Palace of Fine Arts, the Exploratorium, and Fort Mason Center. The main street is Chestnut between Franklin and Lyon, which is lined with shops, cafes, and boutiques.

Cow Hollow   Located west of Van Ness Avenue, between Russian Hill and the Presidio, Cow Hollow is largely residential and occupied by the city's young and yuppie. Its two primary commercial thoroughfares are Lombard Street, known for its many relatively inexpensive motels; and Union Street, a flourishing shopping sector filled with restaurants, pubs, cafes, and shops.

Pacific Heights   The ultra-elite, such as the Gettys and Danielle Steele—and those lucky enough to buy before the real-estate boom—reside in the mansions and homes that make up Pacific Heights. When the rich meander out of their fortresses, they wander down to Union Street, a long stretch of boutiques, restaurants, cafes, and bars.

Japantown   Bounded by Octavia, Fillmore, California, and Geary, Japantown shelters only about 4% of the city's Japanese population, but it's still a cultural experience to explore these few square blocks and the shops and restaurants within them.

Civic Center   Although millions of dollars have been expended on brick sidewalks, ornate lampposts, and elaborate street plantings, the southwestern section of Market Street remains downright dilapidated. The Civic Center, at the "bottom" of Market Street, is an exception. This large complex of buildings includes the domed City Hall, the Opera House, Davies Symphony Hall, and the city's main library.

Haight-Ashbury   Part trendy, part nostalgic, part funky, the Haight, as it's most commonly known, was the soul of the psychedelic and free-loving 1960s and the center of the counterculture movement. Today, the neighborhood straddling upper Haight Street on the eastern border of Golden Gate Park is more gentrified, but the commercial area still harbors all walks of life. You don't need to wear tie-dye to enjoy the Haight—the food, shops, and bars cover all tastes.

The Castro   One of the liveliest streets in town, Castro is practically synonymous with San Francisco's gay community, even though technically it is only a street in the Noe Valley district. Located at the very end of Market Street, between 17th and 18th streets, Castro supports dozens of shops, restaurants, and bars catering to the gay community.

Mission District   The Mexican and Latin American populations, along with their cuisine, traditions, and art, make the Mission District a vibrant area to visit. Although some parts of the neighborhood are poor and sprinkled with homeless, gangs, and drug addicts, many tourists find time to stop into Mission Dolores and cruise by a few of the 200-plus amazing murals. New bars, clubs, and restaurants are popping up on Mission between 18th and 24th streets and Valencia at 16th Street. Don't be afraid to visit this area, but do use caution at night.

2 Getting Around

BY PUBLIC TRANSPORTATION

The San Francisco Municipal Railway, 949 Presidio Ave., better known as **Muni** (☎ 415/673-6864), operates the city's cable cars, buses, and Metro streetcars. Together, these three public transportation services crisscross the entire city, making San Francisco fully accessible to everyone. Buses and Metro streetcars cost $1 for adults, 35¢ for ages 5 to 17, and 35¢ for seniors over 65. Cable cars cost a whopping $2 for all people over 5 ($1 for seniors from 9pm to midnight and from 6 to 7am). Needless to say, they're packed primarily with tourists. Exact change is required on all vehicles except cable cars. Fares quoted here are subject to change.

Muni **discount passes,** called "Passports," entitle holders to unlimited rides on buses, Metro streetcars, and cable cars. A Passport costs $6 for 1 day, and $10 or $15 for 3 or 7 consecutive days. As a bonus, your Passport also entitles you to admission discounts at 24 of the city's major attractions, including the M. H. De Young Memorial Museum, the Asian Art Museum, the California Academy of Sciences, and the Japanese Tea Garden (all in Golden Gate Park);

the Museum of Modern Art; Coit Tower; the Exploratorium; the zoo; and the National Maritime Museum and Historic Ships (where you may visit the USS *Pampanito* and the SS *Jeremiah O'Brien*). Among the places where you can purchase a Passport are the San Francisco Visitor Information Center, the Holiday Inn Civic Center, and the TIX Bay Area booth at Union Square.

BY CABLE CAR   San Francisco's cable cars may not be the most practical means of transport, but these rolling historic landmarks sure are a fun ride. There are only three lines in the city, and they're all condensed in the downtown area. The most scenic, and exciting, is the **Powell-Hyde line,** which follows a zigzag route from the corner of Powell and Market streets, over both Nob Hill and Russian Hill, to a turntable at gaslit Victorian Square in front of Aquatic Park. The **Powell-Mason line** starts at the same intersection and climbs over Nob Hill before descending to Bay Street, just 3 blocks from Fisherman's Wharf. The least scenic is the **California Street line,** which begins at the foot of Market Street and runs a straight course through Chinatown and over Nob Hill to Van Ness Avenue. All riders must exit at the last stop and wait in line for the return trip. The cable-car system operates from approximately 6:30am to 12:30am.

BY BUS   Buses reach almost every corner of San Francisco, and beyond—they travel over the bridges to Marin County and Oakland. Some buses are powered by overhead electric cables; others use conventional gas engines; and all are numbered and display their destinations on the front. Stops are designated by signs, curb markings, and yellow bands on adjacent utility poles, and most bus shelters exhibit Muni's transportation map and schedule. Many buses travel along Market Street or pass near Union Square and run from about 6am to midnight, after which there is infrequent all-night "Owl" service. If you can help it, for safety purposes, avoid taking buses late at night.

Popular tourist routes are traveled by bus nos. 5, 7, and 71, all of which run to Golden Gate Park; 41 and 45, which travel along Union Street; and 30, which runs between Union Square and Ghirardelli Square.

BY METRO STREETCAR   Five of Muni's six Metro streetcar lines, designated J, K, L, M, and N, run underground downtown and on the street in the outer neighborhoods. The sleek railcars make the same stops as BART (see below) along Market Street, including Embarcadero Station (in the Financial District),

Montgomery and Powell streets (both near Union Square), and the Civic Center (near City Hall). Past the Civic Center, the routes branch off in different directions: The J line will take you to Mission Dolores; the K, L, and M lines to Castro Street; and the N line parallels Golden Gate Park. Metros run about every 15 minutes—more frequently during rush hours. Service is offered Monday to Friday from 5am to 12:30am, on Saturday from 6am to 12:20am, and on Sunday from 8am to 12:20am.

BY BART   BART, an acronym for **Bay Area Rapid Transit** (☎ **650/992-2278**), is a high-speed rail network that connects San Francisco with Oakland, Richmond, Concord, and Fremont. Four stations are located along Market Street (see "By Metro Streetcar," above). Fares range from $1 to $3.55. Tickets are dispensed from machines in the stations and are magnetically encoded with a dollar amount. Computerized exits automatically deduct the correct fare. Children 4 and under ride free. Trains run every 15 to 20 minutes, Monday to Friday from 4am to midnight, on Saturday from 6am to midnight, and on Sunday from 8am to midnight.

A $2.5-billion, 33-mile BART extension, currently under construction, includes a southern line that is planned to extend all the way to San Francisco International Airport. It will open, presumably, around the year 2000.

BY TAXI

This isn't New York, so don't expect a taxi to appear whenever you need one. If you're downtown during rush hour or leaving a major hotel, it won't be hard to hail a cab—just look for the lighted sign on the roof that indicates if one is free. Otherwise, it's a good idea to call one of the following companies to arrange a ride: **Veteran's Cab** (☎ 415/552-1300), **Desoto Cab Co.** (☎ 415/673-1414), **Luxor Cabs** (☎ 415/282-4141), **Yellow Cab** (☎ 415/626-2345), or **Pacific** (☎ 415/986-7220). Rates are approximately $2 for the first mile and $1.80 for each mile thereafter.

BY CAR

You don't need a car to explore downtown San Francisco, and in fact, in central areas, such as Chinatown, Union Square, and the Financial District, a car can be your worst nightmare. But if you want to venture outside of the city, driving is the best way to go. If you need to rent a car, see the car-rental information in chapter 2. Before heading outside the city, especially in winter, call for California **road conditions** (☎ 415/557-3755).

FAST FACTS: San Francisco

Airport   See "Getting There," in chapter 2.

American Express   For travel arrangements, traveler's checks, currency exchange, and other member services, American Express has an office at 295 California St., at Battery Street (☎ **415/536-2686**), and at 455 Market St., at First Street (☎ **415/536-2600**), in the Financial District, open Monday to Friday from 8:30am to 5:30pm and Saturday from 9am to 2pm. To report lost or stolen traveler's checks, call ☎ **800/221-7282.** For American Express Global Assist call ☎ **800/554-2639.**

Area Code   The area code for San Francisco is **415;** Oakland, Berkeley, and much of the East Bay use the 510 area code, and the peninsula is generally 650. Most phone numbers in this book are in San Francisco's 415 area code, but there's no need to dial it if you're within city limits.

Baby-sitters   Hotels can often recommend a baby-sitter or child-care service. If yours can't, try **Temporary Tot Tending** (☎ **650/355-7377,** or 650/871-5790 after 6pm), which offers child care by licensed teachers by the hour for children from 3 weeks to 12 years of age. It's open Monday to Friday from 6am to 7pm (weekend service is available only during convention times).

Business Hours   Most banks are open Monday to Friday from 9am to 3pm. Several stay open until about 5pm at least 1 day a week. Many banks also feature 24-hour ATMs.

Most stores are open Monday to Saturday from 10am or 11am to at least 6pm, with restricted hours on Sunday. But there are exceptions: Stores in Chinatown, Ghirardelli Square, and Pier 39 stay open much later during the tourist season; and large department stores, including Macy's and Nordstrom, keep late hours.

Most restaurants serve lunch from about 11:30am to 2:30pm and dinner from 5:30 to 10pm. You can sometimes get served later on weekends. Nightclubs and bars are usually open daily until 2am, when they are legally bound to stop serving alcohol.

Car Rentals   For car-rental information, see chapter 2.

Convention Center   The **Moscone Convention Center,** 774 Howard St. (☎ **415/974-4000**), between Third and Fourth streets, was completed in 1981 and named for slain San Francisco mayor George Moscone. Part of a large revitalization project in the SoMa District, the center contains one of the world's largest column-free exhibition halls.

Drugstores   There are **Walgreens** pharmacies all over town, including one at 135 Powell St. (☎ **415/391-4433**). The store is open Monday to Saturday from 8am to midnight and on Sunday from 9am to 9pm, but the pharmacy has more limited hours: Monday to Friday they're open from 8am to 8pm, Saturday from 9am to 5pm, and Sunday from 10am to 6pm. The branch on Divisadero Street at Lombard (☎ 415/931-6415) has a 24-hour pharmacy. **Merrill's** pharmacy, 805 Market St. (☎ 415/431-5466), is open Monday to Saturday from 9am to 6pm, while the rest of the drugstore is open Monday to Friday from 7am to 8pm, Saturday from 9am to 7pm, and Sunday from 9:30am to 6pm. Both chains accept MasterCard and Visa.

Earthquakes   There will always be earthquakes in California, most of which you'll never notice. However, in case of a significant shaker, there are a few precautionary measures you should know. When inside a building, seek cover; do not run outside. Stand under a doorway or against a wall and stay away from windows. If you exit a building after a substantial quake, use stairs, not elevators. If in your car, pull over to the side of the road and stop—but not until you are away from bridges, overpasses, telephone poles, and power lines. Stay in your car. If you're out walking, stay outside and away from trees, power lines, and the sides of buildings.

Emergencies   Dial ☎ 911 for police, an ambulance, or the fire department; no coins are needed from a public phone. Emergency hot lines include the **Poison Control Center** (☎ 800/523-2222) and **Rape Crisis** (☎ 415/647-7273). **Saint Francis Memorial Hospital,** 900 Hyde St., between Bush and Pine streets on Nob Hill (☎ 415/353-6000), provides emergency-care service 24 hours; no appointment is necessary.

Information   See "Visitor Information," earlier in this chapter.

Liquor Laws   Liquor and grocery stores, as well as some drugstores, can sell packaged alcoholic beverages between 6am and 2am. Most restaurants, nightclubs, and bars are licensed to serve alcoholic beverages during the same hours. The legal age for purchase and consumption is 21; proof of age is required.

Maps   See "City Layout," earlier in this chapter.

Newspapers & Magazines   The city's two main dailies are the *San Francisco Chronicle* and the *San Francisco Examiner;* both are distributed throughout the city. The two papers combine for a massive Sunday edition that includes a pink "Datebook" section— an excellent preview of the week's upcoming events. The free weekly *San Francisco Bay Guardian,* a tabloid of news and listings, is indispensable for nightlife information; it's widely distributed through street-corner dispensers and at city cafes and restaurants.

Of the many free tourist-oriented publications, the most widely read are *Key* and *San Francisco Guide*. Both handbook-size weeklies contain maps and information on current events. They can be found in most hotels and restaurants in major tourist areas.

Police   For emergencies dial ☎ **911** from any phone; no coins are needed. For other matters, call ☎ **415/553-0123.**

Post Office   There are dozens of post offices located all around the city. The closest office to Union Square is inside Macy's department store, 170 O'Farrell St. (☎ **800/275-8777**). You can pick up mail addressed to you and marked "General Delivery" (Poste Restante), at the **Civic Center Post Office Box Unit,** P.O. Box 429991, San Francisco, CA 94142-9991 (☎ **800/275-8777**).

Smoking   If San Francisco is the state's most European city, the comparison stops here. Each year smoking laws are becoming more strict. As of January 1, 1998, smoking is prohibited from restaurants and bars. Although controversial, the law's been enforced in most establishments. Hotels are also offering more nonsmoking rooms, which often leaves smokers out in the cold—literally.

Taxes   An 8.5% sales tax is added at the register for all goods and services purchased in San Francisco. The city hotel tax is a whopping 12%. There is no airport tax.

Taxis   See "Getting Around," earlier in this chapter.

Television   In addition to cable stations, available in most hotels, all the major networks and several independent stations are represented. They include: Channel 2, KTVU (FOX); Channel 4, KRON (NBC); Channel 5, KPIX (CBS); Channel 7, KGO (ABC); and Channel 9, KQED (PBS).

Time Zone   San Francisco is in the Pacific standard time zone, which is 8 hours behind Greenwich mean time and 3 hours behind eastern standard time. To find out the exact time, call ☎ **415/767-8900.**

Transit Information   The San Francisco Municipal Railway (Muni) operates the city's cable cars, buses, and Metro streetcars. For customer service call **Muni** at ☎ **415/673-6864** during the week between 7am and 5pm and on weekends between 9am and 5pm. At other times, recorded information is available.

Useful Telephone Numbers   Tourist info (☎ **415/391-2001**); highway conditions (☎ **415/557-3755**); KFOG Entertainment Line (☎ **415/777-1045**); Movie Phone Line (☎ **415/777-FILM**); Grateful Dead Hot Line (☎ **415/457-6388**).

Weather   Call ☎ **415/936-1212** to find out when the next fog bank is rolling in.

4

Accommodations

*W*hether you want a room with a view or just a room, San Francisco is more than accommodating for its 11 million annual guests. Most of the city's 180 hotels are concentrated around Union Square, but there are also some smaller independent gems scattered around town. When reading over your options, keep in mind that prices listed are hotel rack rates (the published rates) and you should always ask for special discounts or, even better, vacation packages. It's possible that you could get the room you want for $100 less than what's quoted here, except in summer when the hotels are packed and bargaining is close to impossible.

Hunting for hotels in San Francisco can be a tricky business, particularly if you're not a seasoned traveler. What you don't know—and the reservation agent may not tell you—may very well ruin your vacation, so keep the following pointers in mind when it comes time to book a room:

- Prices listed below do not include state and city taxes, which total 14%. Other hidden extras include parking fees and hefty surcharges—up to $1 per local call—for telephone use.
- San Francisco is Convention City, so if you wish to secure rooms at a particular hotel during high season, book well in advance.
- Be sure to have a credit card in hand when making a reservation, and don't be surprised if you're asked to pay for a least 1 night in advance (this doesn't happen often, though).
- Reservations are usually held until 6pm. If you don't tell the hotel you'll be arriving late, you may lose your room.
- Almost every hotel in San Francisco requires a credit card imprint for "incidentals" (and to prevent walkouts). If you don't have a credit card, then be sure to make special arrangements with the management before you hang up the phone, and take down names.

The hotels listed below are classified first by area and then by price, using the following categories: **Very Expensive,** more than $180 per night; **Expensive,** $135 to $180 per night; **Moderate,** $90 to $135 per night; and **Inexpensive,** less than $90 per night. These

Reservation Services

Having reservations about your reservations? Then leave it up to the pros:

Bed-and-Breakfast California, P.O. Box 282910, San Francisco, CA 94128 (☎ **800/677-1500** or 415/696-1690; fax 415/696-1699; Web site: www.bbintl.com; E-mail info@bbintl.com), offers a selection of B&Bs ranging from $60 to $140 per night (2-night minimum). Accommodations range from simple rooms in private homes to luxurious, full-service carriage houses, houseboats, and Victorian homes.

San Francisco Reservations, 22 Second St., San Francisco, CA 94105 (☎ **800/667-1500** or 415/227-1500), arranges reservations for more than 300 of San Francisco's hotels and often offers discounted rates. Ask about their Events and Hotel Packages that include VIP or discount admissions to various San Francisco museums. This service also has a nifty World Wide Web site that allows Internet users to make their reservations on-line. Plug in at http://www.hotelres.com.

categories reflect the price of an average double room during the high season, which runs approximately from April through September. Read each of the entries carefully: Many hotels also offer rooms at rates above and below the price category that they have been assigned in this guidebook. Also note that we do not list single rates. However, some hotels, particularly more budget-oriented establishments, do offer lower rates for singles, so inquire about these if you are traveling alone.

In general, hotel rates in San Francisco are rather inelastic; they don't vary much during the year because the city is so popular year-round. You should always ask about weekend discounts, corporate rates, and family plans; most larger hotels, and many smaller ones, offer them, but many establishments do not mention these discounts unless you make a specific inquiry. You will find nonsmoking rooms available in all of the larger hotels and many of the smaller hotels; establishments that are entirely nonsmoking are listed as such. Nowadays, the best advice for smokers is to confirm a smoking-permitted room in advance.

Most larger hotels will also be able to accommodate guests confined to wheelchairs or those who have other special needs. Ask when you make a reservation to ensure that your hotel of choice will be able to accommodate your needs, especially if you are interested in a bed-and-breakfast.

1 Union Square

VERY EXPENSIVE

✪ **The Clift Hotel.** 495 Geary St. (at Taylor St., 2 blocks west of Union Sq.), San Francisco, CA 94102. ☎ **800/437-8243** in the U.S., or 415/775-4700. Fax 415/441-4621. 357 units. A/C MINIBAR TV TEL. $255–$400 double; from $405 suite. Continental breakfast $12.50 extra. AE, CB, DC, MC, V. Parking $25. Cable car: Powell-Hyde and Powell-Mason lines (2 blocks east). Bus: 2, 3, 4, 30, 38, or 45.

Since Ian Schrager, king of ultrahip hotels such as New York's Royalton and Paramount, Los Angeles's Mondrian, and Miami's Delano, picked up this property almost 2 years ago, we've been waiting to see him put his Midas spin on it. But it wasn't until March 1998 that room renovations began (scheduled to continue through the end of 1998) and while furniture and textiles will be replaced, the hotel's classic style will remain. The Clift is still one of San Francisco's top luxury hotels and won Five-Star and Five-Diamond awards 10 years in a row just before the Schrager takeover. Located in the city's Theater District, 2 blocks from Union Square, the Clift has been known for its staff, who excel at pampering their guests and even manage to be cordial to the droves of tourists who wander slack-jawed through the palatial lobby. Rooms are old-fashioned, with high ceilings, elaborate moldings and woodwork, Georgian reproductions, and marble bathrooms with everything from hair dryers to plush terry-cloth robes. Thoughtful extras include padded hangers, individual climate controls, two-line telephones, and a scale in your dressing room. The windows also open—a nice touch for those guests who appreciate fresh air.

The Clift's "Young Travelers Program" provides traveling families with toys and games, diapers, bottles, children's books, and other amenities to help children and their parents feel at home. The hotel also accepts and pampers pets.

Dining/Diversions: Unless Schrager's team finally creates a new venue, The French Room remains open for breakfast, lunch, and dinner, specializing in seasonally appropriate California-French cuisine. The hotel's dramatic Redwood Room, which opened in 1933 and remains one of San Francisco's most opulent piano bars, has beautiful 22-foot-tall fluted redwood columns and is also famous for its Gustav Klimt murals. The lobby lounge serves cocktails daily and a traditional English tea Monday to Saturday.

Accommodations Near Union Square & Nob Hill

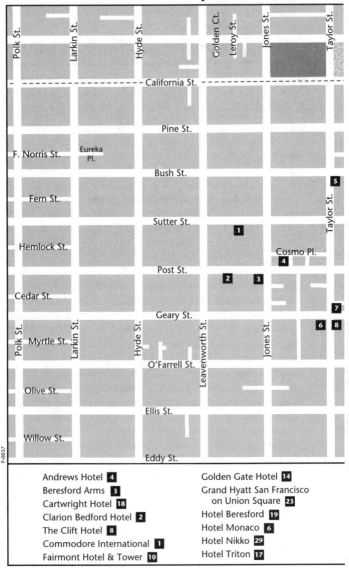

Andrews Hotel **4**	Golden Gate Hotel **14**
Beresford Arms **3**	Grand Hyatt San Francisco
Cartwright Hotel **18**	on Union Square **23**
Clarion Bedford Hotel **2**	Hotel Beresford **19**
The Clift Hotel **8**	Hotel Monaco **6**
Commodore International **1**	Hotel Nikko **29**
Fairmont Hotel & Tower **10**	Hotel Triton **17**

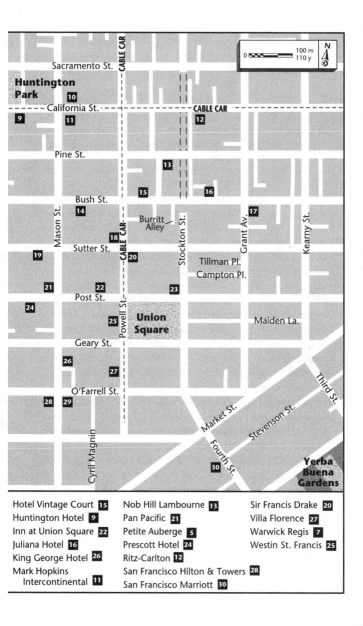

Hotel Vintage Court 15	Nob Hill Lambourne 13	Sir Francis Drake 20
Huntington Hotel 9	Pan Pacific 21	Villa Florence 27
Inn at Union Square 22	Petite Auberge 5	Warwick Regis 7
Juliana Hotel 16	Prescott Hotel 24	Westin St. Francis 25
King George Hotel 26	Ritz-Carlton 12	
Mark Hopkins	San Francisco Hilton & Towers 28	
Intercontinental 11	San Francisco Marriott 30	

Amenities: Concierge, 24-hour room service, overnight laundry and shoe polishing, 1-hour pressing, evening turndown, twice-daily maid service, complimentary in-room fax and computers, extensive fitness facility, 24-hour business center, gift shop.

Grand Hyatt San Francisco on Union Square. 345 Stockton St. (between Post and Sutter sts.), San Francisco, CA 94108. ☎ **800/233-1234** or 415/398-1234. Fax 415/391-1780. 693 units. A/C MINIBAR TV TEL. $189–$290 double (doesn't include breakfast); $224–$325 Regency Club room (including continental breakfast); from $450 suite. Continental breakfast $14.50 extra. AE, CB, DC, JCB, MC, V. Parking $24. Cable car: Powell-Hyde and Powell-Mason lines (2 blocks west). Bus: 2, 3, 4, 30, 38, or 45.

If the thought of a 10-second walk to Saks Fifth Avenue makes you drool and your credit cards start to sweat, this hotel is the place for you. Not only is the Grand Hyatt surrounded by all the downtown shopping, but it also boasts some of the best views in the area. The lobby is indeed grand, with Chinese artifacts and enormous ceramic vases, but sadly the well-kept rooms are little more than upscale basic with a corporate flare. They do have some elbow room and a small table and chairs, and the views from most of the 36 floors are truly spectacular. Accommodations include such amenities as TVs in the bathroom, first-run movies, and a telephone with computer-connection capability. Regency rooms are larger, and prices include continental breakfast and evening hors d'oeuvres. Three floors are also dedicated to Business Plan rooms, which contain private fax, telephone with computer hookup, enhanced lighting, coffeemaker, iron and board, and hair dryer. They also include special services— 24-hour access to compatible printer, photocopier, and office supplies, free local calls and credit-card phone access, and daily newspaper. All for an additional $15.

Dining/Diversions: The brand new 36th floor's Grandviews Restaurant opened in spring of 1998 and serves three meals a day with live jazz on selected evenings.

Amenities: Concierge, room service, free weekday-morning town-car service to the Financial District, fitness center, fully equipped business center, car-rental desk, tour desk.

✪ **Hotel Monaco.** 501 Geary St. (at Taylor St.), San Francisco, CA 94102. ☎ **800/214-4220** or 415/292-0100. Fax 415/292-0111. 210 units. A/C MINIBAR TV TEL. From $175 double; from $295 suite. Call for discounted rates. AE, DC, DISC, JCB, MC, V. Valet parking $24. Bus: 2, 3, 4, 27, or 38.

This remodeled 1910 beaux arts building debuted in June 1995 and is the new diva of Union Square luxury hotels. For $24 million, the Kimpton Group did this place right—from the cozy main lobby with a two-story French inglenook fireplace to the guest rooms with canopy beds, Chinese-inspired armoires, bamboo writing desks, bold stripes, and vibrant color. Everything is fresh, in the best of taste, and as playful as it is serious. The decor, combined with the breathtaking neighboring restaurant, make this our favorite luxury hotel in San Francisco. The only downside is that many of the Hotel Monaco's rooms are too small.

Dining/Diversions: The hotel's restaurant, the Grand Cafe, is the best room downtown (competing only with Kuleto's new Farallon). It is grand, in the true sense of the word, with sky-high ceilings, elaborate 1920s and 1930s style, and an amazing collection of local art. In the past year, chef Denis Soriano has really settled into his kitchen, making the Grand Cafe one seriously hot dining spot (see chapter 5, "Dining," for complete information).

Amenities: Computer; concierge; room service; laundry/dry cleaning; overnight shoe-shine; newspaper delivery; in-room massage; twice-daily maid service; baby-sitting; two-line phones; secretarial services; express checkout; valet parking; courtesy car; complimentary wine-hour nightly; health club with steam room, sauna, and massage; meeting, business, and banquet facilities.

Hotel Nikko. 222 Mason St. (at O'Farrell St.), San Francisco, CA 94102. ☎ **800/645-5687** or 415/394-1111. Fax 415/421-0455. 522 units. A/C MINIBAR TV TEL. $280–$350 double; $525–$2,000 suite. AE, CB, DISC, JCB, MC, V. Parking $25. Cable car: Powell-Hyde and Powell-Mason lines. Bus: 2, 3, 4, 30, 38, or 45.

Part of Japan Airlines's international fleet of superluxury hotels, the 25-story Hotel Nikko combines the luxuries of both Eastern and Western cultures with heavenly results. Work out in the fitness center, take a few laps in the glass-enclosed indoor swimming pool, rest in the Jacuzzi, Japanese sauna, or soaking tub, then top off the morning with a shiatsu massage before starting your day—what more could you ask for?

Ideally located near Union Square and the Theater District, the Nikko's penchant for pampering also carries on to the guest rooms, which feature top-of-the-line amenities such as two-line speaker phones with modem ports, blackout curtains, large windows with views of the city, and huge, marble bathrooms with separate tubs and showers. Suites include separate sitting areas, stereos with CD players, and entry halls (a Japanese tradition). Though the hotel's decor might be a bit too staid for Western tastes—simple furnishings and beige tones predominate—the element of luxury ultimately prevails.

Dining/Diversions: The bistro-style Cafe 222 serves both California and Japanese cuisine for breakfast, lunch, and dinner. On the lobby level is a small sushi bar offering made-to-order sushi, as well as afternoon hors d'oeuvres and live music.

Amenities: Concierge, 24-hour room service, laundry/valet, twice-daily maid service, swimming pool, fitness center, sauna, hot tub, shiatsu massage, tanning booth, business center, gift and other shops.

Pan Pacific. 500 Post St. (at Mason St.), San Francisco, CA 94102. ☎ **800/ 533-6465** or 415/771-8600. Fax 415/398-0267. 329 units. A/C MINIBAR TV TEL. $280–$370 double; from $410 suite. Continental breakfast $12 extra; American breakfast $14.25 extra. AE, DC, DISC, JCB, MC, V. Valet parking $25. Cable car: Powell-Hyde and Powell-Mason lines. Bus: 2, 3, 4, 30, 38, or 45.

The Pan Pacific is 21st century with *Star Wars*–like lighted corridors, artistically glitzy, enormous, and somehow romantic, all at the same time. If this were a Hollywood set, James Bond might hoodwink a villain here, magically drop down the sky-rise's atrium, and disappear into the night. But all is quiet and intimate in the third-floor lobby, even though the skylight ceiling is another 18 floors up. The lobby's marble fountain with four dancing figures and its player piano set the mood for guests relaxing in front of the fireplace. The rooms are rather corporate, but in very good taste, large, and immaculately clean and well stocked with all the luxurious extras, including lavish marble bathrooms with mini-TVs at the sink. In the past year all soft-goods were replaced—from bedspreads to upholstery, drapes, and carpet—with more colorful designs. Other amenities offered are in-room safes, three Touch-Tone phones, fax machines, voice mail, and bathrobes. The hotel is also conveniently located close to Union Square.

Dining: The Pacific dining room serves breakfast, lunch, and dinner featuring excellent California cuisine with Asian and French accents.

Amenities: Concierge, 24-hour room service, laundry/valet, newspaper delivery, in-room massage, twice-daily maid service, baby-sitting, secretarial services, complimentary Rolls Royce transportation in the city, health club, business center, conference rooms.

✪ **Prescott Hotel.** 545 Post St. (between Mason and Taylor sts.), San Francisco, CA 94102. ☎ **800/283-7322** or 415/563-0303. Fax 415/563-6831. 199 units. A/C MINIBAR TV TEL. $205 double; $255 concierge-level double (including breakfast and evening cocktail reception); from $295 suite. AE, CB, DC, MC, V. Valet parking $25. Cable car: Powell-Hyde and Powell-Mason lines (1 block east). Bus: 2, 3, 4, 30, 38, or 45.

The Prescott has always been one of our favorite hotels in San Francisco. The staff treats you like royalty, the rooms are beautiful and immaculate, the location—1 block from Union Square—is perfect, and room service is provided by one of the best restaurants in the city: Postrio. (In fact, it's not unheard of for visitors to check into the Prescott just to get preferred seating.)

Dark tones of green, plum, and burgundy blend well with the cherry-wood furnishings within each of the soundproofed rooms; the view, alas, isn't so pleasant. All bathrooms are supplied with terry-cloth robes and hair dryers, though only the suites have whirlpool bathtubs. "Concierge-level" guests are pampered with free continental breakfast, evening cocktails, and exercise bicycles or rowing machines brought up to your room on request (all for only $20 extra per night).

Dining: The hotel provides preferred seating for guests at Postrio Restaurant. Be sure to make reservations when you book your room (see chapter 5, "Dining," for complete information).

Amenities: Concierge; room service from the Postrio; same-day valet/laundry service; overnight shoe-shine; newspaper delivery; nightly turndown; twice-daily maid service; valet parking; limousine service weekday mornings to the Financial District; complimentary coffee and tea each morning; wine and hors d'oeuvres every evening in the living room; access to off-premises health club ($10), including swimming pool, free weights, and sauna; conference rooms.

San Francisco Hilton & Towers. 333 O'Farrell St. (between Mason and Taylor sts.), San Francisco, CA 94102. ☎ **800/445-8667** or 415/771-1400. Fax 415/771-6807. 1,794 units. A/C MINIBAR TV TEL. $205–$285 double; from $350 suite. Children stay free in parents' room. AE, CB, DC, DISC, MC, V. Parking $27. Cable car: Powell-Hyde and Powell-Mason lines (1 block east). Bus: 2, 3, 4, 30, 38, or 45.

Complete with bustling conventioneers, anxious smokers, and a line to register that resembles airport check-in, the Hilton's lobby is so enormous and busy it feels more like a convention hall than a hotel. It's the Hilton's three connecting buildings (the original 19-story main building, a 46-story tower topped by a panoramic restaurant, and a 23-story landmark with an additional 386 luxurious rooms and suites) that bring the swarms of visitors clamoring for a room. But even during quieter times, the sheer enormity of the place makes the Hilton somewhat overwhelming and its contents mysterious.

After you get past the sweeping grand lobby, jump on an elevator, and wind through endless corridors to your room, you'll find the mystique ends with common, corporate accommodations. Some of the main tower's rooms' floor-to-ceiling views may be memorable, but the decor definitely is not. Room size is simply standard. Unless you're staying in one of the more luxurious abodes, the feel and decor here are impersonal and plain—perfect for the conventioneers, but not for a romantic weekend. One bonus: The Hilton is always upgrading somewhere on the property, and over 400 rooms were renovated in the past year.

Dining: Cityscape, on the 46th floor, serves classic California cuisine with a breathtaking 360° view; the retractable skylight exposes the night sky in all its grandeur. Kiku of Tokyo offers Japanese cuisine. The Mason Street Deli serves breakfast and lunch, and Intermezzo offers Italian-style food to eat in or to go. An elegant sidewalk cafe, The Café on the Square, provides a spot for watching the passing parade.

Amenities: Concierge, room service (6am to midnight), laundry, shoe-shine, swimming pool, health club ($6 fee), business center, tour desk, shopping arcade. Towers-level accommodations offer upgraded services, including separate registration lounge with complimentary breakfast and hors d'oeuvres and daily newspaper.

San Francisco Marriott. 55 Fourth St. (between Market and Mission sts.), San Francisco, CA 94103. ☎ **800/228-9290** or 415/896-1600. Fax 415/777-2799. 1,500 units. A/C MINIBAR TV TEL. $179–$249 double; $350–$2,500 suite. AE, CB, DC, JCB, MC, V. Parking $25. Cable car: Powell-Hyde and Powell-Mason lines (3 blocks west). Muni Metro: All Market St. trams. All Market St. buses.

Some call it a masterpiece, others liken it to the world's biggest parking meter. Regardless, the Marriott is one of the largest buildings in the city, making it a popular stopover for convention-goers and those looking for a room with a view. Fortunately, the controversy does not extend to the newly renovated rooms, so expect pleasant accommodations, floral patterns, large bathrooms and beds, and exceptional city vistas. Upon arrival, enter from Fourth Street, between Market and Mission, to avoid a long trek to the registration area.

Dining/Diversions: Kinoko is a Japanese teppanyaki restaurant and sushi bar. The Garden Terrace, facing the hotel's central fountain, has a breakfast bar and two buffets that prepare made-to-order omelets; there is also a varied lunch-and-dinner menu. You can choose between the Atrium Lounge and the View Lounge, which has a truly panoramic view of the bay and Golden Gate Bridge (assuming there's no fog) as well as live entertainment.

Amenities: Indoor pool and health club, business center, tour desk, car-rental, and gift shop.

✪ **Westin St. Francis.** 335 Powell St. (between Geary and Post sts.), San Francisco, CA 94102. ☎ **800/228-3000** or 415/397-7000. Fax 415/774-0124. 1,275 units. A/C MINIBAR TV TEL. Main building: $229–$405 double; from $395 suite. Tower: $360–$405 double; from $425 suite. Extra person $30. Continental breakfast $12.50 extra. AE, DC, DISC, JCB, MC, V. Valet parking $26. Cable car: Powell-Hyde and Powell-Mason lines (direct stop). Bus: 2, 3, 4, 30, 45, or 76.

Though too massive to offer the personal service you get at the smaller deluxe hotels on Nob Hill, few other hotels in San Francisco can match the majestic aura of the St. Francis. We know it sounds corny, but the St. Francis is so intertwined with the city's past that it truly is San Francisco: Stroll through the vast, ornate lobby and you can feel 100 years of history oozing from its hand-carved redwood paneling. The hotel did a massive $50-million renovation in 1996, replacing the carpeting, furniture, and bedding in every guest room, gussying up the lobby, and restoring the facade, which makes it all the more surprising that pets are welcome here. The older rooms of the main building vary in size and have more old-world charm than the newer tower rooms, but the Tower is remarkable for its great views of the city once you rise above the 18th floor. Even if you stay elsewhere, it's worth a visit if only to partake in high tea at the Compass Rose, one of San Francisco's most enduring and enjoyable traditions.

Dining/Diversions: The lobby-level Dewey's, a sports bar, offers a do-it-yourself luncheon buffet, and burgers and pizzas at night. The St. Francis Cafe, also on the lower level, offers a basic breakfast and dinner menu. The Compass Rose is open daily for lunch and afternoon tea (3 to 5pm), with live music, dancing, champagne, cocktails, and caviar tasting in the evening.

Amenities: Concierge, 24-hour room service, laundry, newspaper delivery, in-room massage, twice-daily maid service, baby-sitting referral, Westin Kids Club (great for families), secretarial services, fitness center, business center, tour and car-rental desks, barber/beauty salon, gift shop.

EXPENSIVE
✪ **Hotel Triton.** 342 Grant Ave. (at Bush St.), San Francisco, CA 94108. ☎ **800/433-6611** or 415/394-0500. Fax 415/394-0555. 147 units. A/C MINIBAR TV TEL. $159–$199 double; $299–$315 suite. AE, DC, DISC, MC, V. Parking $22. Cable car: Powell-Hyde and Powell-Mason lines (2 blocks west).

Executing a bold idea that was long overdue, hotelier magnate Bill Kimpton requisitioned a cadre of local artists and designers to "do their thing" to his latest acquisition, the Hotel Triton. The result was San Francisco's first three-star hotel to finally break the boring barrier. Described as vogue, chic, retro-futuristic, and even neo-Baroque, the Triton begs attention from the Daliesque lobby to the sumptuous designer suites à la Jerry Garcia, Wyland (the ocean artist), and Joe Boxer. Two dozen environmentally sensitive "EcoRooms"—biodegradable soaps, filtered water and air, all-natural linens—were also installed to please the tree-hugger in all of us. A mild caveat: Don't expect perfection; many of the Hotel Triton's rooms could use a little touching up here and there (stained curtains, chipped furniture), and the service isn't as snappy as it could be. If you can live with this, and want to inject a little fun and style into your stay, then come join Dorothy and Toto for a trip far from Kansas.

Dining/Diversions: Café de la Presse, a European-style newsstand and outdoor cafe, serves breakfast, lunch, and dinner. In the hotel lobby, complimentary coffee is served each morning and wine each evening.

Amenities: Room service, same-day laundry, exercise room, business center.

Hotel Vintage Court. 650 Bush St. (between Powell and Stockton sts.), San Francisco, CA 94108. ☎ **800/654-1100** or 415/392-4666. Fax 415/433-4065. 107 units. A/C MINIBAR TV TEL. $129–$169 double; $300 penthouse suite. AE, CB, DC, DISC, MC, V. Parking $21. Cable car: Powell-Hyde and Powell-Mason lines (direct stop). Bus: 2, 3, 4, 30, 45, or 76.

Consistent personal service has prompted a loyal clientele at this European-style hotel located 2 blocks north of Union Square. The lobby, accented with dark wood, deep green, and rose, is welcoming enough to actually spend a little time in, especially when the nightly complimentary California wines are being poured.

But the varietals don't stop at ground level. Each tidy room, renovated in 1995, is named after a winery and mimics a wine-country excursion with its floral bedspreads, matching drapes, and trellised wall-to-wall loop carpeting. Opus One, the deluxe, two-room penthouse suite, includes an original 1912 stained-glass skylight, a wood-burning fireplace, a whirlpool tub, a complete entertainment center, and panoramic views of the city.

Dining/Diversions: The hotel's dining room, Masa's, serving traditional French fare, is one of the top restaurants in San Francisco (see chapter 5, "Dining," for complete information). Breakfast available in the dining room, complementary evening wine service from 5:30 to 7pm features fine California reds and whites.

Amenities: Free morning transportation to the Financial District, tour desk, and car-rental service, access to an off-premises health club at a fee of $10 per day.

Inn at Union Square. 440 Post St. (between Mason and Powell sts.), San Francisco, CA 94102. ☎ **800/288-4346** or 415/397-3510. Fax 415/989-0529. 30 units. TV TEL. $165–$350 double. Rates include continental breakfast. AE, CB, DC, DISC, JCB, MC, V. Valet parking $22. Cable car: Powell-Hyde and Powell-Mason lines. Bus: 2, 3, 4, 30, 38, or 45.

As narrow as an Amsterdam abode, the Inn at Union Square is a veritable antithesis to the big, impersonal hotels that surround Union Square. If you need plenty of elbow room, skip this one. But if you're looking for the type of inn whose staff knows the names of each guest and afternoon tea comes with crisp cucumber sandwiches, then read on. A half block west of the square, the seven-story inn makes up for its small stature by spoiling its guests with a pile of perks. Mornings start with breakfast served at your door along with the *New York Times,* followed by afternoon tea and evening hors d'oeuvres served in adorable little fireplace lounges at the end of each hall. The rooms, each handsomely and individually decorated with Georgian reproductions and floral fabrics, are smaller than average but infinitely more appreciable than the cookie-cutter rooms of most larger hotels.

Amenities: Complete business services available, use of a health club.

Juliana Hotel. 590 Bush St. (at Stockton St.), San Francisco, CA 94108. ☎ **800/328-3880** or 415/392-2540. Fax 415/391-8447. 106 units. A/C MINIBAR TV TEL. $145–$195 double; $179–$225 junior suite; $185–$235 executive suite; $300–$500 2-bedroom suite. Special winter packages available. Continental breakfast $7.95 extra. AE, CB, DC, MC, V. Parking $21. Cable car: Powell-Hyde and Powell-Mason lines (1 block west). Bus: 2, 3, 4, 30, 38, or 45.

We love the lobby at this small, European-style hotel. With its rich, homey surroundings, English prints, and comfy couches facing a blazing fire, which is ensconced in brass and marble, it feels more like a rich friend's study than the entrance to a hotel. With the addition of daily papers hanging on a wooden rack, the Juliana has created a place that makes us want to kick up our feet and stay awhile. And with the complimentary coffee here by day and wine by night, there's no real reason to leave.

The rooms were renovated in 1997, and are a substantial departure from their previous decor. Now surroundings are trendy-bright, with yellow-and-pale-blue-striped wallpaper, candy-striped yellow and red upholstered chairs, floral patterned bedspreads with matching curtains, and blue carpeting. It's vibrant and cheery, for sure, but not the kind of place in which you'd want to nurse a wicked hangover. Extra bonuses are aplenty: irons and ironing boards, in-room faxes, and coffeemakers. The bathrooms were renovated, too, and have lovely golden diamond-patterned wallpaper, a large, well-lit mirror, hair dryer, and a basket of soap and other toiletries. Rooms can be on the small side, but the junior suites have plenty of elbow room and adorable homey touches.

Amenities: Room service, laundry/valet, morning transport to the Financial District, access to an off-premises health club.

Sir Francis Drake. 450 Powell St. (at Sutter St.), San Francisco, CA 94102. ☎ **800/227-5480** or 415/392-7755. Fax 415/391-8719. 417 units. A/C MINIBAR TV TEL. $165–$245 double; $350–$650 suite. AE, CB, DC, DISC, MC, V. Parking $24. Cable car: Powell-Hyde and Powell-Mason lines (direct stop). Bus: 2, 3, 4, 45, or 76.

It took a change of ownership and a multimillion-dollar restoration to save the Sir Francis Drake from becoming a Starbucks, but now this stately old queen is once again housing guests in grand fashion. Granted, this venerable septuagenarian is still showing signs of age (the owners admit there's more work to be done), but the price of imperfection is certainly reflected in the room rate: a good $100 less per night than its Nob Hill cousins. The new Sir Francis Drake is a hotel for people who are willing to trade a chipped bathroom tile or oddly matched furniture for the opportunity to vacation in pseudo-grand fashion. Allow Tom Sweeny, the ever-ebullient (and legendary) Beefeater doorman, to handle your bags as you make your entrance into the elegant, captivating lobby. Sip cocktails at the superchic Starlight Lounge overlooking the city. Dine at Scala's Bistro, one of the hottest restaurants downtown. In short, live like the king or queen of Union Square without all the pomp, circumstance, and credit-card bills.

Dining/Diversions: Scala's Bistro at the lobby level serves excellent Italian cuisine in a stylish setting; Café Expresso, a small Parisian-style corner cafe, does an equally commendable job serving coffees, pastries, and sandwiches daily. The Starlight Room on the 21st floor offers cocktails, entertainment, and dancing nightly with a panoramic view of the city.

Amenities: Concierge, room service, business services, laundry, valet, exercise room, extensive meeting facilities.

Villa Florence. 225 Powell St. (between Geary and O'Farrell sts.), San Francisco, CA 94102. ☎ **800/553-4411** or 415/397-7700. Fax 415/397-1006. 181 units. A/C MINIBAR TV TEL. $145–$185 double; $179–$199 studio king. Continental breakfast $8.50 extra. AE, CB, DC, DISC, MC, V. Valet parking $23. Cable car: Powell-Hyde and Powell-Mason lines (direct stop). Bus: 2, 3, 4, 30, 38, or 45.

Located half a block south of Union Square and fronting the Powell Street cable-car line, the seven-story Villa Florence is parked in one of the liveliest sections of the city (no need to drive, 'cause you're already here). A recent—and sorely needed—renovation has brightened up the rooms considerably. Essentially it's a lower-end replica of the spectacular rooms at the Hotel Monaco (which is owned by the same company), with lots of bold stripes and vibrant colors. You'll like the large, comfortable bed and the bathroom equipped with hand-milled soap and hair dryers. But never mind the rooms: It's the hotel's restaurant that makes it a worthy contender among Union Square's medium-priced inns. As if the location alone weren't reason enough to book a room.

Dining/Diversions: Adjoining the hotel is Kuleto's, one of San Francisco's most popular and stylish Italian restaurants (trust us, you'll want to make a reservation for dinner along with your room). See chapter 5, "Dining," for complete information.

MODERATE

Andrews Hotel. 624 Post St. (between Jones and Taylor sts.), San Francisco, CA 94109. ☎ **800/926-3739** or 415/563-6877. Fax 415/928-6919. 48 units. MINIBAR TV TEL. $89–$119 double; $129 petite suite. Rates include continental breakfast and evening wine. AE, DC, JCB, MC, V. Self-parking $15. Cable car: Powell-Hyde and Powell-Mason lines (3 blocks east). Bus: 2, 3, 4, 30, 38, or 45.

Two blocks west of Union Square, the Andrews was formerly a Turkish bath before its conversion in 1981. As is fitting with Euro-style hotels, the rooms are small but well maintained and comfortable; white lace curtains and fresh flowers in each room add a light touch. Some rooms have shower only, and bathrooms in general tend to be tiny, but for the location—a few blocks from Union Square—and price, the Andrews is a safe bet for an enjoyable stay in the city. An added bonus is the adjoining Fino Bar and Ristorante, which offers complimentary wine to its hotel guests in the evening.

Beresford Arms. 701 Post St. (at Jones St.), San Francisco, CA 94109. ☎ **800/533-6533** or 415/673-2600. Fax 415/929-1535. 144 units. MINIBAR TV TEL. $119 double; $140 Jacuzzi suite; $175 parlor suite. Rates include continental breakfast. Extra person $10. Children under 12 stay free in parents' room. Senior-citizen discount available. AE, CB, DC, DISC, MC, V. Parking $15. Cable car: Powell-Hyde line (3 blocks east). Bus: 2, 3, 4, 27, or 38.

Every time we visit the Beresford Arms, its lobby always seems filled with happy, chatty Europeans. Maybe it's the Jacuzzi whirlpool bathtubs and bidets that keep them smiling, or the "Manager's Social Hour" with free wine and snacks. The price is fair, too: $140 for a large, reasonably attractive (though a bit old-fashioned) suite with a choice of wet bar or fully equipped kitchen—a key for families. Modest business services are available, as is valet or self-parking. The hotel's location, sandwiched between the Theater District and Union Square in a quieter section of San Francisco, is ideal for car-free visitors.

Cartwright Hotel. 524 Sutter St. (at Powell St.), San Francisco, CA 94102. ☎ **800/227-3844** or 415/421-2865. Fax 415/983-6244. 114 units. TV TEL. $119–$149 double or twin; $199–$259 family suite sleeping 4. Rates include continental breakfast and evening wine. AE, CB, DC, DISC, MC, V. Parking $21. Cable car: Powell-Hyde and Powell-Mason lines (direct stop). Bus: 2, 3, 4, 30, or 45.

Diametrically opposed to the hip-hop, happenin' Hotel Triton down the street, the Cartwright Hotel is geared toward the "older, mature traveler" (as hotel marketers like to put it). The hotel management takes pride in its reputation for offering clean, comfortable rooms at fair prices, which explains why most of its guests have been repeat customers for a long time. Remarkably quiet despite its convenient location near one of the busiest downtown corners, the eight-story hotel looks not unlike it did some 80 years ago when it first opened. High-quality antiques collected during its decades of faithful service furnish the lobby, as well as each of the individually decorated rooms. A nice perk usually reserved for fancier hotels is the fully equipped bathrooms, all of which have tubs, shower massages, thick fluffy towels, and terry-cloth robes. *Tip:* Request a room with a view of the backyard; they're the quietest. Guests have access to a nearby health club; complimentary wine, tea, and cookies are served in the small library adjacent to the lobby from 5 to 6pm.

Clarion Bedford Hotel. 761 Post St. (between Leavenworth and Jones sts.), San Francisco, CA 94109. ☎ **800/227-5642** or 415/673-6040. Fax 415/563-6739. 144 units. MINIBAR TV TEL. $119–$169 double; from $175 suite. Continental breakfast $8.50 extra. AE, CB, DC, JCB, MC, V. Parking $18. Cable car: Powell-Hyde and Powell-Mason lines (4 blocks east). Bus: 2, 3, 4, or 27.

For the price and location (3 blocks from Union Square) the 17-story Bedford offers a darn good deal. Your hard-earned dollars will get you a large, spotless, recently renovated room with flowery decor that's not exactly en vogue but definitely in fine taste, as well as service from an incredibly enthusiastic, attentive, and professional staff. Each accommodation is well furnished with king, queen, or two double beds, writing desk, armchair, and well-stocked honor bar with plenty of munchies. Big closets are a trade for the small bathrooms. Most rooms are sunny and bright and have priceless views of the city (the higher the floor, the better the view).

The hotel's bistro, Crushed Tomato's, has a small, beautiful mahogany bar opposite the registration desk. Canvas Café, an enormous eatery located behind the lobby, is under separate management. There's also room service (for breakfast only), dry cleaning, laundry, secretarial services, valet parking, free morning limousine service to the Financial District, and complimentary wine in the lobby each evening from 5 to 6pm.

✪ Commodore International. 825 Sutter St. (at Jones St.), San Francisco, CA 94109. ☎ **800/338-6848** or 415/923-6800. Fax 415/923-6804. 113 units. TV TEL. $99–$119 double or twin. AE, DC, MC, V. Parking $15. Bus: 2, 3, 4, 27, or 76.

If you're looking to pump a little fun and fantasy into your vacation, this is the place. Before its new owners revamped the aging Commodore from top to bottom, it . . . well, okay, it sucked. Then along came San Francisco hotelier Chip Conley who, amped on his success in transforming the Phoenix Hotel into a rocker's retreat, instantly recognized this dilapidated eyesore's potential, added it to his collection, then let his hip-hop decor designers do their magic. The result? One groovy hotel. Stealing the show is the Red Room, a Big Apple–style bar and lounge that reflects no other color of the spectrum but ruby red (you gotta see this one). The stylish lobby comes in a close second, followed by the adjoining Titanic Café, a cute little diner serving buckwheat griddlecakes, Vietnamese tofu sandwiches, and dragon-fire salads. Appealing to the masses, Chip left the Commodore International's first four floors as standard no-frills—though quite clean and comfortable—rooms, while decking out the top two floors in neo-deco overtones (well worth the extra $10 per night).

Hotel Beresford. 635 Sutter St. (near Mason St.), San Francisco, CA 94102. ☎ **800/533-6533** or 415/673-9900. Fax 415/474-0449. 114 units. MINIBAR TV TEL. $109–$119 double. Rates include continental breakfast. Extra person $10. Children under 12 stay free in parents' room. Senior-citizen discounts available. Ask for special rates. AE, CB, DC, DISC, MC, V. Parking $15. Cable car: Powell-Hyde line (1 block east). Bus: 2, 3, 4, 30, 38, or 45.

Small and friendly, the seven-floor Hotel Beresford is a decent, moderately priced choice near Union Square. Rooms have a mish-mash of furniture and stocked fridges, and to block out the street noise, they've recently installed soundproof windows. Everything's well kept, but don't expect much more than a clean place to rest.

The White Horse Tavern, an attractive replica of an old English pub, serves a complimentary continental breakfast, as well as lunch and dinner.

King George Hotel. 334 Mason St. (between Geary and O'Farrell sts.), San Francisco, CA 94102. ☎ **800/288-6005** or 415/781-5050. Fax 415/391-6976. 141 units. TV TEL. $75–$150 double; $225 suite. Special-value packages available seasonally. Continental breakfast $5.75 extra. AE, CB, DC, DISC, JCB, MC, V. Self-parking $16.50. Cable car: Powell-Hyde and Powell-Mason lines (1 block west). Bus: 2, 3, 4, 30, 38, or 45.

Built in 1914 for the Panama-Pacific Exhibition when rooms went for $1 per night, the King George has fared well over the years, continuing to draw a mostly European clientele. The location—surrounded by cable-car lines, the Theater District, Union Square, and dozens of restaurants—is superb, and the rooms are surprisingly quiet for such a busy location. Though the decor is a bit old-fashioned, a recent renovation has upgraded the rooms to new old-fashioned—each one is meticulously neat and clean with full private bathrooms and large beds. A big hit since it started a few years back is the hotel's English afternoon tea, served above the lobby Monday to Saturday from 3 to 6pm.

Services include 24-hour room service, concierge, laundry/valet, baby-sitting, business center, and free access to the nearby 24-hour Nautilus center.

✪ **Petite Auberge.** 863 Bush St. (between Taylor and Mason sts.), San Francisco, CA 94108. ☎ **415/928-6000.** Fax 415/775-5717. 26 units. TV TEL. $110–$160 double; $225 petite suite. Rates include full breakfast. AE, DC, MC, V. Parking $19. Cable car: Powell-Hyde and Powell-Mason lines. Bus: 2, 3, 4, 30, 38, or 45.

The Petite Auberge is so pathetically cute we can't stand it. We want to say it's overdone, that any hotel filled with teddy bears is absurd, but we can't. Bribed each year with fresh-baked cookies from their never-empty platter, we make our rounds through the rooms and ruefully admit to ourselves that we're just going to have to use that word we loath to hear: adorable.

Nobody does French country like the Petite Auberge. Hand-crafted armoires, delicate lace curtains, cozy little fireplaces, adorable (there's that word again) little antiques and knickknacks—no hotel in Provence ever had it this good. Honeymooners should splurge on the Petite suite, which has its own private entrance, deck, spa tub, refrigerator, and coffeemaker. The breakfast room, with its mural of a country market scene, terra-cotta tile floors, French-country decor, and gold-yellow tablecloths, opens onto a small garden. There are complimentary California wines, tea, and hors d'oeuvres served each afternoon.

Warwick Regis. 490 Geary St. (between Mason and Taylor sts.), San Francisco, CA 94102. ☎ **800/827-3447** or 415/928-7900. Fax 415/441-8788. 80 units. MINIBAR TV TEL. $125–$225 double. Rates include continental breakfast. AE, CB, DC, DISC, MC, V. Parking $23. Cable car: Powell-Hyde and Powell Mason lines. Bus: 2, 3, 4, 27, or 38.

Louis XVI may have been a rotten monarch, but he certainly had taste. Fashioned in the style of pre-Revolutionary France (ca. 18th century), the Warwick is awash with pristine French and English antiques, Italian marble, chandeliers, four-poster beds, hand-carved headboards, and the like. The result is an expensive-looking hotel that, for all its pleasantries and perks, is surprisingly affordable when compared to its Union Square contemporaries (singles are as low as $125). Honeymooners should splurge on the Fireplace rooms with canopy beds—ooh la la! Amenities include 24-hour room and concierge service, dry cleaning, laundry, twice-daily maid service, complimentary shoe-shine and newspaper, and valet parking. Adjoining the lobby is fashionable La Scene Café, the perfect place to start your day with a latte and end it with a nightcap.

There's access to a nearby health club, a business center, and conference rooms on the premises.

INEXPENSIVE

Golden Gate Hotel. 775 Bush St. (between Powell and Mason sts.), San Francisco, CA 94108. ☎ **800/835-1118** or 415/392-3702. Fax 415/392-6202. 23 units, 14 with bathroom. TV. $65–$75 double without bathroom; $99–$115 double with bathroom. Rates include continental breakfast. AE, CB, DC, MC, V. Parking $14. Cable car: Powell-Hyde and Powell-Mason lines (1 block east). Bus: 2, 3, 4, 30, 38, or 45.

Among San Francisco's small hotels occupying historic turn-of-the-century buildings are some real gems, and the Golden Gate Hotel is one of them. It's 2 blocks north of Union Square and 2 blocks down (literally) from the crest of Nob Hill, with cable-car stops at the corner for easy access to Fisherman's Wharf and Chinatown (the city's theaters and best restaurants are also within walking distance). But the best thing about the Golden Gate Hotel is that this is a family-run establishment: John and Renate Kenaston are hospitable innkeepers who take obvious pleasure in making their guests comfortable. Each individually decorated room has handsome antique furnishings (plenty of wicker) from the early 1900s, quilted bedspreads, and fresh flowers (request a room with a claw-foot tub if you enjoy a good, hot soak). All rooms have phones, and complimentary afternoon tea is served daily from 4 to 7pm.

2 Nob Hill

VERY EXPENSIVE

Fairmont Hotel & Tower. 950 Mason St. (at California St.), San Francisco, CA 94108. ☎ **800/527-4727** or 415/772-5000. Fax 415/772-5013. 600 units. A/C MINIBAR TV TEL. Main building: $229–$279 double; from $530 suite. Tower: $269–$359 double; from $800 suite. Extra person $30. Continental breakfast $13.50 extra. AE, CB, DC, DISC, MC, V. Parking $27. Cable car: California St. line (direct stop).

The granddaddy of Nob Hill's elite cadre of ritzy hotels, the Fairmont wins top honors for the most awe-inspiring lobby in San Francisco. Even if you're not staying at the Fairmont, it's worth a side trip to gape at its massive, marble Corinthian columns, vaulted ceilings, velvet chairs, gilded mirrors, and spectacular wraparound staircase. Unfortunately, such ostentation doesn't carry over to the guest rooms, which are surprisingly ordinary (aside from the spectacular views from the top floors). In addition to the expected luxuries, guests will appreciate such details as goose-down pillows, electric shoe buffers, bathroom scales, large walk-in closets, and multiline phones with private voice mail.

Dining/Diversions: Masons serves contemporary California cuisine, with live music Tuesday to Sunday. Bella Voce Ristorante features Italian American for breakfast and lunch, while the Crown Room offers deli lunches, dinner buffets, and Sunday brunch, with a panoramic view of the Bay Area. The Tonga Room offers Chinese and Polynesian specialties in a tropical ambiance, as well as dancing and a generous happy hour. Afternoon tea is served daily in the hotel's lobby.

Amenities: 24-hour concierge, 24-hour room service, laundry/valet, complimentary shoe-shine, evening turndown, twice-daily maid service, baby-sitting services, doctor on-call, complimentary morning limousine to the Financial District, health club, business center, barbershop, beauty salon, pharmacy, shopping arcade.

✪ **Huntington Hotel.** 1075 California St. (between Mason and Taylor sts.), San Francisco, CA 94108. ☎ **800/227-4683,** 800/652-1539 in Calif., or 415/

474-5400. Fax 415/474-6227. 140 units. A/C MINIBAR TV TEL. $235–$345 double; from $400–$935 suite. Special packages available. Continental breakfast $11. AE, CB, DC, DISC, MC, V. Valet parking $19.50. Cable car: California St. line (direct stop). Bus: 1.

One of the kings of Nob Hill, the stately Huntington Hotel has long been a favorite retreat for Hollywood stars and political VIPs who desire privacy and security. Family-owned since 1924—an extreme rarity among large hotels—the Huntington eschews pomp and circumstance; absolute privacy and unobtrusive service are its mainstay. Though the lobby, decorated in a grand 19th-century style, is rather petite, the guest rooms are quite large and feature Brunschwig and Fils fabrics and bed coverings, antique French furnishings, and views of the city. The lavish suites, so opulent as to be featured in *Architectural Digest,* are individually decorated with custom-made and antique furnishings. Prices are steep, as you would expect, but special offers such as the Romance Package ($240 per couple, including free champagne, sherry, and limousine service) make the Huntington worth considering for a special occasion.

Dining/Diversions: The Big Four restaurant offers expensive seasonal continental cuisine in one of the city's most handsome dining rooms. Live piano music plays nightly in the lounge.

Amenities: Concierge, room service, laundry, overnight shoeshine, evening turndown, complimentary morning newspaper, twice-daily maid service, complimentary limousine to the Financial District and Union Square, complimentary formal tea or sherry upon arrival, access to off-premises health club and spa ($15).

Mark Hopkins Intercontinental. 1 Nob Hill (at California and Mason sts.), San Francisco, CA 94108. ☎ **800/327-0200** or 415/392-3434. Fax 415/421-3302. 418 units. A/C MINIBAR TV TEL. $220–$320 double; from $450 suite. Breakfast buffet $18 extra. AE, CB, DC, DISC, MC, V. Valet parking $25. Cable car: California St. line (direct stop). Bus: 1.

Built in 1926 on the spot where railroad millionaire Mark Hopkins's turreted mansion once stood, the 19-story Mark Hopkins gained global fame during World War II when it was considered de rigueur for Pacific-bound servicemen to toast their good-bye to the States in the Top of the Mark cocktail lounge. Nowadays, the hotel caters mostly to convention-bound corporate executives who can afford the high rates. Each neoclassical room comes with all the fancy amenities you would expect from a world-class hotel, including custom furniture, plush fabrics, sumptuous bathrooms, and extraordinary views of the city. (*Tip:* The even-numbered rooms on the higher floor overlook the Golden Gate.) A minor caveat with the hotel is that it has only three guest elevators, making a quick trip up to your room difficult during busy periods.

Dining/Diversions: The plush and decidedly formal Nob Hill Restaurant offers international cuisine with a California flair nightly (as well as continental buffet breakfast each morning), while the Nob Hill Terrace, adjacent to the lobby, serves lunch, afternoon tea, cocktails, and dinner daily. The world-renowned Top of the Mark lounge serves cocktails from 4pm to 1:30am daily, Sunday brunch from 10am to 2pm, and dancing to live music Wednesday through Saturday nights.

Amenities: Concierge, room service, laundry, overnight shoe-shine, newspaper delivery, evening turndown on request, in-room massage, twice-daily maid service, baby-sitting, valet parking, courtesy limousine weekday mornings, multilingual guest relations, health club, business center, Executive Club floor, car-rental desk.

✪ **Ritz-Carlton.** 600 Stockton St. (between Pine and California sts.), San Francisco, CA 94108. ☎ **800/241-3333** or 415/296-7465. Fax 415/291-0288. 336 units. A/C MINIBAR TV TEL. $350 double; $450 club-level double; from $550 suite. Weekend discounts and packages available. Continental breakfast $15.25 extra; breakfast buffet $14 extra; Sun brunch $42. AE, CB, DC, DISC, MC, V. Parking $29. Cable car: Powell-Hyde and Powell-Mason lines (direct stop).

Ranked among the top hotels in the world by readers of *Condé Nast Traveler* (as well as the top hotel in the city), the Ritz-Carlton has been the benchmark of San Francisco's luxury hotels since it opened in 1991. A Nob Hill landmark, this former Metropolitan Insurance headquarters stood vacant for years until the Ritz-Carlton company acquired it and embarked on a massive 4-year renovation. The interior was completely gutted and restored with fine furnishings, fabrics, and artwork, including a pair of Louis XVI French, blue marble-covered urns with gilt mounts, and 19th-century Waterford candelabras. The rooms offer every possible amenity and service: Italian-marble bathrooms with double sinks, telephone, and name-brand toiletries, plush terry-cloth bathrobes, and an in-room safe. The more expensive rooms take advantage of the hotel's location—the south slope of Nob Hill—and have good views of the city. Club rooms, located on the eighth and ninth floors, have a dedicated concierge, separate elevator-key access, and complimentary meals throughout the day.

Dining/Diversions: The Ritz-Carlton Dining Room, voted among the nation's top restaurants by several magazines, serves dinner Monday to Saturday (see chapter 5, "Dining," for complete information). The Terrace Restaurant, less formal than the dining room, offers contemporary French cuisine and outdoor dining in the courtyard. The lobby lounge offers afternoon tea and cocktails and sushi daily with low-key live entertainment from 3pm to 1am. Sunday brunch is easily one of the best in town.

Amenities: Concierge, 24-hour room service, same-day laundry/dry cleaning, valet, shoe-shine, complimentary morning newspaper, child care, business center, gift boutique, an outstanding fitness center with pool.

EXPENSIVE

Nob Hill Lambourne. 725 Pine St. (between Powell and Stockton sts.), San Francisco, CA 94108. ☎ **800/274-8466** or 415/433-2287. 20 units. MINIBAR TV TEL. $180 double; $200 executive; $280 suite. Rates include continental breakfast. AE, CB, DC, DISC, MC, V. Valet parking $22. Cable car: California St. line (1 block north).

One of San Francisco's top "business-boutique" hotels, the Nob Hill Lambourne bills itself as an urban health spa, offering on-site massages, facials, body scrubs, aromatherapy, waxing, and yoga lessons to ease corporate-level stress. Even without this "hook," the Lambourne deserves a top-of-the-class rating. Sporting one of San Francisco's most stylish interiors, the hotel flaunts the comfort and quality of its contemporary French design. Top-quality, hand-sewn mattresses and goose-down comforters are complemented by a host of in-room accoutrements that include laptop computers with Internet access, fax machines, irons and ironing boards, VCRs, stereos, kitchenettes, and coffeemakers. Bathrooms contain oversized tubs and hair dryers. Suites include an additional sitting room, plus a choice of treadmill, Lifecycle, or rowing machine. Guests are invited to enjoy a complimentary wine hour starting at 6pm. Smokers should seek a room elsewhere: this place prohibits puffing.

Amenities: Evening turndown, business services, spa treatment room.

3 SoMa

VERY EXPENSIVE

Harbor Court. 165 Steuart St. (between Mission and Howard sts.), San Francisco, CA 94105. ☎ **800/346-0555** in the U.S., or 415/882-1300. Fax 415/882-1313. 131 units. A/C MINIBAR TV TEL. $195–$245 double. Continental breakfast $6.95 extra. AE, CB, DC, MC, V. Parking $19. Muni Metro: Embarcadero. Bus: 14, 32, or 80x.

When the Embarcadero Freeway was torn down after the Big One in 1989, one of the major benefactors was the Harbor Court hotel:

Accommodations Around Town

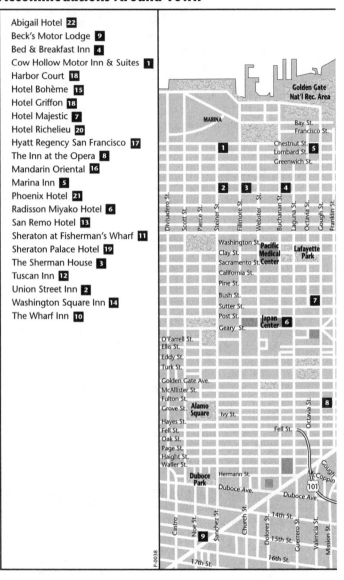

P-0038

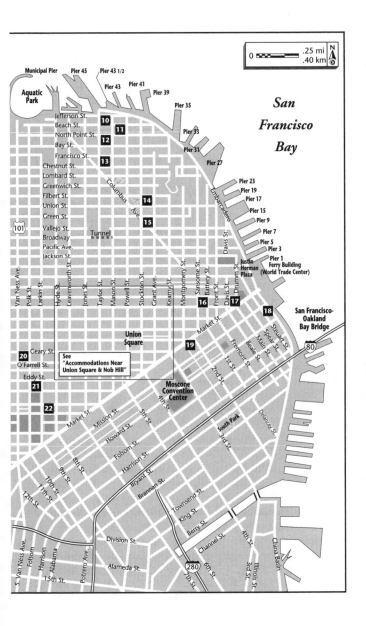

San Francisco Bay

Municipal Pier
Pier 45
Pier 43 1/2
Pier 43
Pier 41
Pier 39
Pier 35
Pier 33
Pier 31
Pier 27
Pier 23
Pier 19
Pier 17
Pier 15
Pier 9
Pier 7
Pier 5
Pier 3
Pier 1
Ferry Building (World Trade Center)

Aquatic Park

Jefferson St.
Beach St.
North Point St.
Bay St.
Francisco St.
Chestnut St.
Lombard St.
Greenwich St.
Filbert St.
Union St.
Green St.
Vallejo St.
Broadway
Pacific Ave.
Jackson St.

Columbus Ave.
Embarcadero
Davis St.
Tunnel

Justin Herman Plaza

Van Ness Ave.
Polk St.
Larkin St.
Hyde St.
Leavenworth St.
Jones St.
Taylor St.
Mason St.
Powell St.
Stockton St.
Grant Ave.
Kearny St.
Montgomery St.
Sansome St.
Battery St.
Front St.
Davis St.
Drumm St.

San Francisco–Oakland Bay Bridge

Union Square

See "Accommodations Near Union Square & Nob Hill"

Market St.

Steuart St.
Spear St.
Main St.
Beale St.
Fremont St.
1st St.

80

Geary St.
O'Farrell St.
Eddy St.

Moscone Convention Center

2nd St.

South Park

Market St.
Mission St.
Howard St.
Folsom St.
Harrison St.
Bryant St.
Brannan St.

3rd St.

Delancey St.

5th St.
4th St.

10th St.
9th St.
8th St.
7th St.
6th St.
12th St.
11th St.

Townsend St.
King St.
Berry St.

Channel St.

280

4th St.
3rd St.
Illinois St.

China Basin

S. Van Ness Ave.
Folsom
Harrison
Alabama
Potrero Ave.

Division St.
Alameda St.
15th St.

101

0   .25 mi
0   .40 km

N

10
11
12
13
14
15
16
17
18
19
20
21
22

Its backyard view went from a wall of cement to a dazzling view of the Bay Bridge (be sure to request a bay-view room, which is $50 extra). Located just off the Embarcadero at the edge of the Financial District, this former YMCA books a lot of corporate travelers, but anyone who prefers stylish, high-quality accommodations—half-canopy beds, large armoires, writing desks, soundproof windows—with a superb view and lively scene will be perfectly content here. A major bonus for health nuts is the free use of the adjoining top-quality fitness club (the Embarcadero YMCA) with indoor, Olympic-size swimming pool.

Dining/Diversions: In the evening the hotel's dark, velvety restaurant, Harry Denton's, transforms into the Financial District's hot spot for hungry singles.

Amenities: Concierge, limited room service, dry cleaning, laundry, secretarial services, excellent fitness club, valet, courtesy car, free refreshments in lobby.

Hotel Griffon. 155 Steuart St. (between Mission and Howard sts.), San Francisco, CA 94105. ☎ **800/321-2201** or 415/495-2100. Fax 415/495-3522. 65 units. A/C MINIBAR TV TEL. $215–$260 double; $315 penthouse suite. Rates include continental breakfast and newspaper. AE, CB, DC, DISC, MC, V. Parking $15. All Market St. buses, BART, and ferries.

After dumping a cool $10 million on a complete rehab in 1989, the Hotel Griffon emerged as a top contender among San Francisco's small hotels. Ideally situated on San Francisco's historic waterfront and only steps from the heart of the Financial District, the Griffon is impeccably outfitted with contemporary features such as whitewashed brick walls, lofty ceilings, marble vanities, window seats, cherry-wood furniture, and art-deco-style lamps (really, this place is smooth). Be sure to request a Bay view room overlooking the Bay Bridge—the added perks and view make it well worth the extra $40—and inquire about the excellent weekend packages the hotel occasionally offers.

Dining/Diversions: Rôti, which has evolved into a prime lunch spot for the nearby Financial District, occupies one side of the lobby, offering California-style food prepared on spit roasts and woodburning ovens, and served from an open kitchen. The dining room and mezzanine contain rich wood accents and a view of the San Francisco Bay and Bay Bridge.

Amenities: Concierge, limited room service, laundry/valet, in-room massage, baby-sitting, secretarial services, free access to nearby deluxe health center.

4 Financial District

VERY EXPENSIVE

Hyatt Regency San Francisco. 5 Embarcadero Center, San Francisco, CA 94111. ☎ **800/233-1234** or 415/788-1234. Fax 415/398-2567. 850 units. A/C TV TEL. $199–$300 double; $349–$450 suite. Continental breakfast $7.95 extra. AE, CB, DC, DISC, MC, V. Valet parking $25. Muni Metro: All Market St. trams. All Market St. buses.

The Hyatt Regency, a convention favorite, rises from the edge of the Embarcadero Center at the foot of Market Street. The structure, with a 1970s, gray-concrete, bunkerlike facade, is shaped like a vertical triangle, serrated with long rows of jutting balconies. The 17-story atrium lobby, illuminated by museum-quality theater lighting, features flowing water and a simulated environment of California grasslands and wildflowers. The hotel was totally renovated in 1993.

Rooms are comfortably furnished. Each also has a hair dryer, voice mail, telephone and VCR; computer ports for modems are available upon request. Rooms for "Gold Passport" members have tea- and coffee-making facilities, and private fax machines are available free upon request. Rooms with two double beds also include a sofa or easy chair. The hotel's 16th and 17th floors house the Regency Club, with 102 larger guest rooms, complimentary continental breakfast, and after-dinner cordials.

Dining/Diversions: The Eclipse Café serves three meals daily; the Thirteen-Views Bar seats about 200 and is open for morning coffee and evening cocktails. The Equinox, which underwent a $500,000 renovation in 1997, is a revolving rooftop restaurant and bar offering 360° city views.

Amenities: Concierge, 24-hour room service, laundry, overnight shoe-shine, newspaper delivery, twice-daily maid service, express checkout, valet parking. Access to off-premises health club, swimming pool, tennis courts, business center, conference room, Avis car-rental desk.

✪ Mandarin Oriental. 222 Sansome St. (between Pine and California sts.), San Francisco, CA 94104. ☎ **800/622-0404** or 415/276-9888. Fax 415/433-0289. 158 units. A/C MINIBAR TV TEL. $325–$415 double; from $475–$520 junior suite. Continental breakfast $18 extra. AE, DC, JCB, MC, V. Parking $25. Muni Metro: Montgomery. All Market St. buses.

We love this hotel because all the rooms are located between the 38th and 48th floors of a downtown high-rise, which allows each of the large accommodations extraordinary panoramic views of the bay and city. Not all rooms have tub-side views, but they do have luxurious marble bathrooms, each stocked with a natural loofah, a large selection of English toiletries, terry- and cotton cloth robes, hair dryer, makeup mirror, and silk slippers. The rooms are less opulent, with a kind of reserved-contemporary decor of light colors, Asian accents, and handsome furnishings, which include a spacious desk and sitting area. Since high rates make this mostly a business hotel, additional amenities include three two-line phones with fax hook-ups, as well as TVs with on-command video access to more than 80 movies.

Dining/Diversions: Silks is a serene dining room that has won rave reviews melding California and Asian ingredients.

Amenities: Concierge; 24-hour room service; laundry/valet; com-plimentary newspaper and shoe-shine; brand-new fitness center with cardio, Nautilus, and free weights; business center.

✪ **Sheraton Palace Hotel.** 2 New Montgomery St. (at Market St.), San Fran-cisco, CA 94105. ☎ **800/325-3535** or 415/392-8600. Fax 415/543-0671. 550 units. A/C MINIBAR TV TEL. $300–$390 double; from $550 suite. Additional person $20. Children under 18 sharing existing bedding stay free in parents' room. Weekend rates and packages available. Continental breakfast $13.50 extra; deluxe continental $15.75 extra. AE, DC, DISC, JCB, MC, V. Parking $22. Muni Metro: All Market St. trams. All Market St. buses.

The original 1875 Palace was one of the world's largest and most luxurious hotels, and every time you walk through the doors, you'll be reminded how incredibly majestic old luxury really is. The hotel was rebuilt after the 1906 quake and renovated in 1991, but the most spectacular attribute here is still the old regal lobby and the Garden Court, a San Francisco landmark that has been restored to its original 1909 grandeur. The court is flanked by a double row of massive Italian-marble Ionic columns, and dangles 10 huge chandeliers. The real heart-stopper, however, is the 80,000-pane stained-glass ceiling. Regrettably, the rooms have that standardized, chain-hotel appearance. The on-site, fourth-floor health club features a skylight-covered lap pool, whirlpool, sauna, and exercise room.

Dining/Diversions: On special holidays the Garden Court serves a $55 brunch worth indulging in, while a scaled-down version takes place on other weekends. Maxfields's Restaurant, a traditional San Francisco grill, has turn-of-the-century charm and is open daily for lunch and dinner. Kyo-ya is an authentic Japanese restaurant with a separate street entrance. The Pied Piper Bar is named after the $2.5-million Maxfield Parrish mural that dominates the room.

Amenities: Concierge, 24-hour room service, laundry/valet, evening turndown, health club, business service center, lobby-level shops.

5 North Beach/Fisherman's Wharf

EXPENSIVE

The Sheraton at Fisherman's Wharf. 2500 Mason St. (between Beach and North Point sts.), San Francisco, CA 94133. ☎ **800/325-3535** or 415/362-5500. Fax 415/956-5275. 524 units. A/C TV TEL. $150–$280 double; from $400 suite. Extra person $20. Continental breakfast $7.95 extra. AE, CB, DC, DISC, MC, V. Parking $14. Cable car: Powell-Mason line (1 block east, 2 blocks south). Bus: 15, 32, or 42.

Built in the mid-1970s, this modern, three-story hotel isn't the most visually appealing of hotels (even their brochure doesn't show it from the outside), but it offers the reliable comforts of a Sheraton within San Francisco's most popular tourist area. In 1995 the hotel spent $4 million renovating the rooms and adding a Corporate Floor catering exclusively to business travelers.

Dining/Diversions: Chanen's is a Victorian-style cafe serving breakfast, lunch, and dinner. Live jazz is played several nights a week along with cocktails and assorted appetizers.

Amenities: Concierge, room service, evening turndown, outdoor heated swimming pool, access to nearby health club, business center, hair salon, car-rental desk, travel desk.

Tuscan Inn. 425 North Point St. (at Mason St.), San Francisco, CA 94133. ☎ **800/648-4626** or 415/561-1100. Fax 415/561-1199. 221 units. A/C MINIBAR TV TEL. $135–$188 double; $198–$258 suite. Rates include coffee, tea, and evening fireside wine reception. AE, DC, DISC, MC, V. Parking $17. Cable car: Powell-Mason line. Bus: 42, 15, 32.

The Tuscan Inn is, in our opinion, the best hotel at Fisherman's Wharf. Like an island of respectability in a sea of touristy schlock, the Tuscan exudes a level of style and comfort far beyond its neighboring competitors. Splurge on parking—cheaper than the wharf's outrageously priced garages—then saunter your way toward the plush lobby warmed by a grand fireplace. Even the rooms, each equipped with writing desks and armchairs, are a definite cut above competing Fisherman's Wharf hotels. The only caveat is the lack of scenic views; a small price to pay for a good hotel in a great location.

Dining/Diversions: The adjoining Cafe Pescatore, open for breakfast, lunch, and dinner, serves standard Italian fare in an airy, partial alfresco setting. (See chapter 5, "Dining," for complete information).

Amenities: Concierge, room service, laundry service

MODERATE

✪ **Hotel Bohème.** 444 Columbus St. (between Vallejo and Green sts.), San Francisco, CA 94133. ☎ **415/433-9111.** Fax 415/362-6292. 15 units. TV TEL. $125 double. AE, CB, DISC, DC, JCB, MC, V. Parking $23 at nearby public garage. Cable car: Powell-Mason line. Bus: 12, 15, 30, 41, 45, or 83.

North Beach romance awaits you at the Bohème. Although located on the busiest strip in North Beach, this recently renovated hotel's style and demeanor are more reminiscent of a prestigious home in upscale Nob Hill. The decor reminisces the beat generation, which flourished here in the 1950s; rooms are small but hopelessly romantic, with gauze-draped canopies and walls artistically accented with lavender, sage green, black, and pumpkin. The staff is ultra-hospitable, and bonuses include hair dryers and complimentary sherry in the lobby each afternoon. Outside the front door, it's a few steps to some of the greatest cafes, restaurants, bars, and shops in the city, and Chinatown and Union Square are within walking distance. *Take note:* While the bathrooms are sweet, they're also absolutely tiny. *Tip:* Request a room off the street side; they're quieter.

The Wharf Inn. 2601 Mason St. (at Beach St.), San Francisco, CA 94133. ☎ **800/548-9918** or 415/673-7411. Fax 415/776-2181. 51 units. TV TEL. $98–$158 double; penthouse $250–$350. AE, CB, DC, DISC, MC, V. Free parking. Cable car: Powell-Mason. Bus: 15, 32, or 42.

Our top choice for budget lodging at Fisherman's Wharf, The Wharf Inn offers above-average accommodations amidst one of the most popular tourist attractions in the world. The newly refurbished rooms, done in handsome tones of forest green, burgundy, and pale yellow, come with all the standard amenities, including complimentary coffee and tea. Its main attribute, however, is its location—right smack-dab in the middle of the wharf, 2 blocks away from Pier 39 and the cable-car turnaround, and within walking distance of the Embarcadero and North Beach. The inn is ideal for car-bound families because parking is free (there's $25-a-day saved) and there's no charge for packing along an extra person.

Washington Square Inn. 1660 Stockton St. (between Filbert and Union sts.), San Francisco, CA 94133. ☎ **800/388-0220** or 415/981-4220. Fax 415/397-7242. 15 units, 2 with bathroom across from the room. TV TEL. $125–$195 double. Rates include continental breakfast. AE, DISC, MC, V. Valet parking $20. Bus: 15, 30, 41, or 45.

Reminiscent of a traditional English inn right down to the cucumber sandwiches served during afternoon tea, this small, comely bed-and-breakfast is ideal for older couples who prefer a more quiet, subdued environment than the commotion of downtown San Francisco. It's located across from Washington Square in the North Beach District—a coffee-craver's haven—and within walking distance of Fisherman's Wharf and Chinatown. Each room is decorated in English floral fabrics with quality European antique furnishings and plenty of fresh flowers; all have private bathrooms. A continental breakfast is included, as are afternoon tea, wine, and hors d'oeuvres. Fax and VCRs are available upon request.

INEXPENSIVE

✪ **San Remo Hotel.** 2237 Mason St. (at Chestnut St.), San Francisco, CA 94133. ☎ **800/352-REMO** or 415/776-8688. Fax 415/776-2811. E-mail: info@sanremohotel.com. 63 units, 1 with bathroom. $60–$70 double; $125 suite. AE, DC, JCB, MC, V. Parking $8–$12. Cable car: Powell-Mason line. Bus: 15, 22, 30 or 42.

This small, European-style pensione is one of the best budget hotels in San Francisco. Located in a quiet North Beach neighborhood and within walking distance of Fisherman's Wharf, the San Remo originally served as a boardinghouse for dockworkers displaced by the great fire of 1906. As a result, the rooms are small and bathrooms are shared, but all is forgiven when it comes time to pay the bill. Rooms are decorated in a cozy country style with brass and iron beds, oak, maple, or pine armoires, and wicker furnishings; most have ceiling fans. The shared bathrooms, each one immaculately clean, feature claw-foot tubs and brass pull-chain toilets with oak tanks and brass fixtures. If the penthouse is available, book it: you won't find a more romantic place to stay in San Francisco for so little money.

6 Pacific Heights/Cow Hollow

VERY EXPENSIVE

✪ **Sherman House.** 2160 Green St. (between Webster and Fillmore sts.), San Francisco, CA 94123. ☎ **800/424-5777** or 415/563-3600. Fax 415/563-1882. 14 units. TV TEL. $310–$395 double; from $650 suite. Continental breakfast $15 extra. AE, CB, DC, MC, V. Valet parking $16. Cable car: Powell-Hyde line. Bus: 22, 41, or 45.

How expensive is a night at the Sherman House? Put it this way: If you have to ask, you can't afford it. Built in 1876 by philanthropist/music publisher Leander Sherman, this magnificent Pacific Heights

Victorian doubled as his home and playhouse for such guest stars as Enrico Caruso, Lillian Russell, and Victor Herbert. After years of neglect, it took 4 years and a small fortune to restore the estate to its original splendor. Today the Sherman House sets the standard in San Francisco for privacy, personal service, and sumptuous furnishings. All rooms are individually decorated with authentic antiques in French Second Empire, Biedermeier, or English Jacobean style and contain queen-size canopy featherbeds along with ultrarich tapestry fabrics and down comforters; all except one have fireplaces. Rooms also feature TVs, VCRs, and stereos, and black granite bathrooms complete with bathrobes and whirlpool bathtubs. The English-style Hyde Park room offers a fine bay view from its cushioned window seat. The Jacobean-style Paderewski suite was formerly the billiards room, and it retains the dark wainscoting and beamed ceiling. The least expensive room (no. 203) is a twin furnished with English antiques, but it lacks a fireplace. The most expensive suite is the Thomas Church Garden suite, which consists of two rooms with 1 1/2 bathrooms, with an adjoining sunken garden terrace with gazebo and pond.

Dining/Diversions: The dining room has a very fine reputation, but because of a zoning dispute, it has lost its license to serve food to nonguests and is now open only to residents; this change may affect the standards. Currently, a fixed-price menu, without wine, is available for $75, main courses from the à la carte items run from about $29 to $35. Although prices are steep, the meal is quite elaborate.

Amenities: Concierge, room service, butler (who will discreetly unpack luggage), dry cleaning/laundry, complimentary newspaper delivery, massage, twice-daily maid service, baby-sitting, secretarial services, personalized shopping, private chauffeuring.

EXPENSIVE

✪ **Union Street Inn.** 2229 Union St. (between Fillmore and Steiner sts.), San Francisco, CA 94123. ☎ **415/346-0424.** Fax 415/922-8046. http://www.unionstreetinn.com. 5 units, 1 cottage. TV TEL. $135–$195 standard double; $245 cottage. Rates include breakfast, hors d'oeuvres, and evening beverages. AE, MC, V. Parking $15. Bus: 22, 41, 45, or 47.

Who would have guessed that one of the most delightful B&Bs in California would be in San Francisco? This two-story Edwardian may front the perpetually busy (and trendy) Union Street, but it's quiet as a church on the inside. All individually decorated rooms are comfortably furnished, and most come with canopied or brass beds with down comforters, fresh flowers, bay windows (beg for one with a view of the garden), and private bathrooms (a few even have Jacuzzi tubs). An extended continental breakfast is served either in the parlor, in your room, or on an outdoor terrace overlooking a lovely English garden. The ultimate honeymoon retreat is the private carriage house behind the inn, but any room at this warm, friendly inn is guaranteed to please.

MODERATE

✪ **Bed & Breakfast Inn.** 4 Charlton Court (off Union St., between Buchanan and Laguna sts.), San Francisco, CA 94123. ☎ **415/921-9784.** Fax 415/921-0544. 13 units, 4 with shared bathroom. $70–$90 double without bathroom, $115–$140 double with bathroom; $190–$275 suite. Rates include continental breakfast. No credit cards. Parking $10 a day at nearby garage. Bus: 41 or 45.

San Francisco's first bed-and-breakfast is composed of a trio of Victorian houses all gussied up in English-country style, hidden in a culde-sac just off Union Street. While it doesn't have quite the casual ambiance of neighboring Union Street Inn, the Bed & Breakfast Inn is loaded with charm. Each room is uniquely decorated with family antiques, original art, and a profusion of fresh flowers. The Garden Suite—highly recommended for families or groups of four—comes with a fully stocked kitchen, a living room with fireplace, two bedrooms, two bathrooms (one with a Jacuzzi tub), a study, and French doors leading out into the garden. Breakfast (freshly baked croissants; fresh fruit; orange juice; and coffee, tea, or cocoa) is either brought to your room on a tray with flowers and a morning newspaper, or served in a sunny Victorian breakfast room with antique china.

INEXPENSIVE

Cow Hollow Motor Inn & Suites. 2190 Lombard St. (between Steiner and Fillmore sts.), San Francisco, CA 94123. ☎ **415/921-5800.** Fax 415/922-8515. 130 units. A/C TV TEL. $82 double, $8 extra per person; from $185 suite, $10 extra person. AE, DC, MC, V. Free parking. Bus: 28, 43, or 76.

If you're less interested in being downtown and more into playing in and around the beautiful bay-front marina, check out this modest brick hotel smack in the middle of busy Lombard Street. There's no fancy theme here, but each room comes loaded with such amenities as cable TV, free local phone calls, free covered parking, and in-room coffeemakers. All the rooms were renovated in 1996, so you'll be sure to sleep on a nice firm mattress surrounded by clean, new carpeting and drapes. Families will appreciate the Cow Hollow Motor Inn's one- and two-bedroom suites, which have full kitchens and dining areas.

⭘ **Marina Inn.** 3110 Octavia St. (at Lombard St.), San Francisco, CA 94123. ☎ **800/274-1420** or 415/928-1000. Fax 415/928-5909. 40 units. TV TEL. Nov 1–Feb 29 $55–$95 double; Mar 1–May 31 $65–$105 double; June 1–Oct 31 $75–$115 double. Rates include continental breakfast, afternoon sherry, and turndown service. AE, MC, V. Bus: 28, 43, 76.

The Marina Inn is, without question, the best low-priced hotel in San Francisco. How they offer so much for so little is mystifying. Each guest room within this 1924 four-story Victorian looks as if it has been culled from a Country Furnishings catalog, complete with rustic pine-wood furnishings, a four-poster bed with silk-soft comforter, pretty wallpaper, and soothing tones of rose, hunter green, and pale yellow. There's even high-class touches that many of the city's expensive hotels don't include, such as new remote-control televisions discreetly hidden in pine cabinetry, full bathtubs with showers, and nightly turndown service with chocolates on your pillow—all for as little as *$65 a night* ($55 in the winter). Combine that with complimentary continental breakfast, afternoon sherry, friendly service, and an armada of shops and restaurants within easy walking distance, and there you have it: Our number 1 choice for Best Overall Value.

7 Japantown & Environs

EXPENSIVE

⭘ **Hotel Majestic.** 1500 Sutter St. (between Octavia and Gough sts.), San Francisco, CA 94109. ☎ **800/869-8966** or 415/441-1100. Fax 415/673-7331. 60 units. TV TEL. $135–$195 double; from $315 suite. Group, government, corporate, and relocation rates available. Continental breakfast $8.50 extra. AE, CB, DC, DISC, MC, V. Valet parking $18.

Both tourists and business travelers adore the Majestic because it covers every professional need while retaining the ambiance of a luxurious old-world hotel. It was built in 1902 and thankfully retains its original integrity—the lobby alone will sweep guests into another era with an overabundance of tapestries, tasseled brocades, Corinthian columns, and intricate, lavish detail.

Rooms are furnished with French and English antiques, the centerpiece of each being a large four-poster canopy bed; you'll also find custom-made, mirrored armoires and antique reproductions. All drapes, fabrics, carpet, and bedspreads were replaced in 1997, which ensures you'll rest not only in style, but in freshness as well. Conveniences include a full-size, well-lit desk and clock-radio; extra bathroom amenities include bathrobes. Some rooms also have fireplaces.

Dining/Diversions: Café Majestic and Bar serves California/Asian fare in a romantic setting and continues to intrigue a local clientele. Cocktails are offered in the adjacent bar complete with French mahogany marble-topped bar and a collection of African butterflies.

Amenities: Concierge, room service, valet, dry cleaning, laundry service, complimentary newspaper, in-room massage, baby-sitting, secretarial service, courtesy car on weekdays, and afternoon sherry and fresh-baked cookies from 6 to 8pm nightly.

Radisson Miyako Hotel. 1625 Post St. (at Laguna St.), San Francisco, CA 94115. ☎ **800/533-4567** or 415/922-3200. Fax 415/921-0417. 218 units. A/C MINIBAR TV TEL. $199–$209 double or twin; from $299 suite. Children 12 and under stay free in parents' room. Continental breakfast $7.50 extra; breakfast buffet $12.50 extra. AE, CB, DC, DISC, MC, V. Valet parking $15; self-parking $10. Bus: 2, 3, 4, or 38.

Japantown's Miyako is a tranquil alternative to staying downtown (and it's only about a mile away). The 15-story tower and five-story Garden Wing overlook the Japan Center, which is home to the city's largest complex of Japanese shops, restaurants, and a huge movie complex, but the hotel manages to maintain a feeling of peace and quiet you'd expect somewhere much more remote. Rooms are Zen-like with East-meets-West decor plus such amenities as an iron and ironing board and hair dryer; the Western-style (don't think cowboy) rooms are fine, but romantics and adventurers should opt for the traditional-style Japanese rooms with tatami mats and futons, *yukatas* (cotton robes), a *tokonoma* (alcove for displaying art), and Shoji screens that slide away to frame views of the city. Two futon luxury suites have Japanese rock gardens and deep-tub Japanese bathrooms. Added bonus: Fillmore Street's upscale boutiques are a few blocks away.

Dining/Diversions: YOYO Bistro, the hotel's restaurant, offers fantastic food, including "Tsumami," Japanese-style cocktail food, in an intimate dining area. See chapter 5, "Dining," for complete details.

Amenities: Limited concierge and room service, dry cleaning, newspaper delivery, evening turndown, in-room shiatsu massage, on-call baby-sitting, express checkout, valet parking, limited exercise room and access to nearby health club, business center, conference rooms, gift shop, car-rental desk.

8 Civic Center

EXPENSIVE

✪ **The Inn at the Opera.** 333 Fulton St. (at Franklin St.), San Francisco, CA 94102. ☎ **800/325-2708** or 415/863-8400. Fax 415/861-0821. 48 units.

MINIBAR TV TEL. $165–$190 double; from $235 suite. Extra person $15. Rates
include European buffet breakfast. AE, DC, MC, V. Parking $19. Bus: 5, 21, 47,
or 49.

From the minute you walk in through the mullioned front door to
a lobby decorated with silk and damask, upholstered antique chairs,
hand-painted French screen, and loads of marble, you know you're
about to be spoiled with sumptuousness. But don't take our word
for it; Luciano Pavarotti, Placido Domingo, Mikhail Baryshnikov,
and dozens of other stars of the stage throw their slumber parties
here regularly, requisitioning the inn's luxurious restaurant and
lounge, Ovation at the Opera, along with a floor or two of rooms.
Queen-size beds with huge stuffed pillows are standard in each
pastel-hued guest room, along with elegant furnishings, minibars,
microwave ovens, refrigerators, and bouquets of fresh flowers. Suite
bathrooms include hair dryers, scales, terry-cloth robes, and French
milled soaps. The larger rooms and suites are especially recommended for those who need elbow room; typical of small hotels, the
least expensive "standard" rooms are short on space.

Dining/Diversions: Ovation at the Opera, the hotel's fine-
dining room, provides an intimate setting for dinner, while the adjacent lounge with its leather chairs, glowing fire, and soft piano
music is a favorite city meeting place.

Amenities: Concierge, 24-hour room service, laundry/valet, complimentary light pressing and overnight shoe-shine, morning newspaper, evening turndown, staff physician, complimentary limousine
service to the Financial District, business center.

MODERATE

Hotel Richelieu. 1050 Van Ness (at Geary Blvd.), San Francisco, CA 94109.
☎ **800/295-RICH** or 415/673-4711. Fax 415/673-9362. 168 units. MINIBAR
(nonalcoholic) TV TEL. Nov–Mar $109–$119 double; Apr–Oct $129 double.
Suites $139–$189. AE, DC, DISC, MC, V. AAA and other discounts available.
Parking $13. Bus: 2, 3, 4, 38, 42, 47, 49, 76.

Considering all the extras, this place offers one heck of a bargain. At
one time, the Richelieu must have been a high-end contender: the
1908 building has a grand, welcoming lobby and was built with
enough rooms to house a small army. But in modern times its
location on Van Ness, the city's street-level Highway 101 thoroughfare, has made it a less desirable spot. Nonetheless, the Richelieu has
all kinds of things going for it. For starters, with all the discounts
they offer, most guests pay far below $100 per night. Further, the
rooms—which are all different—can be quite large and have decent
dark-wood furnishings; colorful, newish textiles; in-room safes; irons

and ironing boards (in most rooms); spotless bathrooms; and hair dryers. An added bonus is the new adjoining restaurant—one of our favorite late-night burger joints, wonderfully greasy Mel's Diner. Renovations of the already suitable rooms were completed in spring '98, which means the rooms are even more spiffy and the new lobby, where complimentary coffee and afternoon cookies are served, is looking especially dapper. Its location, 2 blocks from the California Street cable car and near the Opera House, is safer. One bummer: local calls are 60¢ even if your party doesn't answer the phone. *Tip:* Noisier rooms are facing Van Ness. Request something facing the courtyard for a quieter room.

✪ **Phoenix Hotel.** 601 Eddy St. (at Larkin St.), San Francisco, CA 94109. ☎ **800/248-9466** or 415/776-1380. Fax 415/885-3109. 44 units. TV TEL. $99–$119 double; $149 suite. Rates include continental breakfast. AE, DC, MC, V. Free parking. Bus: 19, 31, or 38.

Situated on the fringes of San Francisco's less-than-pleasant Tenderloin District, this retro 1950s-style hotel has been described by *People* as the hippest hotel in town, a gathering place for visiting rock musicians, writers, and filmmakers who crave a dose of southern California—hence the palm trees and pastel colors—on their trips to San Francisco. The focal point of the Palm Springs–style hotel is a small, heated outdoor pool adorned with a paisley mural by artist Francis Forlenza and ensconced by a modern-sculpture garden.

The rooms, while far from plush, were upgraded in 1998 are comfortably equipped with bamboo furnishings, potted plants, and original local art. In addition to the usual amenities, the inn offers VCRs and movies upon request. Services include an on-site massage therapist, concierge, laundry/valet, and—whoo hoo!—free parking. Adjoining the hotel is Backflip (formerly Miss Pearl's Jam House), a superhip and oh-so-blue cocktail lounge serving tapas and Caribbean-style appetizers and a heck of a lot of San Francisco attitude.

INEXPENSIVE

Abigail Hotel. 246 McAllister St. (between Hyde and Larkin sts.), San Francisco, CA 94102. ☎ **800/243-6510** or 415/861-9728. Fax 415/861-5848. 60 units. TV TEL. $79 double standard; $89 deluxe; $149 suite. Extra person $10. Rates include continental breakfast. AE, CB, DC, MC, V. Parking $12.50. Muni Metro: All Market St. trams. All Market St. buses.

The Abigail is one of San Francisco's rare sleeper hotels: Though it doesn't get much press, this is one of the better medium-priced hotels in the city. Built in 1925 to house celebrities performing at the world-renowned Fox Theater, what the Abigail lacks in luxury is more than made up in charm. The rooms, while on the small side, are clean, cute, and comfortably furnished with cozy antiques and down comforters. Morning coffee, pastries, and complimentary newspapers greet you in the beautiful faux-marble lobby designed by Shawn Hall, while dinner is served downstairs in the "organic" restaurant, Millennium. Access to a nearby health club ($10) and laundry and massage services are available upon request.

9   The Castro

Though everyone is welcome, most hotels in the Castro cater to a gay and lesbian clientele. Unfortunately, there are few choices, and their amenities don't really compare to most of the better hotels in the city. However, if you'd like to stay in the heart of the Castro, the following is an option.

INEXPENSIVE

Beck's Motor Lodge. 2222 Market St. (at 15th St.), San Francisco, CA 94114. ☎ **800/227**-4360 in the U.S., except Calif.; 415/621-8212 (if in Calif., call collect to make reservations). Fax 415/241-0435. 57 units. TV TEL. $75–$125. Rates include parking. AE, CB, DC, DISC, MC, V. Bus: 8, 37; Muni Metro: F.

In a town where D.I.N.K. (double income, no kids) tourists happily spend fistfuls of money, you'd think someone would create a gay luxury hotel—or even a moderate hotel for that matter. But absurdly, the most commercial and modern accommodation in the ever-touristy Castro district is this run-of-the-mill motel. Standard, but contemporary, the ultratidy rooms include coffeemakers, refrigerators, free HBO, and access to coin-operated washing machines, a sundeck overlooking upper–Market Street, and free parking. Unless you're into the homey B&Bs, this is really your only choice in the area—fortunately, it's very well maintained.

5

Dining

*R*estaurants are to San Franciscans as bagels are to New Yorkers: indispensable. At last count, city residents had more than 3,300 reasons to avoid cooking at home, and actually spent more money on dining out than those of any other city in the nation.

As one of the world's cultural crossroads, San Francisco is blessed with a cornucopia of cuisines. Afghan, Cajun, Burmese, Jewish, Moroccan, Persian, Cambodian, Vegan—whatever you're in the mood for tonight, this town has got it covered. All you need is money, reservations, and an adventurous palate, because half the fun of visiting San Francisco is the rare opportunity to sample the flavors of the world in one fell swoop.

While dining in San Francisco is almost always a hassle-free experience, there are a few things you should keep in mind your next time out:

- If you want a table at the expensive restaurants with the best reputations, you will probably need to book six to eight weeks ahead for weekends and several weeks ahead for a table during the week.
- If there's a long wait for a free table, ask if you can order at the bar, which is often faster and more fun.
- Don't leave *anything* valuable in your car while dining (particularly in or near high-crime areas), and only give the valet the key to your car, *not* your hotel room or house key.
- *Remember:* It is against the law to smoke in any restaurant in San Francisco, even if it has a separate bar or lounge area. You're welcome to smoke outside, however.

The restaurants below are divided first by area, then by price, using the following guide: **expensive,** more than $45 per person; **moderate,** $25 to $45 per person; **inexpensive,** less than $25 per person. These categories reflect the price of the majority of dinner menu items and include an appetizer, main course, coffee, dessert, tax, and tip.

1 Restaurants by Cuisine

AMERICAN

Beach Chalet Brewery &
Restaurant (Richmond/
Sunset Districts, *M*)
Bix (North Beach, *E*)
Boulevard (SoMa, *E*)
Doidge's (Pacific Heights/
Cow Hollow, *I*)
Fog City Diner (North Beach/
Telegraph Hill, *M*)
Hamburger Mary's (SoMa, *I*)
Hard Rock Café (Nob Hill/
Russian Hill, *M*)
Harris' (Pacific Heights/Cow
Hollow, *E*)
Mel's Diner (Pacific Heights/
Cow Hollow, *I*)
Postrio (Union Square, *E*)
Sears Fine Foods (Union
Square, *I*)

ASIAN/FRENCH

YOYO Bistro (Japan Center
& Environs, *M*)

CALIFORNIA

Bix (North Beach, *E*)
Café Flore (Castro, *I*)
Cliff House (Richmond/
Sunset Districts, *M*)
Farallon (Union Square, *E*)
Hawthorne Lane (SoMa, *E*)
Moose's (North Beach, *E*)
One Market (Financial
District, *E*)
Rumpus (Union Square, *M*)
2223 (Castro, *M*)

CALIFORNIA/FRENCH

Grand Cafe (Union Square, *M*)

Jardinière (Civic Center, *E*)
Ritz-Carlton Dining Room
(Nob Hill, *E*)

CAJUN/CREOLE

The Elite Café (Pacific
Heights/Cow Hollow, *M*)

CALIFORNIA/FRENCH/
MEDITERRANEAN

PlumpJack Café
(Pacific Heights/
Cow Hollow, *M*)

CARIBBEAN

Cha Cha Cha (Haight-
Ashbury, *M*)

CHINESE

Brandy Ho's Hunan Food
(Chinatown, *M*)
Harbor Village (Financial
District, *E*)
House of Nanking
(Chinatown, *I*)
Tommy Toy's (Financial
District, *E*)

CHINESE/DIM SUM

Hong Kong Flower Lounge
(Richmond/Sunset
Districts, *M*)
Ton Kiang (Richmond/
Sunset Districts, *M*)
Yank Sing (Financial District,
M)

CONTINENTAL

Carnelian Room (Financial
District, *E*)
Lulu (SoMa, *M*)

Abbreviations Key: *E*=Expensive, *M*=Moderate, *I*=Inexpensive

CREPES

Ti Couz (Mission District, *I*)

EAST-WEST FUSION

Eos (Haight-Ashbury, *M*)

FRENCH

Charles Nob Hill (Nob Hill, *E*)

Fringale Restaurant (SoMa, *M*)

La Folie (Pacific Heights/Cow Hollow, *E*)

Masa's (Union Square, *E*)

South Park Café (SoMa, *I*)

FRENCH/ITALIAN

Bizou (SoMa, *M*)

INDIAN

North India Restaurant (Pacific Heights/Cow Hollow, *M*)

ITALIAN

A. Sabella's (Fisherman's Wharf, *E*)

Cafe Pescatore (Fisherman's Wharf, *M*)

Caffè Sport (North Beach, *E*)

Il Fornaio (North Beach/Telegraph Hill, *M*)

Kuleto's (Union Square, *M*)

L'Osteria del Forno (North Beach, *I*)

Mario's Bohemian Cigar Store (Mission District, *M*)

Pauline's (Mission District, *M*)

Pane e Vino (Pacific Heights/Cow Hollow, *M*)

Rose Pistola (North Beach, *M*)

Splendido (Financial District, *M*)

Stinking Rose (North Beach, *M*)

Zinzino (Pacific Heights/Cow Hollow, *M*)

JAPANESE

Ace Wasabi's (Pacific Heights/Cow Hollow, *M*)

Sanppo (Japan Center & Environs, *I*)

MEDITERRANEAN

Bruno's (Mission District, *M*)

Enrico's (North Beach, *M*)

Firewood Café (The Castro, *I*)

Mecca (Castro, *M*)

Moose's (North Beach, *E*)

Zuni Café (Civic Center, *M*)

MEXICAN

La Canasta (Pacific Heights/Cow Hollow, *I*)

Taquerias La Cumbre (Mission District, *I*)

Zona Rosa (Haight-Ashbury, *I*)

SEAFOOD

A. Sabella's (Fisherman's Wharf, *E*)

Aqua (Financial District, *E*)

Cliff House (Richmond/Sunset Districts, *M*)

Farallon (Union Square, *E*)

Swan Oyster Depot (Nob Hill/Russian Hill, *I*)

Tadich Grill (Financial District, *M*)

SOUTHEAST ASIAN

Betelnut (Pacific Heights/
Cow Hollow, *M*)

SPANISH

Thirsty Bear Brewing Com-
pany (SoMa, *M*)

SUSHI

Ace Wasabi's (Pacific
Heights/Cow Hollow, *M*)

THAI

Khan Toke Thai House
(Richmond/Sunset
Districts, *M*)

Manora's (SoMa,
I)
Thep Phanom (Haight-
Ashbury, *M*)

VEGETARIAN

Greens Restaurant, Fort
Mason (Pacific Heights/
Cow Hollow, *M*)

VIETNAMESE

The Slanted Door (Mission
District, *M*)

2 Union Square

EXPENSIVE

✪ **Farallon.** 450 Post St. (between Mason and Powell sts.). ☎ **415/956-6969.** Reservations recommended. Main courses $18.75–$26. AE, DC, DISC, MC, V. Daily noon–midnight. Bus: 2, 3, 4, 38. Valet parking $7. COASTAL CUISINE/SEAFOOD.

If there is one hot new restaurant that's a must-visit, this is it. Here the multimillion-dollar attraction is seafood, from the outrageous decor to the stellar "coastal" cuisine. Handblown Jellyfish lamps, kelp-bed–like back-lit columns, glass clam shells, sea-urchin light fixtures, a sea-life mosaic floor, and a tentacle-encircled bar sets the scene. Thankfully, during designer Pat Kuleto's impressive renovation of this 1924 building, the original gothic arches were left intact, making the main dining room one of the most impressive in the entire city. (Though the bright and busy front room and intimate and incognito balcony aren't exactly shabby either.) If you think the atmosphere is undeniably appealing and lavish, wait till you try the food. Chef Mark Franz, who opened Stars with Jeremiah Tower, is at the helm of the $5-million kitchen, offering starters ranging from the expected (oysters) to the more ambitious—iced Atlantic and Pacific shellfish indulgence, a cornucopia of oysters, clams, crayfish, prawns, mussels, and scallops with a horseradish mignonette ($16.75 per person); spot prawn, sea scallop, and lobster pyramid (the only mildly disappointing dish of the evening); and knockout main lobster and prawns with potato gnocchi. While most main courses, such as the ginger-steamed wild salmon and striped bass "pillows" with prawn mousse, napa cabbage, and foie-gras coulis, stick with the sea-side theme, meat and game eaters are also honored with grilled squab breast stuffed with mushrooms and served with braised Swiss chard and grilled fillet of beef with truffled potatoes, cara-melized torpedo onions and wild-mushroom sauce. While the whimsy-meets-sophistication does extend to the food, the service and wine list (over 300 by the bottle; 24 by the glass) are seriously professional. This place has been quite the scene since it opened in mid-1997, so reserve well in advance. And if it's available, don't miss the huckleberry bombolini, a refreshingly different dessert.

Masa's. In the Hotel Vintage Court, 648 Bush St. (at Stockton St.). ☎ **415/ 989-7154.** Reservations required; accepted up to 21 days in advance. Fixed-price dinner $72–$77. AE, CB, DC, DISC, MC, V. Tues–Sat 6–9:30pm. Closed 1st 2 weeks in Jan and 1st week in July. Cable car: Powell-Mason and Powell-Hyde lines. Bus: 2, 3, 4, 30, or 45. FRENCH.

Either fixed-price or à la carte, dinner is a memorable expense-be-damned experience from start to finish. If you wish, you can sim-ply leave the decisions up to the kitchen. The restaurant's passion for using only the highest-quality ingredients accounts for the restaurant's four-star ranking—and budget-busting prices. A typical dinner may begin with the Sonoma foie gras in a Madeira truffle sauce, or poached lobster with potatoes, fried leek, and a truffle vinaigrette. Main entrees may include medaillons of New Zealand fallow deer with zinfandel sauce and caramelized green apples, or the Atlantic black bass with a saffron sauce. Dessert, as you would imag-ine, is heavenly.

✪ **Postrio.** 545 Post St. (between Mason and Taylor sts.). ☎ **415/776-7825.** Reservations required. Main courses $6–$15 breakfast, $14–$15 lunch, $19–$30 dinner. AE, CB, DC, DISC, MC, V. Mon–Fri 7–10am, 11:30am–2pm, and 5:30–10:30pm; Sat 9am–2pm and 5:30–10:30pm; Sun 9am–2pm and 5:30–10pm; bar daily 11:30am–2am. Cable car: Powell-Mason and Powell-Hyde lines. Bus: 2, 3, 4, or 38. AMERICAN.

They say the higher you climb, the longer it takes to fall, and that's certainly the case with Postrio. Ever since chefs Anne and David Gingrass left the kitchen to start their own enterprise, rumors have been flying that San Francisco's top restaurant isn't what it used to be (poor execution from the line tops the list). If its owners are cry-ing, however, they're crying all the way to the bank, because it's a rare night when the kitchen doesn't perform to a full house.

Eating, however, is only half the reason one comes to Postrio. After squeezing through the perpetually swinging bar—which, in its

Union Square, Nob Hill & Financial District Dining

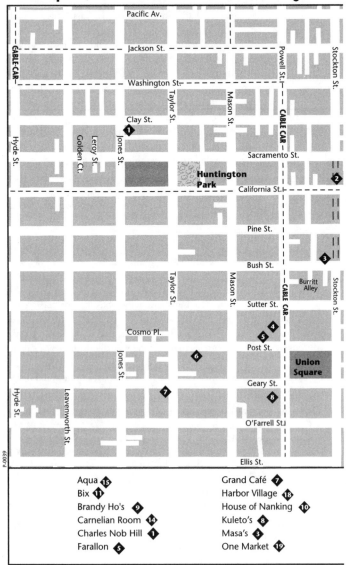

Aqua 🕔
Bix ⑪
Brandy Ho's ⑨
Carnelian Room ⑭
Charles Nob Hill ❶
Farallon ❺

Grand Café ❼
Harbor Village ⑱
House of Nanking ⑩
Kuleto's ❽
Masa's ❸
One Market ⑲

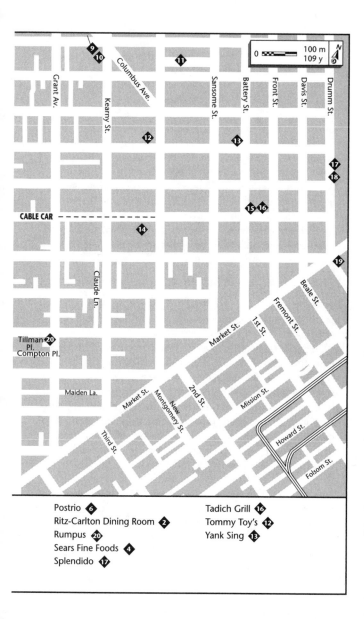

Postrio ◆6
Ritz-Carlton Dining Room ◆2
Rumpus ◆20
Sears Fine Foods ◆4
Splendido ◆17

Tadich Grill ◆16
Tommy Toy's ◆12
Yank Sing ◆13

own right, dishes out excellent tapas and pizzas from a wood-burning oven in the corner—guests are forced to make a grand entrance down the antebellum staircase to the cavernous dining room below (it's everyone's 15 seconds of fame, so make sure your fly is zipped). Pure Hollywood, for sure, but fun.

The menu, prepared by brothers Mitchell and Steven Rosenthal, combines Italian, Asian, French, and California styles with mixed results. When we last visited Postrio, the sautéed salmon, for example, was a bit overcooked, but the accompanying plum glaze, wasabi mashed potatoes, and miso vinaigrette were outstanding. Again with the grilled squab: It lacked flavor, but the accompaniment—a sweet potato foie-gras spring roll—was pure genius. The desserts, each artistically sculpted by pastry chef Janet Rikala, were the highlight of the evening. Despite the prime-time rush, service was friendly and infallible, as was the presentation.

MODERATE

✪ **Grand Cafe.** 501 Geary St. (at Taylor St., adjacent to the Hotel Monaco). ☎ **415/292-0101.** Reservations accepted. Main courses $13–$24. AE, CB, DC, DISC, MC, V. Daily 7am–2:30pm; Sun–Thurs 5:30–10pm (cafe menu until 11pm); Fri–Sat 5:30–11pm (cafe menu until midnight). Valet parking $7 for 3 hrs. Bus: 2, 3, 4, 27, or 38. CALIFORNIA/FRENCH.

With the exception of Farallon restaurant, the Grand Cafe has the most stunningly beautiful dining room in San Francisco. The cocktail area alone is impressive, but the *pièce de résistance* is the enormous turn-of-the-century grand ballroom, a magnificent combination of old Europe and art nouveau. From every angle you'll see playful sculptures, original murals, and a cadre of dazzling deco chandeliers. Until recently, the fare had never quite lived up to the view, but chef Denis Soriano and his crew have finally worked out the kinks and are now enjoying that most coveted of clientele: the repeat customer. On a recent visit, seated in a plush booth with deep brown velvet and framed in walnut, we feasted on poached mussels in a savory celery-and-saffron sauce, a tender, pan-seared duck leg confit with cabbage-walnut dressing, and a tender baby-spinach salad with sliced pears, feta, walnuts, and fresh raspberry vinaigrette. Recommended entrees are the roasted duck breast with mission figs and huckleberry sauce, and the grilled filet mignon in a mushroom-shallot sauce—the most tender cut of meat we've ever encountered. Service was both friendly and prompt, making the entire dining experience a pleasure. *Note:* The bar area has it's own exhibition kitchen and menu, offering similar dishes for about half the price.

Impressions

[San Francisco is] the city that knows how.
—President William Howard Taft

[San Francisco is] the city that knows chow.
—Trader Vic, Restaurateur

The pizzas from the wood-burning oven are excellent, as is the grilled marinated skirt steak with whipped potatoes and red-wine sauce.

Kuleto's. 221 Powell St. (between Geary and O'Farrell sts., in the Villa Florence Hotel). ☎ **415/397-7720.** Reservations recommended. Breakfast $5–$10; main courses $8–$18. AE, CB, DC, DISC, MC, V. Mon–Fri 7–10:30am; Sat and Sun 8–10:30am; daily 11:30am–11pm. Cable car: Powell-Mason and Powell-Hyde lines. Muni Metro: Powell. Bus: 2, 3, 4, or 38. ITALIAN.

Story has it the owners of this popular downtown bistro were so delighted with the design of their new restaurant that they named it after the architect, Pat Kuleto. Whatever the reason, Kuleto's is a beautiful place filled with beautiful people who are here to see and be seen (don't come underdressed). The best plan of action is to skip the wait for a table, muscle a seat at the antipasto bar, and fill up on appetizers (which are often better than the entrees). For a main course, try the penne pasta drenched in a tangy lamb-sausage marinara sauce, the clam linguini (generously overloaded with fresh clams), or any of the fresh-fish specials grilled over hardwoods. If you don't arrive by 6pm, expect to wait—this place fills up fast.

Rumpus. 1 Tillman Place (off Grant Ave., between Sutter and Post sts.). ☎ **415/421-2300.** Reservations recommended. Main courses $11.95–$19.95. AE, DC, MC, V. Mon–Sat 11:30am–2:30pm; Sun–Thurs 5:30–10pm; Fri–Sat 5:30–11pm. Bus: 2, 3, 4, 30, 45, 76. Cable car: Powell-Hyde and Powell-Mason lines. CALIFORNIA.

Tucked into a small cul-de-sac off Grant Avenue you'll find Rumpus, a fantastic restaurant serving well-prepared California fare at reasonable prices. The perfect place for a business lunch, shopping break, or dinner with friends, Rumpus is architecturally playful, colorful, and buzzing with conversation. The menu is affordable, offering a delight of flavorful options, such as the pan-roasted chicken whose crispy and flavorful crust is almost as delightful as the perfectly cooked chicken and mashed potatoes beneath it; and the quality cut of New York steak comes with savory mashed potatoes. If nothing else, make sure to stop in here for one of the best desserts we've ever had: the puddinglike chocolate brioche cake. (We've introduced it to out-of-town guests, and they've cursed us ever since because they now know it exists and can't get it at home.)

INEXPENSIVE

Sears Fine Foods. 439 Powell St. (between Post and Sutter sts.). ☎ **415/986-1160.** Reservations for parties of 6 or more. Breakfast $3–$8; salads and soups $3–$18; main courses $5–$10. No credit cards. Daily 6:30am–2:30pm. Cable car: Powell-Mason and Powell-Hyde lines. Bus: 2, 3, 4, or 38. AMERICAN.

Sears would be the perfect place for breakfast on the way to work, but you can't always guarantee you'll get in the door before 9am. It's not just another pink-tabled diner run by motherly matrons—it's an institution, famous for its crispy, dark-brown waffles, light sourdough French toast, and Swedish, silver-dollar–sized pancakes. As the story goes, Sears was founded in 1938 by Ben Sears, a retired clown. It was his Swedish wife Hilbur, however, who was responsible for the legendary pancakes, which are still whipped up according to her family's secret recipe. Keeping up with the nineties trend, the menu also offers a "healthy-heart menu."

3   Financial District

EXPENSIVE

✪ **Aqua.** 252 California St. (between Battery and Front sts.). ☎ **415/956-9662.** Reservations recommended. Main courses $26–$35; 6-course tasting menu $65; vegetarian tasting menu $45. AE, DC, MC, V. Mon–Fri 11:30am–2:15pm; Mon–Sat 5:30–10:30pm. All Market St. buses. SEAFOOD.

Without question, Aqua is San Francisco's finest seafood restaurant, light years beyond the genre of shrimp cocktails and lemon-butter sauce. Heralded Chef Michael Mina dazzles his customers with a bewildering juxtaposition of earth and sea in his seasonally changing menus. The poached steelhead salmon, for example, rests in a bed of potato and leek purée infused with Dungeness crab, beurre blanc, and oxtre caviar. The miso glazed black cod steak in vegetable jus is another work of art, perfectly paired with rock shrimp and vegetable strudel. Mina's passion for exotic mushrooms pervades most dishes, for taste as well as for show (Mina is, to a fault, amazingly adept at the art of presentation). Desserts are equally impressive, particularly the Aqua soufflé-of-the-day. Steep prices prevent most people from making a regular appearance, but for special occasions or billable lunches, Aqua is highly recommended.

Carnelian Room. 555 California St. (at Montgomery St.). ☎ **415/433-7500.** Reservations recommended. Main courses $22–$39; Sun brunch $27 adults,

$13 children. AE, CB, DC, DISC, MC, V. Daily 6pm–9:30pm; Sun brunch 10am–1:30pm. Cable car: California. Self-parking $7. Bus: 1, 15, 9, or 42. CONTINENTAL.

By day, the Carnelian Room is the exclusive Banker's Club, accessible only to members or by invitation, but at night anyone with a big-enough bankroll can dine among the clouds. Soaring 52 stories above San Francisco's Financial District on the top floor of the Bank of America building, the Carnelian Room is a definite contender for "Best View." Dark oak paneling, brass railings, and huge picture windows reek with romanticism, particularly if you're fortunate enough to get a window table. The upscale menu used to cater to old-style banker's tastes—expensive meat dishes with rich, thick sauces—but the recent trend toward healthier eating has rounded out the menu considerably, and now you can find numerous fish, fowl, and pasta dishes along with such Carnelian classics as prime rib and thick-cut New York steak. A recommended dish is the smoked sturgeon with caviar-whipped potatoes, though it's hard to pass up the rack of lamb with port wine and rosemary sauce. A wine cellar of some 36,000 bottles and the restaurant's accomplished sommelier all but guarantee the proper vintage to accompany your meal.

Harbor Village. 4 Embarcadero Center, lobby level (at Drumm St. between Sacramento and Clay sts.). ☎ **415/781-8833.** Reservations recommended. Main courses $9–$32. AE, DC, MC, V. Mon–Fri 11am–2:30pm; Sat 10:30am–2:30pm; Sun 10am–2:30pm; daily 5:30–9:30pm. Bus: 15, 45, or 76. CHINESE.

Voted best Chinese restaurant in town by *San Francisco* magazine, this is one of the city's most upscale Chinese restaurants, serving primarily Cantonese dishes along with spicy Szechuan specials.

The courteous staff will guide you through the extensive menu, which includes some 30 seafood dishes alone, such as striped bass steamed with ginger and scallions. If you've never had shark-fin soup, this is the place to try it. Unique appetizers include shredded spicy chicken and minced squab in lettuce cups. Stir-fried garlic prawns, beggar's chicken cooked in a clay pot, and sizzling beef in black-pepper sauce are excellent main-course choices. Dim-sum lunch is served daily (from 11am weekdays, 10:30am on Sat, and 10am on Sun) and is definitely worth trying (although the Hong Kong Flower Lounge is better if you don't mind venturing to the Richmond District). The wait staff brings trays full of steaming hot appetizers (they will happily explain what they are) from which you can choose what you like. Try the Shanghai-style steamed pork dumplings flavored with ginger and scallions, the rice-paper dumplings filled with sweet shrimp, taro cake, or the curried beef wonton.

The restaurant offers validated parking at all the Embarcadero Center garages (located at the foot of Clay Street). It'll cost you a few dollars during weekdays, but it's free after 5pm Monday to Friday and all day on weekends and holidays.

One Market. 1 Market St. (at Steuart across from Justin Herman Plaza). ☎ **415/777-5577.** Reservations recommended. Main courses $18–$30. AE, DC, MC, V. Mon–Thurs 11:30am–2pm and 5:30–9pm; Fri 11:30am–2pm and 5:30–10pm; Sat 5–10pm. All Market St. buses. Valet parking $7. CALIFORNIA.

The enormous restaurant's decor, which is both cosmopolitan and folk-artsy, has been recently fine-tuned to complement executive-chef George Morrone's (previously at Aqua) farm-fresh menu. Amidst tapestry, banquettes, mahogany, and slate floors, there's seating for 170 in the main dining area. The bar, which features gold walls and sponge-painted mustard columns, displays a prominent colorful mural of a market scene. The menu changes frequently to reflect the freshest local ingredients. Start with a dozen of the Skookum and Fanny Bay oysters with homemade cocktail sauce and chili malt vinegar dressing, followed by the maple-glazed day-boat scallops with pumpkin ravioli. Main courses range from wild steelhead with foie-gras mashed potatoes and green-apple jus to herb-poached baby chicken with white-pepper dumplings, bouillon, and turnip greens. Whatever you choose, you're bound to find a perfectly accompanying wine from the "cellar," which has over 500 selections of American vintages. A corporate crowd convenes from 5 to 7pm weeknights for $1 beers. The room picks up with live jazz nightly.

Tommy Toy's. 655 Montgomery St. (at Columbus Ave. and Washington St.). ☎ **415/397-4888.** Main courses $14.95–$28. Fixed-price dinner $39.50. AE, DC, DISC, JCB, MC, V. Mon–Fri 11:30am–2:30pm; daily 6–9:30pm. Closed Thanksgiving and Christmas. Valet parking $3.50 (dinner only). CHINESE.

Tommy Toy's turned Chinese from a take-out affair to a dress-up affair when he created his $1.5 million dark and opulent Asian fine-dining room. The atmosphere, created after the 19th-century empress dowager's reading room, is accented with dimly lit candelabras and ancient paintings. Most evenings, the restaurant is crowded with tourists and some locals who come for the five-course fixed-price meal, which usually includes minced squab in lettuce leaves, lobster bisque soup served in a coconut and topped with puffed pastry, a whole lobster sautéed with peanuts and mushrooms, duck served with plum sauce, medaillons of beef, and finally a light dessert of peach mousse. The à la carte menu flaunts vanilla prawns and other such delicacies. On the two occasions we've been here, once the food was very good, the next time it was just okay, and both times the portions were substantial. If you want romantic Chinese, this is as good as it gets in the US of A.

MODERATE

Splendido. 4 Embarcadero Center (at Clay and Drumm sts.). ☎ **415/ 986-3222.** Main courses $11–$26. AE, DC, DISC, MC, V. Mon–Fri 11:30am– 2:30pm; bar menu 2:30pm–5:30pm; daily 5:30–10pm. Bus: 15, 45, or 76. CONTEMPORARY ITALIAN.

Warm olive wood, flickering candles, rustic stone walls, hand-painted tiles, and hand-hewn beams create the illusion of an old Mediterranean getaway in the middle of metropolitan Embarcadero Four.

But it's not the decor alone that procures kudos from *Gourmet* and other culinary magazines. The food is beautifully presented, lovingly prepared, and consistently tasty. Starters might include a light and flavorful Mediterranean seafood soup and crab cakes, which are large but too bready for our tastes. Main courses, which are served on colorful, individually decorated plates, might include a wonderful grilled salmon with pearl-onion carrot confit, which is cooked to perfection and accompanied by a crisp, subtle broth; or oven-roasted pork loin with braised cabbage, onions, and a lentil salad. Dessert is a decadent affair, with such belt-busters as an amaretto-and-espresso tiramisu and ever-popular house-made profiteroles with warm chocolate sauce. When the weather is pleasant, you can eat under a canopy on the outdoor patio, or choose the seating in front of the open kitchen. Be sure to glance in the exhibition bakery near the entrance, where you might see chefs rolling fresh pasta.

✪ **Tadich Grill.** 240 California St. (between Battery and Front sts.). ☎ **415/ 391-1849.** Reservations not accepted. Main courses $12–$18. MC, V. Mon–Fri 11:30am–9:30pm; Sat 11:30am–9:30pm. Muni Metro: All Market St. trams, BART. All Market St. buses. SEAFOOD.

This famous, venerated California institution arrived with the gold rush in 1849 and claims to be the very first to broil seafood over mesquite charcoal, back in the early 1920s. The original mahogany bar extends the entire length of the restaurant while no-nonsense white-linen–draped tables are topped with big plates of sourdough bread. Power-lunchers get one of the seven enclosed, private booths.

For a light meal, try one of the delicious seafood salads, such as shrimp or prawn Louis. Hot dishes include baked avocado with shrimp diablo, baked casserole of stuffed turbot with crab and shrimp à la Newburg, and charcoal-broiled petrale sole with butter

Dining Around Town

A. Sabella's **29**
Ace Wasabi's **3**
Beach Chalet **17**
Betelnut **10**
Bizou **50**
Boulevard **44**
Bruno's **28**
Cafe Flore **24**
Cafe Pescatore **30**
Caffe Sport **37**
Cha Cha Cha **53**
Cliff House **12**
Doidge's **9**
Elite Cafe **11**
Enrico's **39**
Eos **55**
Firewood Cafe **23**
Fog City Diner **41**
Fringale **49**
Greens Restaurant, Fort Mason **1**
Hamburger Mary's **52**
Hard Rock Cafe **42**
Harris' **32**
Hawthorne Lane **46**
Hong Kong Flower Lounge **13**
Il Fornaio **40**
Jardiniere **19**
Khan Toke Thai House **13**
La Canasta **7**
La Folie **31**

L'Osteria del Ferno **34**
Lulu **47**
Manora's **51**
Mario's Bohemian Cigar Store **33**
Mecca **22**
Mel's Diner **4** **13**
Moose's **36**
North India Restaurant **5**
Pane e Vino **8**
Pauline's Pizza **26**
Plumpjack Café **6**
Rose Pistola **35**
Sanppo **16**
The Slanted Door **27**
South Park Café **48**
Stinking Rose **38**
Swan Oyster Depot **43**
2223 **25**
Taquerias La Cumbre **27**
Thep Phanom **21**
Thirsty Bear Brewing Company **45**
Ti Couz **27**
Ton Kiang **14**
Yo Yo Bistro **15**
Zinzino **2**
Zona Rosa **54**
Zuni Cafe **20**

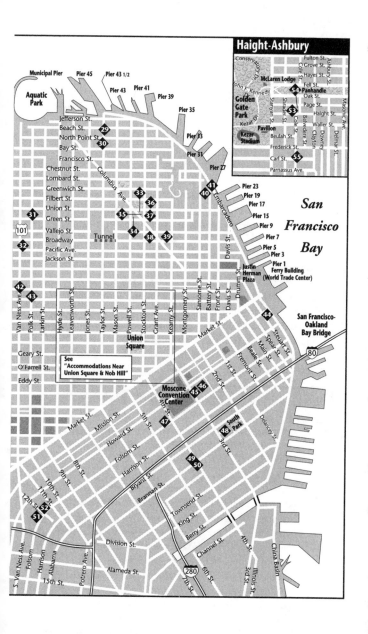

Haight-Ashbury

Conservatory Dr.
Fulton St.
Grove St.
Hayes St.
McLaren Lodge
John F. Kennedy Dr.
Fell St.
Oak St.
Golden Gate Park
Page St.
Haight St.
Waller St.
Kezar Dr.
Pavilion
Beulah St.
Kezar Stadium
Frederick St.
Carl St.
Parnassus Ave.

Conservatory Dr.
Cole St.
Shrader St.
Stanyan St.
Belvedere St.
Clayton St.
Cole St.
Ashbury St.
Masonic Ave.
Downey
Delmar St.

54
53
55

Municipal Pier
Pier 45
Pier 43 1/2
Pier 43
Pier 41
Pier 39
Aquatic Park
Pier 35
Jefferson St.
Beach St.
29
North Point St.
30
Bay St.
Pier 33
Francisco St.
Chestnut St.
Pier 31
Lombard St.
Pier 27
Greenwich St.
Filbert St.
33
Union St.
36
31
Green St.
35
37
Vallejo St.
Broadway
Tunnel
34
38
39
Pacific Ave.
Jackson St.

Columbus Ave.

101
32

Pier 41
Pier 40
Pier 23
Pier 19
Pier 17
Pier 15
Pier 9
Pier 7
Pier 5
Pier 3
Pier 1
Ferry Building
(World Trade Center)

Embarcadero
Davis St.
Drumm St.
Justin Herman Plaza

San Francisco Bay

42
43
Van Ness Ave.
Polk St.
Larkin St.
Hyde St.
Leavenworth St.
Jones St.
Taylor St.
Mason St.
Powell St.
Stockton St.
Grant Ave.
Kearny St.
Montgomery St.
Sansome St.
Battery St.
Front St.
Davis St.

44

San Francisco-Oakland Bay Bridge

Union Square

Market St.

See "Accommodations Near Union Square & Nob Hill"

Geary St.
O'Farrell St.
Eddy St.

Steuart St.
Spear St.
Main St.
Beale St.
Fremont St.
1st St.
2nd St.

80

Market St.
Mission St.
5th St.
Howard St.
Folsom St.
Harrison St.
Bryant St.
Brannan St.

Moscone Convention Center
45 **46**
47
48
South Park
49
50
3rd St.
Delancey St.

8th St.
9th St.
10th St.
11th St.
12th St.
52
51

Townsend St.
King St.
Berry St.
Channel St.
4th St.
China Basin

S. Van Ness Ave.
Folsom
Harrison
Alabama
15th St.

Division St.

Alameda St.

280

6th St.
7th St.
Illinois St.
3rd St.

81

sauce, a local favorite. Almost everyone gets a side order of big, tasty french fries.

Yank Sing. 427 Battery St. (between Clay and Washington sts.). ☎ **415/781-1111.** Dim sum $2.30–$5 for 3 to 4 pieces. AE, DC, MC, V. Mon–Fri 11am–3pm; Sat–Sun 10am–4pm. Cable car: California St. line. Bus: 1 or 42. CHINESE/DIM SUM.

Loosely translated as "a delight of the heart," Yank Sing does dim sum like no other Chinese restaurant we've visited. Poor quality of ingredients has always been the shortcoming of all but the most expensive Chinese restaurants, but Yank Sing manages to be both affordable and excellent. Confident, experienced servers take the nervousness out of novices—they're good at guessing your gastric threshold. Most dim-sum dishes are dumplings, filled with tasty concoctions of pork, beef, fish, or vegetables. *Congees* (porridges), spareribs, stuffed crab claws, scallion pancakes, shrimp balls, pork buns, and other palate-pleasers complete the menu. Like most good dim-sum meals, at Yank Sing you get to choose the small dishes from a cart that's continually wheeled around the dining room. While the food is delicious, the location makes this the most popular tourist spot. A second location is at 49 Stevenson St., off First Street (☎ **415/541-4949**). Ideally, we still prefer the Richmond's Hong Kong Flower Lounge. *Tip:* Sit by the kitchen and you're guaranteed to get it while it's hot.

4 Nob Hill/Russian Hill

EXPENSIVE

✪ **Charles Nob Hill.** 1250 Jones St. (at Clay St.). ☎ **415/771-5400.** Main courses $25–$35. AE, MC, V. Tues–Sun 5:30–10pm. Cable car: California St. and Powell–Hyde lines. Bus: 1, 12, 27, or 83. FRENCH.

We never knew beef could actually melt in your mouth until Aqua owner Charles Condy bought historic restaurant "Le Club" and introduced us to Chef Ron Seagal's culinary magic (it really did melt!). The "classically inspired light French fare," as he prefers to call it, is served in two dining rooms with velvet banquettes, fresh floral arrangements, and the loud buzz of the older socialite crowd. Start with a bowl of the soup of the day, which, when we dined here, was a spinach-and-roasted-garlic soup with cumin-scented rock shrimp and crumbled bacon that was surprisingly beautiful, electric green, and overflowing with flavor. Scallop-and-black-truffle pot pie is another must-try. And for the main course, you might choose the Poele of beef tenderloin with wild-mushroom and potato torte, balsamic glazed onions, and foie gras, or a flavorful squab with veal sweetbread, lentils, and mushroom fricassee. Better yet, opt for the $65 six-course tasting menu and let the chef's preference lead you through the meal. Although the room itself is romantic, the atmosphere and noise level are too convivial for real intimacy. Wrap up the evening with the outstanding pear-and-Roquefort tart. *Tip:* No matter what, don't drive here unless you can pay the valet; you may spend over an hour looking for parking.

✪ **Ritz-Carlton Dining Room.** 600 Stockton St. (at California St.). ☎ **415/ 296-7465.** Reservations recommended. Fixed-price menus $55–$69. AE, CB, DC, DISC, MC, V. Mon–Sat 6–9:30pm. Valet parking $9. Cable car: Powell-Hyde and Powell-Mason lines (direct stop). Bus: 1. CALIFORNIA/FRENCH.

The Ritz-Carlton Hotel is renowned for pampering its guests as if they were royalty, and the Dining Room is no exception. On our last visit, no less then five tuxedoed wait staff were surreptitiously attending to our needs (no half-empty water glasses in this joint) as we fussed over the wine list and debated the proper pronunciation of "tatin." The setting, as you would imagine, is quite regal and sumptuous: crystal chandeliers, rich brocade, elegant table settings, cushy high-backed chairs, and live harp music reek of formality. Unfortunately, celebrity chef Gary Danko—winner of the 1995 James Beard Award, the Academy Award of the food world—is no longer with the Ritz; his replacement, chef Sylvain Portay, now runs the kitchen with similar aplomb, but the loss is noticeable—dishes such as the roast Maine lobster and striped-bass fillet were quite good, but certainly not of the four-star caliber Danko's fans are accustomed to. A few dishes, however, were outstanding, particularly crayfish bisque (one of the best dishes we have ever tasted) and the risotto with butternut squash and roasted squab. Dessert, alas, was also deigned for mere mortals, though the warm port-poached pear in vanilla sauce was superb. The menu, which changes monthly, offers a choice of three-, four-, or five-course dinners ranging from $55 to $69, the latter of which includes wine pairing per course by master-sommelier Emmanuel Kemiji for an additional $43. The Dining Room also features the country's only "rolling" cheese cart, laden with at least two dozen individually ripened cheeses.

MODERATE

Hard Rock Café. 1699 Van Ness Ave. (at Sacramento St.). ☎ **415/ 885-1699.** Reservations accepted for groups of 15 or more. Main courses $6–$16. AE, DC, MC, V. Sun–Thurs 11:30am–11pm; Fri–Sat 11:30am–midnight. Valet $4.25 for 2 hrs. Cable car: California St. line. Bus: 1. AMERICAN.

Like its affiliated restaurants around the world, this loud, nostalgia-laden place offers big portions of decent food at moderate prices and plenty of blaring music to an almost exclusively tourist clientele. The real draw, of course, is the merchandise shop, which often has as long a line as the restaurant.

The cafe is decorated with a profusion of framed gold records, musical instruments, signed rock-star photos, historic front pages, and the usual "Save the Planet" montage. The menu offers burgers, fajitas, baby-back ribs, grilled fish, chicken, salads, and sandwiches; we usually go for the chicken sandwich with a side of onion rings, both of which are pretty darn good. Although it's nothing unique to San Francisco, the Hard Rock is a fine place to bring the kids and grab a bite.

✪ **Swan Oyster Depot.** 1517 Polk St. (between California and Sacramento sts.). ☎ **415/673-1101.** Reservations not accepted. Seafood cocktails $5–$8; clams and oysters on the half shell $6–$7.50 per half dozen. No credit cards. Mon–Sat 8am–5:30pm. Bus: 27. SEAFOOD.

Pushing 90 years of faithful service to Bay Area chowder-heads, the Swan Oyster Depot is classic San Francisco; a unique dining experience you shouldn't miss. Opened in 1912, this tiny hole in the wall run by the city's friendliest and vivacious servers is little more than a narrow fish market that decided to slap down some bar stools. There are only 20 or so seats jammed cheek by jowl along a long marble bar. Most patrons come for a quick cup of chowder or a plate of half-shelled oysters that arrive chilling on crushed ice. The menu is limited to fresh crab, shrimp, oyster, and clam cocktails, Maine lobster, and Boston-style clam chowder, all of which are exceedingly fresh. *Note:* Don't let the lunchtime line dissuade you—it moves fast.

5 South of Market (SoMa)

EXPENSIVE

✪ **Boulevard.** 1 Mission St. (at Embarcadero and Steuart St.). ☎ **415/543-6084.** Reservations recommended. Main courses $19–$27. AE, CB, DC, DISC, MC, V. Mon–Fri 11:30am–2pm; bistro 2:30–5:15pm; dinner Mon–Wed and Sun 5:30–10pm, Thurs–Sat 5:30–10:30pm. Bus: 15, 30, 32, 42, or 45. Valet parking $6. AMERICAN.

Master restaurant designer Pat Kuleto and chef Nancy Oaks teamed up to create one of San Francisco's most exciting restaurants, and though it's been over 5 years since its debut, it's still as popular as ever. What's the winning combination? The dramatically artistic belle-epoch interior with vaulted brick ceilings, floral-design banquettes, a mosaic floor, and fluid, tulip-shaped lamps combined with Oaks's equally impressive sculptural and mouth-watering dishes. Start with the delicate crab and mascarpone ravioli with truffle beurre blanc and tomato cream, then embark on such wonderful concoctions as grilled wild king salmon with leek and sweet corn mashed potatoes, French beans, and herb salad (she makes a mean honey-cured pork loin, too). Vegetarian items, such as wild-mushroom risotto with fresh chanterelles and Parmesan, are also offered. Three levels of formality—bar, open kitchen, and main dining room—keep things from getting too snobby. Though steep prices prevent most from making Boulevard a regular gig, you'd be hard-pressed to find a better place for a special, fun-filled occasion.

❂ **Hawthorne Lane.** 22 Hawthorne Lane (at Howard St. between Second and Third sts.). ☎ **415/777-9779.** Reservations recommended. Jacket appropriate but not required. Main courses $9.50–$13 lunch, $18–$25 dinner. CB, DC, DISC, JCB, MC, V. Mon–Fri 11:30am–2pm; Sun–Thurs 5:30–10pm; Fri–Sat 5:30–10:30pm. BART: Montgomery Station. Muni Metro: F, J, K, L, M, or N. Bus: 12, 30, 45, or 76. CALIFORNIA.

Anne and David Gingrass, who hailed from Postrio, preside over the kitchen at Hawthorne Lane, their SoMa restaurant strategically located a block away from the Museum of Modern Art. Anne and David are a culinary team who prepare their menu based on the best and freshest ingredients available. Menus change with the seasons and reflect the Asian and European influences that made them famous under Wolfgang Puck.

The bar area is comfortable and inviting, with both cocktail tables and bar seating; continue on to the dining room, where earthquake reinforcement beams divide the room in a way that is not only functional, but is also decorative and creates the illusion that each section is a more intimate environment. Even the decor is just right: not too fancy or pretentious, but well-lit and decorated with bright artwork, fresh floral arrangements, and a leaf motif throughout.

But where the Gingrass's expertise really shines is in the food. The bread basket that arrives at your table is overflowing with fresh-baked goods of all tastes and types. Each dish arrives beautifully presented without being too contrived, but usually with a whimsical accent, such as a leaf-shaped pastry or a bird made of a carrot sliver. Dishes are remarkably well balanced, and accompaniments are often more exciting than the main course itself. If it's on the menu, don't pass up the black-cod appetizer served with a miso glaze and spinach rolls. The light, flaky lobster tempura with a vegetable salad is another show-stopper, as is the main course of quail glazed with maple and perched on the most delightful potato gratin. Desserts are as good to look at as they are to eat.

MODERATE

Bizou. 598 Fourth St. (at Brannan St.). ☎ **415/543-2222.** Reservations recommended. Main courses $12.50–$21. AE, MC, V. Mon–Fri 11:30am–2:30pm; Mon–Thurs 5:30–10pm; Fri–Sat 5:30–10:30pm. Bus: 15, 30, 32, 42, or 45. FRENCH/ITALIAN.

Around town, almost everyone sings Bizou's praises and with good reason: The restaurant's golden-yellow walls and terra-cotta ceiling are warmly lit by antique light fixtures and art-deco wall sconces, and provide an atmosphere perfect for a first date or an evening out with Mom. The wait staff is friendly and professional, and all the ingredients are fresh and in creative combinations. Our only complaint is that literally every dish is so rich and powerfully flavorful (including the salads), it's a bit of a sensory overload. The menu's starters include an Italian flat bread with caramelized onions, fresh herbs, and Parmesan cheese, Sonoma duck-liver terrine, and baked shrimp with white beans, tomato, and feta. The main courses may include a grilled veal chop with broccoli-rabe potato gratin or stuffed chicken with celeriac, apple, and goat cheese. All main-course portions are substantial here, so don't overindulge on appetizers. And save a little room for dessert—the meringue covered in chocolate and topped with coffee ice cream and candied almonds is quite a treat. Too bad there are no cots in a back room here—after your meal, you'll need a nap.

✪ Fringale Restaurant. 570 Fourth St. (between Brannan and Bryant sts.). ☎ **415/543-0573.** Reservations recommended. Main courses $4–$12 at lunch, $11–$19 at dinner. AE, MC, V. Mon–Fri 11:30am–3pm; Mon–Sat 5:30–10:30pm. Bus: 30 or 45. FRENCH.

One of San Francisco's best restaurants for the money, Fringale—French colloquial for "sudden urge to eat"—has enjoyed a weeklong waiting list since the day chef/co-owner Gerald Hirigoyen first opened this small SoMa bistro. Sponged, eggshell-blue walls and other muted sand and earth tones provide a serene dining environment, which is all but shattered when the 18-table room inevitably fills with Hirigoyen's fans. For starters, try the steamed mussels with roasted red pepper, basil, and vinaigrette, or the sheep's-milk cheese and prosciutto tureen with figs and greens. Among the dozen or so main courses on the seasonally changing menu you might find rack of lamb with potato gratin or pork tenderloin confit with onion and apple marmalade. Desserts are worth savoring, too, particularly the hazelnut-and-roasted-almond mousse cake or the signature crème brûlée with vanilla bean. The mostly French waiters provide uncharacteristically charming service, and prices are surprisingly reasonable for such high-quality cuisine. It's one of our favorites.

Lulu. 816 Folsom St. (at Fourth St.). ☎ **415/495-5775.** Reservations recommended. Main courses $7–$13 lunch, $9–$17 dinner. AE, MC, V. Sun–Thurs 11:30am–10:30pm; Fri–Sat 11:30am–11pm. Bus: 15, 30, 32, 42, or 45. CONTINENTAL.

After reigning for 4 years as one of San Francisco's top restaurants, the celebrity staff left to open Rose Pistola, taking a good chunk of its status along with it. The energy within the enormous dining room, however, still radiates as the cadre of cooks, communicating via headsets, slide bubbling plates of pizza and shellfish in and out of the open kitchen's wood-fired ovens. Watching the carefully orchestrated chaos makes dining here something of an event. The main room seats 170, but even as you sit amidst a sea of stylish diners, the room somehow feels warm and convivial. And then there's the food, which is consistently delicious. Locals return again and again for the roasted mussels piled high on an iron skillet; the chopped salad with lemon, anchovies, and tomatoes; the pork loin with fennel, garlic, and olive oil; and any of the other wonderful dishes. Everything is served family-style and is meant to be shared. Save room for dessert; opt for the gooey chocolate cake, which oozes with chocolate to be scooped up with the side of melting ice cream. The adjoining cafe serves the same menu, with the addition of gourmet sandwiches, on a first-come, first-served basis.

✪ Thirsty Bear Brewing Company. 661 Howard St. (1 block east of the Moscone Center). ☎ **415/974-0905.** Reservations recommended. Main courses $10–$17. AE, DC, MC, V. Mon–Sun 11:30am–1am. Bus: 12, 15, 30, 45, or 76. SPANISH.

Despite the dumb name, the Thirsty Bear Brewing Company has quickly become a favorite of the Financial District/SoMa crowd, who come as much for the excellent house-made brews as they do for chef Daniel Olivella's outstanding Spanish food. A native of Catalunia, Spain, Olivella is a master of paella. His Paella Valenciana—a sizzling combo of chicken, shrimp, sausage, shellfish, and saffron-laden rice served in a cast-iron skillet—is the best we've had outside of Barcelona. Upscale pub grub includes a variety of hot and cold tapas, a few of our favorites being the Escalivada (Olivella's mother's version of roasted vegetables—spicy caramelized onions are wild—served at room temperature) and the Espinacas à la Catalana (spinach sautéed with garlic, pine nuts, and raisins). Ask the waiter which brews best accompany the dishes. Olivella's signature dessert is his La Sagrada Familia—twin towers of sugar cones (fans of Gaudí will recognize them immediately) filled with chocolate mousse that rest upon a bed of Chantilly cream and fresh berries. Almost as impressive as the food is the costly conversion from a high-ceilinged brick warehouse to a two-level industrial-chic brew pub complete with pool tables, dart boards, and live music (including jazz, flamenco, blues, alternative, and classical).

INEXPENSIVE

Hamburger Mary's. 1582 Folsom St. (at 12th St.). ☎ **415/626-5767.** Reservations recommended. Breakfast $5–$9; main courses $6–$10. AE, DC, DISC, MC, V. Mon–Thurs 11:30am–1am; Fri 11:30am–2am; Sat 10am–2am; Sun 10am–1am. Bus: 9, 12, 42, or 47. AMERICAN.

San Francisco's most . . . alternative burger joint, Hamburger Mary's is a popular hangout for gays, lesbians, and just about everyone else eschewing society's norms. The restaurant's kitsch decor includes thrift-shop floral wallpaper, family photos, garage-sale prints, stained glass, religious drawings, and Oriental screens. You'll get to know the bar well—it's where you'll stand with the tattooed masses while you wait for a table. Don't despair: They mix a good drink, and people-watching is what you're here for anyway. Sandwiches, salads, and vegetarian dishes provide an alternative to their famous greasy burgers, served on healthful nine-grain bread (like it makes a difference). *Tip:* Go with the home fries over the french fries. In the morning, Hamburger Mary's doubles as a breakfast joint, a good stop for a three-egg omelet or French toast.

✪ **Manora's.** 1600 Folsom St. (at 12th St.). ☎ **415/861-6224.** Main courses $5.95–$11. MC, V. Mon–Fri 11:30am–2:30pm and 5–10:30pm; Sat 5:30–10:30pm; Sun 5:30–10pm. Bus: 9, 12, or 47. THAI.

Manora's cranks out some of the best Thai in town and is well worth a jaunt to its SoMa location. But this is no relaxed dining affair. It's perpetually packed (unless you come early), and you'll be seated sardinelike at one of the cramped but well-appointed tables. During the dinner rush, the noise level can make conversation almost impossible among larger parties, but the food is so darn good, you'll probably prefer to turn your head toward your plate and stuff your face. Start with a Thai iced tea or coffee and one of the tangy soups or the chicken satay, which comes with a decadent peanut sauce. Follow up with any of the wonderful dinner dishes—which should be shared—and a side of rice. There are endless options, including a vast array of vegetarian plates. Every remarkably flavorful dish arrives seemingly seconds after you order it, which is great if you're hungry, a bummer if you were planning a long, leisurely dinner. Come before seven or after nine if you don't want a loud, rushed meal.

South Park Café. 108 S. Park Ave. (between Brannan and Bryant sts.). ☎ **415/495-7275.** Reservations recommended. Main courses $11.50–$17. AE, MC, V. Mon–Fri 7:30am–10pm; Sat 6–10pm. Bus: 15, 30, 32, 42, 45, or 76. FRENCH.

Whenever we get the urge to dump everything and fly to Paris (which is about every day), we drive across town to the South Park Café—it's not quite the same thing as a bistro on Boulevard Montparnasse, but it's close. Usually we're content with an espresso and pastry; a splurge involves the saffron mussels or blood sausage served with sautéed apples. For the ultimate romantic intention, bring a blanket and dine *sur l'herbe* at the adorable park across the street. Beware of the midweek lunch rush, though.

6 Chinatown

MODERATE

Brandy Ho's Hunan Food. 217 Columbus Ave. (at Pacific Ave.). ☎ **415/788-7527.** Reservations accepted. Main courses $8–$13. AE, DC, DISC, MC, V. Sun–Thurs 11:30am–11pm; Fri–Sat 11:30am–midnight. Bus: 15 or 41. CHINESE.

Fancy black-and-white granite tabletops and a large, open kitchen give you the first clue that the food here is a cut above the usual Hunanese fare. Take our advice and start immediately with the fried dumplings (in the sweet-and-sour sauce) or cold chicken salad. Next, move on to the fish-ball soup with spinach, bamboo shoots, noodles, and other goodies. The best main course is Three Delicacies, a combination of scallops, shrimp, and chicken with onion, bell pepper, and bamboo shoots, seasoned with ginger, garlic, and wine, and served with black-bean sauce. Most dishes here are quite hot and spicy, but the kitchen will adjust the level to meet your specifications. There is a small selection of wines and beers, including plum wine and sake.

INEXPENSIVE

House of Nanking. 919 Kearny St. (at Columbus Ave.). ☎ **415/421-1429.** Reservations accepted for 6 or more. Main courses $4.95–$8.95. No credit cards. Mon–Fri 11am–10pm; Sat noon–10pm; Sun 4–10pm. Bus: 9, 12, 15, or 30. CHINESE.

To the unknowing passerby, the House of Nanking has "greasy dive" written all over it. To its legion of fans, however, the wait—sometimes up to an hour—is worth what's on the plate. Located on the edge of Chinatown just off Columbus Avenue, this inconspicuous little diner is one of San Francisco's worst-kept secrets. When the line is reasonable, we drop by for a plate of pot stickers (still the best we've ever tasted) and chef/owner Peter Fang's signature shrimp-and-green-onion pancake served with peanut sauce. Trust the waiter when he recommends a special, or simply point to what looks good on someone else's table. Even with a new expansion that's doubled the elbow room, seating is tight, so prepare to be bumped around a bit, and don't expect good service—it's all part of the Nanking experience.

7 North Beach/Telegraph Hill

EXPENSIVE

Bix. 56 Gold St. (between Sansome and Montgomery sts.). ☎ 415/
433-6300. Reservations recommended. Main courses $7–$14 lunch, $15–$25 dinner. AE, CB, DC, DISC, MC, V. Mon–Thurs 11:30am–11pm; Fri 11:30am–midnight; Sat 5:30pm–midnight; Sun 6–10pm. Bus: 15, 30, 41, or 45. CLASSIC AMERICAN/CALIFORNIA.

If you feel like dressing up and hittin' the town, this suave little back-alley bar and restaurant is a good place to start. Fashioned after a 1920s supper club, Bix is better known for its martinis than for its menu. Curving Honduran mahogany, massive silver columns, and art-deco–style lighting set the stage for dancing to live music, though most locals settle for chatting with the friendly bartenders and noshing on appetizers. While the ultrastylish setting tends to overshadow the food, Bix actually serves some pretty good grub. The fresh fettuccine with seared day-boat scallops, wild mushrooms, butternut squash, and tomato fondue is the undisputed favorite, followed by the grilled filet mignon with mushrooms and chicken hash à la Bix. And for that special occasion, how can you say no to a round of $118 Beluga caviar on toast?

Caffè Sport. 574 Green St. (between Grant and Columbus aves.). ☎ 415/
981-1251. Reservations accepted only for parties of 4 or more. Main courses $15–$24. No credit cards. Tues–Thurs noon–2pm; Fri–Sat noon–2:30pm; Tues–Thurs seatings at 5, 6:30, 8:30, and 10pm; Fri–Sat at 6:30, 8:30, and 10pm. Bus: 15, 30, 41, or 45. ITALIAN.

People either love or hate this stodgy Sicilian eatery. Cluttered with hanging hams, fishnets, decorative plates, dolls, mirrors, and 2 decades worth of dust, Caffè Sport is better known for its surly staff and eclectic ambiance than for its food. Owner/chef/artiste Antonio Latona serves up healthy portions of attitude along with garlic-laden pasta dishes and is happy to report that this is Senator Dianne

Feinstein's favorite North Beach hangout. Lunch is tame in comparison to dinner, when the Sport is mobbed and lively. Disregard the framed menu that sits on each table and accept the waiter's "suggestions." Whatever arrives—whether it be a dish of calamari, mussels, and shrimp in tomato-garlic sauce, or pasta in pesto sauce—it's bound to be *bene.* Bring a huge appetite, but above all, don't be late if you have a reservation.

Moose's. 1652 Stockton St. (between Filbert and Union sts.). ☎ **415/ 989-7800.** http://www.mooses.com. Reservations recommended. Main courses $13–$26. AE, CB, DC, JCB, MC, V. Mon–Thurs 11:30am–11pm; Fri–Sat 11:30am–midnight; Sun 10:30am–11pm. Valet parking $9 for 3 hrs. Bus: 15, 30, 41, or 45. MEDITERRANEAN/CALIFORNIA.

You'll see the big blue neon Moose out front long before you pass through the doors, and once inside you'll notice you're in the largest dining room in North Beach. This is where Nob Hill socialites and local politicians come to dine and be seen, but Moose's is not just an image—in fact, the dining room itself is rather sparse and unintimate. The food, however, well *that's* a different story. Everything that comes out of Moose's kitchen is way above par. The appetizers are innovative, fresh, and well balanced (try the Mediterranean fish soup with rouille and croutons that's cooked in the wood-fired oven), and the main courses (especially the meats) are perfectly prepared. The menu changes every few months and might include a grilled veal chop with potato galette and a variety of pasta, chicken, and fish dishes.

The bar, separated from the main dining room by a low, frosted-glass partition, remains busy long after the kitchen closes. Jazz featuring piano and bass is played there nightly, as well as during Sunday brunch.

MODERATE

Enrico's. 504 Broadway (at Kearny St.). ☎ **415/982-6223.** Reservations recommended. Main courses $8–$13 lunch, $13–$19 dinner. AE, DC, DISC, MC, V. Mon–Sun 11:30–11pm; Fri–Sat 11:30–midnight; bar daily noon–2am. Bus: 12, 15, 30, or 83. MEDITERRANEAN.

Though it's taking its sweet time, North Beach's bawdy stretch of Broadway is on the road to rehabilitation. Helping things along is the newly refurbished version of Enrico's, a glitzy sidewalk restaurant and supper club that was once the place to hang out before Broadway took its seedy downward spiral. Families may want to skip this one, but anyone with an appreciation for live jazz (played nightly), late-night noshing, and weirdo-watching from the outdoor patio would be quite content spending an alfresco evening under the heat lamps. Chewy brick-oven pizza, zesty tapas, and thick steaks are hot items on the monthly changing menu. The best part? No cover charge, killer burgers served until midnight on weekends, and valet parking.

Fog City Diner. 1300 Battery St. (at Lombard St.). ☎ **415/982-2000.** Reservations accepted. Main courses $12–$18. CB, DC, DISC, MC, V. Sun–Thurs 11:30am–11pm; Fri–Sat 11:30am–midnight. Bus: 42. AMERICAN.

Now more popular because of its Visa commercial than its food, Fog City has become a tourist destination, with a few locals straggling in for business lunches. The restaurant looks like a genuine American metallic diner—but only from the outside. Inside, dark polished woods, inspired lighting, and a well-stocked raw bar tell you this is no hash-slinger.

Dressed-up dinner dishes include gourmet chili dogs, salads, sandwiches, burgers, pork chops, and pot roast. Fancier fish and meat meals include grilled catches of the day and thick-cut steaks. Lighter eaters can make a meal out of the long list of "small plates" that include crab cakes or quesadilla with chili peppers and almonds. The place is cute and the food is fine, but if your heart is set on coming here, do so at lunch—you'll be better off elsewhere if you want a special dinner.

Il Fornaio. Levi Plaza, 1265 Battery St. (bounded by Sansome, Battery, Union, and Greenwich sts.). ☎ **415/986-0100.** Main courses $9–$18. AE, DC, MC, V. Mon–Fri 7am–11pm; Sat–Sun 9am–11pm. Bus: 12, 32, or 42. Valet parking $5. ITALIAN.

While we can't say Il Fornaio would be our choice if we could only eat at one spot for the rest of our lives, it's one of our favorite standbys, producing consistently good Italian fare at decent prices. Located in Levi Plaza a few minutes away from Pier 39, this trattoria has great atmosphere: It bustles, it's big, and though a little cramped, the decor is not overwhelming but smart Italian. By day it is buzzing with Financial District types and socialites, by night, with couples and gathering friends.

Stacks of fresh-baked Italian cookies behind glass greet you when you first walk through the door. If you don't have a reservation and can't wait to eat, pull up a stool at the marble-topped bar, where the view of the open kitchen and dining room is unobstructed. Better yet, on a sunny day, grab a patio table that looks onto Levi Plaza's fountain. The divided dining room, with high ceilings and enormous, Italian-style paintings, is also warm and convivial. The first of many delights is the basket of fresh-baked breads and breadsticks that arrive at your table accompanied by a dipping dish of olive oil. Complement them with any of the delicious salads or the daily soup (especially if it's carrot), then venture onward to any of the pastas, pizzas, or main courses. Our favorite is the rotisserie duck in balsamic vinegar, which Il Fornaio somehow serves without all the fat you'd expect from duck and all the crispy skin you wish for. Parents especially appreciate the "bambini" menu, which features pint-size fare for under $6. Desserts are decadent and wonderful. Try the tiramisu and a glass of rose grappa—a perfect way to end the meal. Breakfasts here are a treat as well.

○ **Rose Pistola.** 532 Columbus Ave. (at Union and Green sts.). ☎ **415/ 399-0499.** Reservations highly recommended. Main courses $6.95–$18.50 lunch; most dishes $9–$21.50 dinner. AE, MC, V. Sun–Thurs 11:30am–10:30pm with late-night menu until midnight; Fri–Sat 11:30am–11:30pm with late-night menu until 1am. Valet parking $5 lunch, $8 dinner. Bus: 15, 30, 41, or 45. ITALIAN.

Undoubtedly the hottest new restaurant in 1997, Rose Pistola was created by the masterminds behind the ultrasuccessful SoMa restaurant Lulu. Like its North Beach neighborhood, the atmosphere is of a smart, bustling bistro. Although it's a larger dining room than most in the area, it's divided so it doesn't feel impersonal (though you'll want to avoid the tables next to the bar). Sidewalk seating is favored on sunny afternoons, but inside there's plenty to see as chefs crank out the eclectic food from the open kitchen. Fare here is meant to be shared, and aside from sandwiches, comes à la carte. The appetizer list features a barrage of hot and cold antipasti, which are reasonably priced between $2.75 and $7.50 but tend to be in small portions. We opted for fried chickpeas, an innovative and tasty new way to enjoy the seed; lemon, prosciutto, sweet pea, and mozzarella risotto fritters, which were wonderful but pricey for four golfball-size morsels ($4.75); and a boring—and again pricey—chopped salad ($5.50).

Along with meats and foul, you'll find a variety of fish choices on the menu. We tried mussels in a rich tomato broth, which was so flavorful we kept it around to soak up our bread long after the shellfish had been devoured. Our favorite dish, however, was the whole Arctic char, which came bathing in fennel and tapenade in a big iron skillet. The fish was crispy and perfectly seasoned on the outside, tender and juicy on the inside—definitely worth writing home about. The "flaming cream" dessert, three fried crème-brûlée–type diamonds that arrived afire with a Bacardi-and-apricot sauce, was creative and very tasty, but not worth the $7.50 asking price. Still, overall, we agree that Rose Pistola is hot for the right reasons: It's the place to be, the food is great, and the menu is varied enough for all tastes and budgets.

Stinking Rose. 325 Columbus Ave. (between Vallejo and Broadway). ☎ **415/781-7673.** Reservations accepted. Main courses $12–$18. AE, DC, JCB, MC, V. Sun–Thurs 11am–11pm; Fri–Sat 11am–midnight. Bus: 15, 30, 41, or 45. ITALIAN.

Garlic, of course, is the "flower" from which this restaurant gets its name. From soup to ice cream, the supposedly healthful herb is a star ingredient in most every dish. ("We season our garlic with food," exclaims the menu.) From a strictly gourmet point of view, the Stinking Rose is unremarkable. Pizzas, pastas, and meats smothered in simple, overpowering garlic sauces are tasty, but memorable only for their singular garlicky intensity. That said, this is a fun place; the restaurant's lively atmosphere and odoriferous aroma combine for good entertainment. Black-and-white floors, gray marble tables, and large windows overlooking the street help maintain the high energy. The best dishes here include garlic-steamed clams and mussels, garlic pizza, and 40-clove garlic chicken (served with garlic mashed potatoes, of course).

INEXPENSIVE

♦ **L'Osteria del Forno.** 519 Columbus Ave. (between Green and Union sts.). ☎ **415/982-1124.** Sandwiches $5–$6; pizzas $10–$13; main courses $6–$8.25. No credit cards. Mon–Wed 11:30am–10pm; Fri–Sat 11:30am–10:30pm; Sun 1–10pm. Bus: 15 or 41. ITALIAN.

L'Osteria del Forno may be only slightly larger than a walk-in closet, but it's one of the top-three Italian restaurants in North Beach. Peer in the window facing Columbus Avenue, and you'll probably see two Italian women with their hair up, sweating from the heat of their brick-lined oven that cranks out the best focaccia (and focaccia sandwiches) in the city. There's no pomp or circumstance involved: locals come here strictly to eat. The menu features a variety of superb pizzas and fresh pastas, plus a few daily specials (pray for the roast pork braised in milk). Small baskets of warm focaccia bread keep you going till the entrees arrive, which should always be accompanied by a glass of Italian red.

Mario's Bohemian Cigar Store. 566 Columbus Ave. ☎ **415/362-0536.** Sandwiches $5–$6.25. No credit cards. Daily 10am–midnight. Closed Dec 24–Jan 1. Bus: 15, 30, 41, or 45. ITALIAN.

Across the street from Washington Square is one of North Beach's most popular neighborhood hangouts: Mario's. The century-old bar—small, well worn, and perpetually busy—is best known for its focaccia sandwiches, including meatball or eggplant. Wash it all down with an excellent cappuccino or a house Campari as you watch the tourists stroll by. And yes, they do sell cigars.

Note: A new, larger location has opened at 2209 Polk St., between Green and Vallejo streets (☎ **415/776-8226**).

8 Fisherman's Wharf

EXPENSIVE

A. Sabella's. Fisherman's Wharf, 2766 Taylor St. (at Jefferson St.), 3rd floor. ☎ **415/771-6775.** Reservations accepted. Main courses $12–$47. AE, CB, DC, DISC, MC, V. Daily 11am–10:30pm. Cable car: Powell-Mason line. ITALIAN/ SEAFOOD.

The Sabella family has been serving seafood in San Francisco since the turn of the century and has operated A. Sabella's restaurant on the wharf continuously since 1920. Catering heavily to the tourist trade, the menu offers something for everyone—steak, lamb, sea-food, chicken, and pasta dishes, all made from scratch with fresh local ingredients. Where A. Sabella's really shines, however, is in the shellfish department. Its 1,000-gallon saltwater tank allows for fresh crab, abalone, and lobster year-round, which means no restaurant in the city can touch A. Sabella's when it comes to feasting on fresh Dungeness crab and abalone out of season. A nice touch is the live piano music played nightly in the spacious and rather chic dining room overlooking the wharf.

MODERATE

Cafe Pescatore. 2455 Mason St. (at North Point St.). ☎ **415/561-1111.** Reservations recommended. Main courses $3.95–$7.95 breakfast, $10–$16 lunch or dinner. AE, DC, DISC, MC, V. Mon–Thurs 11:30am–10pm; Fri 11:30am–11pm; Sat 5–11pm; Sun 5–10pm; Sat–Sun 7am–3pm brunch, 3–5pm cafe menu. Cable car: Powell-Mason line. Bus: 42, 15, or 39. ITALIAN.

Though San Francisco locals are a rarity at Cafe Pescatore, most agree that if they had to dine at Fisherman's Wharf, this cozy trattoria would be their first choice. Two walls of sliding glass doors offer pseudo-side-walk seating when the weather's warm, although heavy vehicular traf-fic can detract from the alfresco experience. The general consensus is to order anything that's cooked in the open kitchen's wood-fired oven, such as the pizzas and roasts. A big hit with tourists is the *polenta al forno*—oak-roasted cheese polenta with marinara sauce and fresh pesto. The verde pizza (pesto-flavored prawns and spinach) and huge serving of roast chicken are also safe bets.

9 Pacific Heights/Cow Hollow

EXPENSIVE

Harris'. 2100 Van Ness Ave. (at Pacific Ave.). ☎ **415/673-1888.** Reservations recommended. Main courses $18–$34. AE, CB, DC, DISC, MC, V. Mon–Thurs 5:30–9:30pm; Fri 5:30–10:30pm; Sat 5–10:30pm; Sun 5–9:30pm. Bus: 38 or 45. STEAK HOUSE.

Every big city has a great steak restaurant, and in San Francisco it's Harris'—a comfortably elegant establishment sporting a handsome wood-paneled dining room with curving banquettes and stately waiters. Proprietor Ann Lee Harris knows steaks; she grew up on a cattle ranch and married the owner of the largest feedlot in California. In 1976, the couple opened the Harris Ranch Restaurant on Interstate 5 in central California, where they built a rock-solid reputation up and down the coast. The steaks, which can be seen hanging in a glass-windowed aging room off Pacific Avenue, are cut thick—either New York–style or T-bone—and are served with a baked potato and seasonal vegetables. Harris' also offers lamb chops, fresh fish, lobster, and roast duckling, as well as venison, buffalo, and other types of game when in season.

✪ **La Folie.** 2316 Polk St. (between Green and Union sts.). ☎ **415/776-5577.** Reservations recommended. Main courses $24–$32; 5-course tasting menu $65; vegetarian tasting menu $50. AE, CB, DC, DISC, MC, V. Mon–Sat 5:30–10:30pm. Bus: 19, 41, 45, 47, 49, or 76. FRENCH.

For fantastic French food without the highbrow attitude, La Folie is the place to feast. The minute you walk through the door you'll know why this is many locals' favorite restaurant. The country-French decor is tasteful but not too serious, with whimsical chandeliers and a cloudy sky painted overhead. The staff is friendly, knowledgeable, and very accommodating, and the food is truly outstanding. Unlike many renowned chefs, La Folie's Roland Passot is in the kitchen nightly, and it shows. Each of his California-influenced French creations is an architectural and culinary masterpiece. Best of all, they're served in a relaxed and comfortable environment. Start with an appetizer such as the roast quail and foie gras with salad, wild mushrooms, and roasted garlic—it's guaranteed to melt in your mouth. Main courses are not petite as in many French restaurants, and all are accompanied by flavorful and well-balanced sauces. Try the rôti of quail and squab stuffed with wild mushrooms and wrapped in crispy potato strings, or the roast venison with vegetables, quince, and huckleberry sauce. Finish off with any of the delectable desserts.

MODERATE

Ace Wasabi's. 3339 Steiner St. (at Chestnut St.). ☎ **415/567-4903.** Reservations not accepted. Main courses $4–$9. AE, MC, V. Mon–Thurs 5:30–10:30pm, Fri–Sat 5:30–11pm, Sun 5–10pm. Bus: 30. JAPANESE/SUSHI.

Yeah, more sushi, but this time with a twist. What differentiates this Marina hot spot (formerly known as Flying Kamikazes) from the usual sushi spots around town are the unique combinations, the varied menu, and the young, hip atmosphere. Ace Wasabi's innovative rolls are a nice welcome to those bored with the traditional styles, though they may be too much adventure for some (don't worry, there's plenty of nonsea and nonraw items on the menu). Don't miss the rainbow "Three Amigos" roll or the "Rock and Roll" with cooked eel, avocado, and cucumber. The buckwheat-noodle-and–julienne-vegetable salad is also a treat. The service could be improved—on busy nights you'll wait forever for your server to pour your Sapporo—but the staff is friendly and the atmosphere is fun, so nobody seems to mind.

Betelnut. 2030 Union St. (at Buchanan St.). ☎ **415/929-8855.** Reservations recommended. Main courses $9–$16. CB, DC, DISC, MC, V. Sun–Thurs 11:30am–11pm; Fri–Sat 11:30am–midnight. Bus: 22, 41, or 45. SOUTHEAST ASIAN.

While San Francisco is teeming with Asian restaurants, few offer the posh, fashionable dining environment of this restaurant on upscale Union Street. As the menu explains, the restaurant is themed after "Pejui Wu," a traditional Asian beer house offering local brews and savory dishes. But with the bamboo paneling, red Formica countertops, and low-hanging lamps, the place feels less like an authentic harbor restaurant and more like a set out of Madonna's movie *Shanghai Surprise*. Still, the atmosphere is en vogue, with dimly lit booths, ringside seating overlooking the bustling stir-fry chefs, sidewalk tables (weather permitting), and body-to-body flirting at the cramped but festive bar. Starters include sashimi and tasty salt-and-pepper whole gulf prawns; main courses offer orange-glazed beef with asparagus, and oyster mushrooms and Singapore chili crab. While prices seem reasonable, it's the incidentals such as white rice ($1.50 per person) and tea ($3.50 per pot) that rack up the bill. Many locals and tourists absolutely adore this place, so we're hesitant to bash it. Unfortunately, when we've come here the food was merely fair and the wait staff so inattentive, the experience was ruined. In our minds, the main reason to choose this restaurant over others is the atmosphere and their heavenly signature dessert: a mouth-watering tapioca pudding with sweet red adzuki beans.

The Elite Café. 2049 Fillmore St. (between Pine and California sts.). ☎ **415/ 346-8668.** Reservations not accepted. Main courses $10.95–$24. AE, DC, DISC, MC, V. Mon–Sat 5–11pm; Sun 10am–3pm and 5–10pm. Bus: 41 or 45. CAJUN/ CREOLE.

If the shellfish in the window doesn't get you in the door, the festive atmosphere will. This place is always bustling with Pacific Heights's beautiful people who come for fresh oysters, blackened filet mignon with Cajun butter, jambalaya, redfish with crab and Creole cream sauce, or any of the other well-spiced Cajun dishes. The high-backed booths provide more-intimate dining than the crowded tables and bar. Brunch is good, too, when all kinds of egg dishes—Benedict, sardou, Hangtown fry, and many more—are offered along with such goodies as bagels and lox and smoked chicken sausage.

Greens Restaurant, Fort Mason. Building A, Fort Mason Center (enter Fort Mason opposite the Safeway at Buchanan and Marina sts.). ☎ **415/ 771-6222.** Reservations recommended 2 weeks in advance. Main courses $11– $15; fixed-priced dinner $40; brunch $8–$11. DISC, MC, V. Mon 5:30–9:30pm; Tues–Fri 11:30am–2pm and 5:30–9:30pm; Sat 11:30am–2:30pm and 5:30– 9pm; Sun brunch 10am–2pm. Bakery Mon–Sat 8am–4:30pm; Sun 9:30am– 3:30pm. Bus: 28 or 30. VEGETARIAN.

Knowledgeable locals swear by Greens, where executive-chef Annie Somerville (author of *Fields of Greens*) cooks with the seasons, using produce from Green Gulch Farm and other local organic farms. Located in an old warehouse, with enormous windows overlooking the bridge and the bay, the restaurant is both a pioneer and a legend. A weeknight dinner might feature such appetizers as tomato, white-bean, and sorrel soup, or grilled asparagus with lemon, Parmesan cheese, and watercress, followed by such choices as spring-vegetable risotto with asparagus, peas, shiitake and crimini mushrooms, and Parmesan cheese, or Sri Lankan curry made of new potatoes, cauliflower, carrots, peppers, and snap peas stewed with tomatoes, coconut milk, ginger, and Sri Lankan spices.

A special five-course dinner is served on Saturday only. A recent example began with grilled asparagus, yellowfin potatoes, and peppers with blood-orange beurre blanc, followed by shiitake and crimini mushroom lasagna with leeks and mushroom port sauce. Desserts are equally adventuresome—try the chocolate pave with mint crème anglaise or the espresso ice cream with chocolate sauce (*Insider tip:* A "Late Evening Desert" is served Mon to Thurs from 9:30 to 11pm.). Lunch and brunch are somewhat simpler, but equally as inventive.

Like the restaurant, the adjacent bakery is also operated by the Zen Center. It sells homemade breads, sandwiches, soups, salads, and pastries to take home.

North India Restaurant. 3131 Webster St. (at Lombard St.). ☎ **415/931-1556.** Reservations recommended. Main courses $14.50–$19.95; fixed-price dinner $12.95. AE, DC, MC, V. Mon–Fri 11:30am–2:30pm; daily 5–10pm. Bus: 41 or 45. INDIAN.

While many Indian establishments lack atmosphere, chef Parvesh Sahi's full Indian menu is served in a plush, dimly lit dining room, providing the perfect ambiance for an intimate evening out with some ethnic flair. Start by ordering a cup of the sweet and spicy chai tea, and the oversized, moist samosas (spiced potatoes and green peas served in a crisp pocket), then venture onward with any of the tandoori specials, such as the mixed seafood dish with sea bass, jumbo prawns, and calamari. There are plenty of vegetarian dishes as well, ranging from *aloo gobi* (cauliflower and potatoes in curry sauce) to *baingan aloo masala* (eggplant, potatoes, tomatoes, ginger, garlic, green onions, and spices). All these tasty feasts are accompanied by bottomless pots of delicious mango chutney and cucumber-dill sauce. Anything you order here will be fresh, well prepared, and served by courteous waiters wearing vests adorned with Indian-style mirrors and gold embroidery. Although expensive for Indian food, it's worth the extra bucks if you want to be ensured good quality and atmosphere. Arrive between 5 and 7pm and you can opt for the very affordable fixed-price dinner for $12.95.

✪ **Pane e Vino.** 3011 Steiner St. (at Union St.). ☎ **415/346-2111.** Reservations recommended. Main courses $8.50–$19.95. MC, V. Mon–Thurs 11:30am–2:30pm and 5–10pm; Fri–Sat 11:30am–10:30pm; Sun 5–10pm. Bus: 41 or 45. ITALIAN.

Pane e Vino is one of San Francisco's top and most authentic Italian restaurants, as well as our personal favorite. The food is consistently excellent (careful not to fill up on the outstanding breads served upon seating), the prices reasonable, and the mostly Italian-accented staff always smooth and efficient under pressure (you'll see). The two small dining rooms, separated by an open kitchen that eminates heavenly aromas, offer only limited seating, so expect a wait even if you have a reservation. The menu offers a wide selection of appetizers, including a fine carpaccio, *vitello tonnato* (sliced roasted veal and capers in a lemony tuna sauce), and the hugely popular chilled artichoke stuffed with bread and tomatoes and served with a vinaigrette. Our favorite, the antipasti of mixed grilled vegetables, always spurs a fork fight. A similar broad selection of pastas is available, including a flavorful *pennette alla boscaiola* with porcini mushrooms and pancetta in a tomato cream sauce. Other specialties are grilled fish and meat dishes, including a chicken breast marinated in lime juice and herbs. Top dessert picks are any of the Italian ice creams, the crème caramel, and (but, of course) the creamy tiramisu.

PlumpJack Café. 3127 Fillmore St. (between Filbert and Greenwich sts.). ☎ **415/563-4755.** Reservations recommended. Main courses $15–$22. AE, MC, V. Mon–Fri 11:30am–2pm; Mon–Sat 5:30–10:30pm. Bus: 41 or 45. CALIFORNIA/FRENCH/MEDITERRANEAN.

Wildly popular among San Francisco's style-setters, this small Cow Hollow restaurant quickly became the "in" place to dine. This is partly due to the fact that it's run by one of the Getty clan (as in J. Paul), but mostly because Chef Maria Helm's food is just plain good and the whimsical decor is a veritable work of art.

Though the menu changes weekly, you might find such appetizers as smoked salmon with two kinds of caviar, or a salad of watercress and Belgian endive with kumquats, toasted pine nuts, shaved reggiano, and champagne vinaigrette. Main dishes range from risotto with spring onions, asparagus, pancetta, and chèvre to roasted duck-breast confit with potato rosti and thyme-roasted apples. Top it off with bittersweet chocolate soufflé or cinnamo-scented Alsatian apple cake. The extraordinarily extensive California wine list—gleaned from the PlumpJack wine shop down the street—is sold at next to retail, with many wines available by the glass.

✪ **Zinzino.** 2355 Chestnut St. (at Divisadero St.). ☎ **415/346-6623.** Reservations accepted. Main courses $9–$16.50. AE, MC, V. Mon–Thurs 6–10pm; Fri–Sat 5:30–11pm; Sun 5:30–9:30pm. Bus: 22 or 30. ITALIAN.

Owner Ken Zankel and Spago-sired chef Andrea Rappaport have combined forces to create one of the city's top Italian restaurants. Zinzino may look like a tiny trattoria from the outside, but you could fit a small nuclear sub in the space from the sun-drenched facade to the shaded back patio of this former Laundromat.

Italian movie posters, magazines, antiques, and furnishings evoke memories of past vacations, but we rarely recall the food in Italy being this good (and certainly not this cheap). Start off with the crispy calamari with a choice of herbed aioli or tomato sauces (second only to Scala's Earth and Surf), the roasted jumbo prawns wrapped in crisp pancetta and bathed in a tangy balsamic reduction sauce, or the peculiar-tasting shaved-fennel-and-mint salad—or try them all. Rappaport is giving Zuni Café a run for its money with her version of roasted half chicken, the most tender bird we've ever tasted ("It's all the wood-fired oven," she admits); the accompanying goat-cheese salad and potato frisee were also superb. New to the menu are Rappaport's weekly rotating specials, such as her roasted shellfish platter, oven-roasted half lobster, or baby lamb chops.

INEXPENSIVE

✪ **Doidge's.** 2217 Union St. (between Fillmore and Steiner sts.). ☎ **415/921-2149.** Reservations accepted and essential on weekends. Breakfast $4.50–$10; lunch $5–$8. MC, V. Mon–Fri 8am–1:45pm; Sat–Sun 8am–2:45pm. Bus: 41 or 45. AMERICAN.

Doidge's is sweet, small, and always packed, serving up one of the better breakfasts in San Francisco since 1971. Doidge's fame is based on eggs Benedict; eggs Florentine, prepared with thinly sliced Motherlode ham, runs a close second. Invariably, the menu includes a gourmet omelet packed with luscious combinations, and to delight the kid in you, hot chocolate comes in your very own teapot. The six seats at the original mahogany counter are still the most coveted by locals.

La Canasta. 2219 Filbert St. (at Fillmore St.). ☎ **415/921-3003.** Main courses $2.80–$6.15. No credit cards. Mon–Sat 11am–10pm. Bus: 22, 41, or 45. MEXICAN.

Unless you forge to the Mission District, burritos don't get much better (or bigger) than those served here at this tiny take-out establishment where you can stuff yourself with a huge chicken burrito for around $5 (the meat's grilled fresh to order). There are no seats here, though, so you'll just have to find another place to devour your grub; fortunately, the Marina Green is a short walk away and offers a million-dollar view no other restaurant can boast. A second location is at 3006 Buchanan St., at Union Street (☎ **415/474-2627**).

Mel's Diner. 2165 Lombard St. (at Fillmore St.). ☎ **415/921-3039.** Reservations accepted. Main courses $4–$5.50 breakfast, $6–$8 lunch, $8–$12 dinner. No credit cards. Sun–Thurs 6am–3am; Fri–Sat 24 hr. (Lombard location only). Bus: 22, 43, or 30. AMERICAN.

Sure, it's contrived, touristy, and nowhere near healthy, but when you get that urge for a chocolate shake and banana cream pie at the stroke of midnight, no other place in the city comes through like Mel's Diner. Modeled after a classic 1950s diner right down to the nickel jukebox at each table, Mel's harks back to the halcyon days when cholesterol and fried foods didn't stroke your guilty conscience with every greasy, wonderful bite. Too bad the prices don't reflect the fifties; a burger with fries and a coke runs about $8, and they don't take credit. There's another Mel's at 3355 Geary at Stanyan Street (☎ 415/387-2244).

10 Civic Center

EXPENSIVE

Jardinière. 300 Grove St. (at Franklin St.). ☎ **415/861-5555.** Reservations recommended. Main courses $19–$29; 3-course dinner (before 7pm only) $35; 5-course tasting menu $65. AE, DC, DISC, MC, V. Daily 5:30–10:30pm regular menu; 10:30–midnight late menu. Bus: 19, 21. FRENCH/CALIFORNIA.

One of the hottest new restaurants in town, Jardinière is also the favored pre- and postsymphony alternative to Jeremiah Tower's Stars. The hoopla is a result of a culinary dream team: owner/chef Traci Des Jardins, who packed up her pots and pans at Rubicon to go solo; owner/designer Pat Kuleto, who created the swank ambiance; and general manager Doug Washington, who's good looks and unswerving charm won him local fame at Vertigo. Now the two-story brick structure is abuzz with the "in" crowd who sip cocktails at the centerpiece mahogany bar or watch the scene discreetly from the upstairs circular balcony. The restaurant's champagne theme is integrated via twinkling lights and fun ice buckets built into the balcony railing, making the atmosphere conducive to throwing back a few in the best of style—especially when there's live jazz. Actually, cocktailing is our recommended reason to visit here. While the daily changing menu is good, many locals argue that its way pricey, tiny in portion, and not exactly memorable. We're in partial agreement; when we dined here the food was good, but didn't pack the surprise punches necessary to impress us jaded San Francisco diners (although restaurant critic Michael Bauer would disagree). But anyone simply in search of a quality meal will not be disappointed. The sweet onion tart with cured salmon and herb salad, lobster, leek, and chanterelle strudel was tasty and the crisped chicken with chanterelles, ozette potatoes, and apple-wood–smoked bacon; striped bass with lobster saffron broth, fennel, and potatoes; and fillet of beef with sunchoke gratin, mushrooms, and red-wine sauce are also recommended. A bonus for theatergoers is the "Staccato Menu," which is a three-courser that includes an appetizer, main course, and dessert and is available before 7pm. Late diners can also come here for a limited menu served from 10:30pm to midnight. We also have to give kudos to the great wine selection—many by the glass and over 300 bottles.

MODERATE

✪ **Zuni Café.** 1658 Market St. (at Franklin St.). ☎ **415/552-2522.** Reservations recommended. Main courses $15–$22.50. AE, MC, V. Tues–Sat 11:30am–midnight; Sun 11am–11pm. Valet parking $5. Muni Metro: All Market St. trams. Bus: 6, 7, 71, or 75. MEDITERRANEAN.

Even factoring in the sometimes snotty wait staff, Zuni Café is still one of our favorite places in the city to have lunch. Its expanse of windows and prime Market Street location guarantee good people-watching—a favorite San Francisco pastime—and chef Judy Rodgers's Mediterranean-influenced menu is wonderfully diverse and satisfying. For the full effect, sit at the bustling, copper-topped bar and peruse the foot-long oyster menu (a dozen or so varieties are on hand at all times); you can also sit in the stylish, exposed-brick dining room or on the outdoor patio. Though the changing menu always includes meat, such as New York steak with Belgian endive gratin, and fish—either grilled or braised in the kitchen's brick oven—the proven winners are Rodgers's brick-oven–roasted chicken for two with Tuscan-style bread salad, the polenta appetizer with mascarpone, and the hamburger on grilled rosemary focaccia bread (a strong contender for the city's best burger). Whatever you decide, be sure to order a side of the shoestring potatoes.

11 Japan Center & Environs

MODERATE

YOYO Bistro. In the Miyako Hotel, 1611 Post St. (at Laguna St.). ☎ **415/ 922-7788.** Reservations not necessary. Main courses $9–$14; continental breakfast buffet $7.50–$18. AE, CB, DC, JCB, MC, V. Daily 6:30am–11am, 11:30am–2:30pm, and 5:30–10pm. Parking in Japan Center garage; a fee is charged. Bus: 2, 3, 22, or 38. ASIAN/FRENCH.

You'd be wise to venture out of downtown for dinner in YOYO's dark, 50-person dining room, which is surrounded by authentic shoji screens. Previously Elka, the restaurant changed hands in 1996 and is now run by ex-Elka employees, who have put a great deal of care into creating a quality dining experience. The room and the food combine contemporary and ancient, Asian and French. One of the best times to come is between 5:30 and 10pm for *tsumami* (Japanese tapas) where you can order à la carte or choose four dishes for $14. These scrumptious little creations are anything from fresh oysters to pork ribs, and all come with outstanding sauces. Main courses from the dinner menu will include fresh fish, duck, and chicken—all very well prepared.

INEXPENSIVE

Sanppo. 1702 Post St. (at Laguna St.). ☎ **415/346-3486.** Reservations not accepted. Main courses $6–$15; combination dishes $10–$17. MC, V. Mon–Sat 11am–10pm; Sun 11:30am–10pm. Bus: 2, 3, 4, or 38. JAPANESE.

Simple and unpretentious though it is, Sanppo, across from the Japan Center, serves excellent, down-home Japanese food. You may be asked to share one of the few tables that surround a square counter in the small dining room. Lunches and dinners all include miso soup, rice, and pickled vegetables. At lunch you might have an order of fresh, thick-cut sashimi, teriyaki, tempura, beef donburi, or an order of *gyoza* (dumplings filled with savory meat and herbs) for $5 to $12. The same items are available at dinner for about $1 additional. Combination dishes, including tempura, sashimi, and gyoza, or tempura and teriyaki, are also available. Beer, wine, and sake are also served.

12 Haight-Ashbury

MODERATE

✪ **Cha Cha Cha.** 1801 Haight St. (at Shrader St.). ☎ **415/386-5758.** Reservations not accepted. Tapas $4.50–$7.75; main courses $9–$13. MC, V. Daily 11:30am–4pm; Sun–Thurs 5–11pm; Fri–Sat 5–11:30pm. Muni Metro: N. Bus: 6, 7, 66, 71, or 73. CARIBBEAN.

This is one of our all-time favorite places to come for dinner, but it's not for everybody. Cha Cha Cha is not a meal, it's an experience. Put your name on the mile-long list, crowd into the minuscule bar, and drink sangria while you wait (and try not to spill when you get bumped by all the young, attractive patrons who are also waiting). When you do finally get seated (it usually takes at least an hour), you'll dine in a loud—and we mean loud—dining room with Santeria altars, banana trees, and plastic tropical tablecloths. The best thing to do is order from the tapas menu and share the dishes family-style. The fried calamari, fried new potatoes, Cajun shrimp, and mussels in saffron broth are all bursting with flavor and are accompanied by rich, luscious sauces—but whatever you choose, you can't go wrong. This is the kind of place where you take friends in a partying mood, let your hair down, and make an evening of it. If you want all the flavor without the festivities, come during lunch.

✪ **Eos.** 901 Cole (at Carl St.). ☎ **415/566-3063.** Reservations recommended. Main courses $16–$26. AE, MC, V. Mon–Sat 5:30–11pm; Sun 5–11pm. Muni Metro: N. Bus: 6, 33, or 43. EAST-WEST FUSION.

Named after the Greek goddess of dawn, Eos is certainly basking in the spotlight thanks to chef/proprietor Arnold Wong, a master of texture and taste who perfected his craft while working at Masa's and Silks. It's not without a twinge of guilt that one mars the artistic presentation of each dish, such as the tender breast of Peking duck, smoked in ginger-peach tea leaves and served with a plum-kumquat chutney, or the blackened Asian catfish atop a bed of lemongrass risotto. For starters, try the almond-encrusted soft-shell crab dipped in spicy plum ponzu sauce. Unfortunately, the stark, industrial-deco decor does little to dampen the decibels, making a romantic outing nearly impossible unless you're into shouting. There is, however, a quiet, casual wine bar around the corner (same name) which stocks more than 400 vintages from around the globe.

✪ **Thep Phanom.** 400 Waller St. (at Fillmore St.). ☎ **415/431-2526.** Reservations recommended. Main courses $5.95–$10.95. AE, CB, DC, DISC, MC, V. Daily 5:30–10:30pm. Bus: 6, 7, 22, 66, or 71. THAI.

By successfully incorporating flavors from India, China, Burma, Malaysia, and more recently the West, Thep Phanom has risen the heady ranks to become one of the best Thai restaurants in San Francisco. Case in point: There's almost always a line out the front door. Start with the signature dish, ped swan—boneless duck in a light honey sauce served on a bed of spinach. The *larb ped* (minced duck salad), velvety basil-spiked seafood curry served on banana leaves, and spicy *yum plamuk* (calamari salad) are also recommended. Its Haight Street location attracts an eclectic crowd and informal atmosphere, though the decor is actually quite tasteful. Reservations are advised, and don't leave anything even remotely valuable in your car.

INEXPENSIVE

Zona Rosa. 1797 Haight St. (at Shrader St.). ☎ **415/668-7717.** Burritos $3.90–$4.90. No credit cards. Daily 11am–11pm. Muni Metro: N. Bus: 6, 7, 66, 71, or 73. MEXICAN.

This is a great place to stop and get a cheap (and healthful) bite. The most popular items here are the burritos, which are made to order and include your choice of beans (refried, whole pinto, or black), meats, or vegetarian ingredients. You can sit on a stool at the window and watch all the Haight Street freaks strolling by, relax at one of five colorful interior tables, or take it to go and head to Golden Gate Park (it's just 2 blocks away). Zona Rosa is one of the best burrito stores around.

13 Richmond/Sunset Districts

MODERATE

Beach Chalet Brewery & Restaurant. 1000 Great Hwy. (at the west end of Golden Gate Park near Fulton St.). ☎ **415/386-8439.** Reservations accepted. Lunch appetizers $5–$7.50; main courses $8–$12.50 at lunch, $12.50–$18 at dinner. MC, V. Mon–Thurs 11:30am–10pm (bistro menu 3–5:30pm); Fri–Sat 11:30am–11pm (bistro menu 3–5:30pm); Sun 10am–10pm. (Bar open until 2am nightly.) Bus: 18, 31, or 38. AMERICAN.

Since reopening on New Year's Eve 1996, the Beach Chalet has been one of the most popular reasons to make it out to the breakers. The restaurant occupies the upper floor of a historic public lounge that originally opened in 1900, was rebuilt in 1925, and, after being closed for more than 15 years, was recently renovated. Today the main floor's wonderful restored WPA frescoes and historical displays on the area are enough to lure tourists and locals, but upstairs is something altogether different. The only thing harking back to yesteryear is the timeless view of the great Pacific Ocean. While the place is bright and cheery, we agree with the critics: The restaurant should have been more reminiscent of its heritage. Dinner is pricey and the view disappears with the sun, so come for lunch or bistro snacks, when you can eat your grilled pizzetta with peppers, artichokes, mozzarella, and basil, or smoked-ham–and-brie sandwich or herb-crusted rotisserie chicken with garlic mashed potatoes with one of the best vistas around. After dinner it's a more local thing, especially on Friday, Saturday, and Sunday when live blues accompany the cocktails and house-made brews. *Note:* Be careful getting into the parking lot (only accessible from the northbound side of the highway); it's a quick, sandy turn.

Cliff House. 1090 Point Lobos (at Merrie Way). ☎ **415/386-3330.** Two dining areas: upstairs and main room. Reservations recommended for upstairs and brunch only. Main courses $7–$11 upstairs breakfast; $7–$11 upstairs lunch, $7.50–$18 main lunch; $12–$19 main and upstairs dinner. AE, CB, DC, MC, V. Upstairs: Mon–Fri 9am–3:30pm and 5–10pm; Sat–Sun 8:30am–4pm and 5–10pm. Main room: Mon–Sat 11am–10:30pm; Sun 10am–3pm and 3:30–10:30pm. Bus: 38 or 18. SEAFOOD/CALIFORNIA.

Back in the old days (we're talking way back) the Cliff House was the place to go for a romantic night on the town. Nowadays, this aging San Francisco landmark caters mostly to tourists who arrive by the busloads to gander at the Sutro Bath remains next door.

Three restaurants in the main, two-story building give diners a choice of how much they wish to spend. Phineas T. Barnacle is the least expensive; sandwiches, salads, soups and such are served

Hofbrau–style across from the elaborate saloon-style bar, after which you can seat yourself at the window-side tables overlooking the shore or beside the fireplace if you're chilled. A step up from the P.T.B. (literally) is Upstairs at the Cliff House, a slightly more formal setting that's best known for its breakfast omelets, and the main room, known as the Seafood and Beverage Co., the fanciest of the lot. Refurbished back to its glory days near the turn of the century, it offers superb ocean views, particularly at sunset, when the fog lets up; unfortunately, the food is a distant second to the scenery. The best M.O. is to arrive before dusk, request a window seat, order a few appetizers and cocktails, and enjoy the view, or opt for the elaborate Sunday brunch served from 10am to 3pm in the newly renovated Terrace Room.

✪ **Hong Kong Flower Lounge.** 5322 Geary Blvd. (between 17th and 18th aves.). ☎ **415/668-8998.** Most main dishes $7.95–$14.95; dim-sum dishes $1.80–$3.50. Mon–Fri 11am–2:30pm; Sat–Sun 10am–2:30pm; daily 5–9:30pm. Bus: 1, 2, or 38. CHINESE/DIM SUM.

If you come for dim sum, be prepared to stand in line because you're not the only one who's heard this is the best in town. The Hong Kong Flower Lounge has been one of our very favorite restaurants for years now. It's not the pink and green decor or the live fish swimming in the tank, or even the beautiful marble bathrooms; it's simply that every little dish that comes our way is so darn good. Don't pass up taro cake, salt-fried shrimp, shark-fin soup, and shrimp or beef crepes.

Khan Toke Thai House. 5937 Geary Blvd. ☎ **415/668-6654.** Reservations recommended. Main courses $6–$11; fixed-price dinner $16.95. AE, MC, V. Daily 5–10pm. Bus: 38. THAI.

Khan Toke Thai is so traditional you're asked to remove your shoes before being seated. Popular for special occasions, this Richmond Distinct fixture is easily the prettiest Thai restaurant in the city; lavishly carved teak interiors evoke the ambiance of a Thai temple.

To start, order the *tom yam gong* lemongrass shrimp with mushroom, tomato, and cilantro soup. Follow with such well-flavored dishes as ground pork with fresh ginger, green onion, peanuts, and lemon juice; prawns with hot chilies, mint leaves, lime juice, lemongrass, and onions; or the chicken with cashew nuts, crispy chilies, and onions. For a real treat, have the deep-fried pompano topped with sautéed ginger, onions, peppers, pickled garlic, and yellow-bean sauce; or deep-fried red snapper with "three-flavors" sauce and hot basil leaves. A complete dinner including appetizer, soup, salad, two main courses, dessert, and coffee is a great value.

MODERATE

○ **Ton Kiang.** 5821 Geary Blvd. (between 22nd and 23rd aves.) ☎ **415/387-8273.** Reservations not accepted. Dim sum $1.80–$4.50. Daily 10:30am–10pm. AE, MC. V. Bus: 38. DIM SUM.

We still love the Hong Kong Flower Lounge, but Ton Kiang is justifiably the number-one place in the city to do dim sum. Wait in the never-ending line (which is out the door anytime between 11am and 1:30pm), get a table on either the first or second floor, and get ready to party with your palate. From stuffed crab claws, roast Peking duck, and a gazillion dumpling selections (including scallop and vegetable, shrimp, and beef) to the delicious and hard-to-find "doa miu" (a.k.a. snow pea sprouts, which are flash sautéed with garlic and peanut oil), shark-fin soup, and a mesmerizing mango pudding, every tray of morsels coming from the kitchen is an absolute delight. This is definitely one of our favorite places to do lunch, and it happens to have an unusually friendly staff. Their second location (3148 Geary Blvd., at Spruce St., ☎415/752-4440), which is closer to downtown, does not serve dim sum but is known for its low prices, delicious Hakka cuisine, and clay-pot dishes.

14 The Castro

While you will see gay and lesbian singles and couples at almost any restaurant in San Francisco, the following spots cater particularly to the San Francisco gay community, though being gay is certainly not a requirement for enjoying them.

MODERATE

○ **Mecca.** 2029 Market St. (between Duboce and Church sts.). ☎ **415/621-7000.** Reservations recommended. Main courses $12.75–$18. AE, DC, MC, V. Mon–Wed and Sun 6–11pm; Thurs–Sat 6pm–midnight. Muni Metro: F, K, L, or M. Bus: 8, 22, 24, or 37. MEDITERRANEAN.

In 1996, Mecca entered the scene in a decadent swirl of chocolate-brown velvet, stainless steel, cement, and brown Naugahyde, unveiling the kind of industrial-chic supper club that makes you want to order a martini just so you'll match the ambiance. And cocktail they do—that eclectic city clientele (with a heavy dash of same-sex couples) who mingle at the oval centerpiece bar. A night here promises a dose of live jazz, and a tasty, though sometimes unpredictable, California meal, which is served at tables tucked into several dining nooks. Menu options include such starters as pomegranate-glazed quail on endive and watercress, and herb-skewered prawns with romesco sauce and roasted potatoes. Main courses include the popular mustard-seed–crusted halibut, duck breast with roasted fig and huckleberry sauce and potatoes, and a veal chop with wild-mushroom potato cake. The food is very good, but it's that only-in-San-Francisco vibe that makes this place the smokin' hot spot to dine in the Castro.

2223. 2223 Market St. (between Sanchez and Noe sts.). ☎ **415/431-0692.** Reservations recommended. $12.95–$19.95. AE, MC, V. Sat–Sun 10am–2pm; Sun–Thurs 5:30–10pm; Fri–Sat 5:30–midnight. Muni Metro: F, L, K, or M. Bus: 8, 22, 24, or 37. CALIFORNIA.

Run by the owners of the renowned Cypress Club, the decor here is substantially less opulent than its counterpart, but the energy level is definitely more lively. Surrounded by hardwood floors, candles, streamlined modern light fixtures and loud music, festive gays and straights come here to cocktail on the heavy-handed specialty drinks and dine on grilled pork chops or the ever popular roasted chicken with garlic mashed potatoes. Along with Mecca, this is currently the dining and schmoozing spot in the area.

INEXPENSIVE

Café Flore. 2298 Market St. (at Noe St.). ☎ **415/621-8579.** Reservations not accepted. American breakfast $5.95; main courses $4.50–$10. No credit cards. Sun–Thurs 7am–11:30pm; Fri–Sat 7am–midnight. Muni Metro: F. Bus: 8. CALIFORNIA.

Sheathed with glass on three sides, and overlooking Market Street, Noe Street, and a verdant patio in back, Café Flore attracts young, bright, and articulate members of the gay (mostly male) community. Local wits refer to it as a place where body piercing is encouraged but not mandatory, although this kind of exhibitionism tends to be more prevalent in the evening rather than during the daytime.

Many of the menu items are composed of mostly organic ingredients, and include a succulent version of roasted (sometimes free-range) chicken, soups, pastas, and steaks. Café latte costs $2 a cup. Plan on hearing a lot of noise and possibly seeing a handsome young man sending not particularly furtive glances your way. Those with late-night munchies take heed: while the place stays open later, the kitchen closes at 10:30pm.

✪ **Firewood Café.** 4248 18th St. (at Diamond St.). ☎ **415/252-0999.** Main courses $5.25–$7. MC, V. Sun–Thurs 11am–11pm; Fri–Sat 11am–midnight. Muni Metro: F, K, L, or M line. Bus: 8, 33, 35, or 37. MEDITERRANEAN.

It shouldn't take a genius to realize that aesthetics count even in cheap restaurants. But apparently it did, because until just recently, finding budget gourmet food and attractive decor together were about as likely as seeing Newt Gingrich dancing through the Castro wearing chaps. But times they are a-changin', and this restaurant is setting the standard. One of the sharpest rooms in the neighborhood, the colorful Firewood put its money in the essentials and eliminated extra overhead. There are no waiters or waitresses here; everyone orders at the counter, then relaxes at either the single, long family-style table or one of the small tables facing the huge streetside windows. Where they didn't skimp is with the cozy-chic atmosphere and inspired-but-limited Mediterranean menu: The fresh salads, which are all less than $5, come with a choice of three "fixin's" ranging from caramelized onions to spiced walnuts and three gourmet dressing options. Then there's the pastas—four tortellini selections, such as roasted chicken and mortadella—and gourmet pizzas: the calamari with lemon-garlic aioli is a winner. Or how about an herb-roasted half or whole chicken ($5.25 or $9.95, respectively) with roasted new potatoes? Wines cost $3.25 by the glass and a reasonable $16 to $18 by the bottle. Draft and bottled beers are also available, and desserts top off at $2.25. (Thank goodness *someone* realized that $6 for an after-dinner treat is bordering on ridiculous.)

15 Mission District

MODERATE

Bruno's. 2389 Mission St. (between 19th and 20th sts.). ☎ **415/550-7455.** Reservations recommended. Main courses $14–$21. DC, MC, V. Tues–Thurs 6:30–11pm; Fri–Sat 6:30pm–midnight. Parking in back lot $5. ECLECTIC.

When the new owners scraped 60 years worth of grease and cigar smoke from the wood-paneled bar, added live music, and began serving flavorful fare in the fifties-style dining room, the hipsters came in droves. But even two years after its opening, crowds are still coming to this Mission District restaurant. The reason? Aside from people-watching, the food here actually competes with the ambiance. House specialties include apple salad, grilled boneless quail, and oxtail with mashed potatoes. After dinner, meander into the bar and beyond, where bands liven the crowd. *Note:* While the dining room is closed on Monday, you can still order appetizers and dessert at the bar.

✪ Pauline's. 260 Valencia St. (between 14th St. and Duboce Ave.). ☎ **415/552-2050.** Reservations recommended. Main courses $10.50–$21.50. MC, V. Tues–Sat 5–10pm. Bus: 14, 26, or 49. PIZZA.

The perfect pizza? Quite possibly. At least it's the best we've ever had. Housed in a cheery double-decker yellow building that stands out like a beacon in a somewhat seedy neighborhood, Pauline's only does two things—pizzas and salads—but does them better than any other restaurant in the city. It's worth running the gauntlet of panhandlers for a slice of Pauline's Italian sausage pizza on handmade thin-crust dough. The eclectic toppings range from house-spiced chicken to French goat cheese, roasted eggplant, Danish fontina cheese, and tasso (spiced pork shoulder). The salads are equally amazing: certified organic, hand-picked by California growers, and topped with fresh and dried herbs (including edible flowers) from Pauline's own gardens in Berkeley. The wine list offers a smart selection of low-priced wines, and service is excellent. Yes, prices are a bit steep (small pizzas start at $10.50), but what a paltry price to pay for perfection.

The Slanted Door. 584 Valencia St. (at 17th St.). ☎ **415/861-8032.** Reservations recommended. Lunch main courses $5.25–$16.50; most dinner dishes $5.75–$16.50. MC, V. Daily 11:30am–3:30pm; Sun–Thurs 5:30pm–10pm; Fri–Sat 5:30pm–10:30pm. Bus: 22, 26, 33, 49 or 53; BART: 16th St. station. VIETNAMESE.

We've tried, but the fact is, we just don't get why this place is all the rage. Sure, the food is fresh and well priced, and the room is certainly the most stylish one serving Vietnamese. But in our minds that doesn't make the spot a destination restaurant. It is, however, a great place to dine if you're in the neighborhood. Pull up a modern, color-washed chair in the industrial-but-colorful space and order anything from clay-pot catfish or green papaya salad to one of the inexpensive lunch rice dishes, which come in a large ceramic bowl and are topped with such options as grilled shrimp, curry chicken, or stir-fried eggplant. Dinner items, which change seasonally, may range from steamed chicken with black-bean sauce, long beans with shrimp to vegetarian noodles sautéed with mushrooms, lily buds, tofu, bamboo, and shiitake mushrooms. There's also an eclectic collection of teas, which come by the pot for $3 to $5. Perhaps one of the best elements to this restaurant is its eclectic clientele; since everyone thinks this is the place to be these days, it actually is.

INEXPENSIVE

✪ **Taquerias La Cumbre.** 515 Valencia St. (between 16th and 17th sts.). ☎ **415/863-8205.** Tacos and burritos $2–$4.25; dinner plates $5–$7. No credit cards. Mon–Sat 11am–10pm; Sun noon–9pm. BART: Mission. Bus: 14, 22, 33, 49, or 53. MEXICAN.

If San Francisco commissioned a flag honoring its favorite food, we'd probably all be waving a banner of the Golden Gate Bridge bolstering a giant burrito—that's how much we love these mammoth tortilla-wrapped meals. And while most restaurants gussy up their gastronomic goods with million-dollar decor and glamorous gimmicks, the burrito needs only to be craftily constructed of fresh pork, steak, chicken, or vegetables, plus cheese, beans, rice, salsa, and maybe a dash of guacamole or sour cream, and practically the whole town will drive to the remotest corners to taste it. In this case, the fact that it's served in a cafeterialike brick-lined room with overly shellacked tables and chairs is all the better: There's no mistaking the attraction here.

Ti Couz. 3108 16th St. (at Valencia St.). ☎ **415/252-7373.** Crepes $1.95–$8.25. MC, V. Mon–Fri 11am–11pm; Sat 10am–11pm; Sun 10am–10pm. BART: Mission. Bus: 14, 22, 33, 49, or 53. CREPES.

With fierce culinary competition around every corner, many restaurants try to invent new gourmet gimmicks to hook the hungry. Unfortunately, the results are often creative concoctions that verge on palate pandemonium. Not true for Ti Couz (say "Tee Cooz"), one of the most architecturally stylish and popular restaurants in the Mission. Here the headliner is simple: a delicate, paper-thin crepe. And while its fillings aren't exactly original, they're excellently executed and infinite in their combinations. The menu advises how to enjoy these wraps: Order a light crepe as an appetizer, a heftier one as a main course, and a drippingly sweet one for dessert. Recommended combinations are listed, but you can build your own from the 15 main-course selections (such as smoked salmon, mushrooms, sausage, ham, scallops, and onions) and 19 dessert options (caramel, fruit, chocolate, Nutella, and more). Soups and salads solicit the less adventurous palate but are equally stellar; the sensational seafood salad, for example, is a compilation of shrimp, scallops, and ahi tuna with veggies and five kinds of lettuce. Ciders and beer complement the cuisine.

What to See & Do in San Francisco

*S*an Francisco's parks, museums, tours, and landmarks are favorite haunts for travelers the world over and offer an array of activities to suit every visitor. But it's not any particular activity or place that makes the city the most popular tourist destination in the world. It's San Francisco itself—its charm, its atmosphere, its perfect blend of big metropolis with small-town hospitality. No matter what you do while you're here—whether you spend all your time in central areas like Union Square or North Beach or explore the intricacies of outer neighborhoods—you're bound to collect a treasure of vacation memories that can only be found in this culturally rich, strikingly beautiful City by the Bay.

1 Famous San Francisco Sights

✪ **Alcatraz Island.** Pier 41, near Fisherman's Wharf. ☎ **415/773-1188** (for info only; no ferry reservations accepted at this number). Admission (includes ferry trip and audio tour) $11 adults, $9.25 seniors 62 and older, $5.75 children 5–11. Winter daily 9:15am–2:30pm; summer daily 9:15am–4:15pm. Advance purchase advised. Ferries depart every half hour, at 15 and 45 min. after the hour on the weekends, and every 45 min. throughout the week. Arrive at least 20 min. before sailing time.

Visible from Fisherman's Wharf, Alcatraz Island (a.k.a. "The Rock") has seen a checkered history. It was discovered in 1775 by Juan Manuel Ayala, who named it after the many pelicans that nested on the island. From the 1850s to 1933, when the army vacated the island, it served as a military post protecting the bay shoreline. In 1934, the buildings of the military outpost were converted into a maximum-security prison. Given the sheer cliffs, treacherous tides and currents, and frigid temperatures of the waters, it was believed to be a totally escape-proof prison. Among the famous gangsters who were penned in cell blocks A through D were Al Capone; Robert Stroud, the so-called Birdman of Alcatraz (because he was an expert in ornithological diseases); Machine Gun Kelly; and Alvin Karpis. It cost a fortune to keep them imprisoned here because all supplies,

Major San Francisco Sights

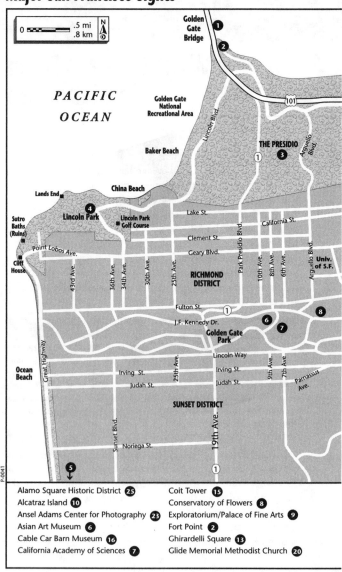

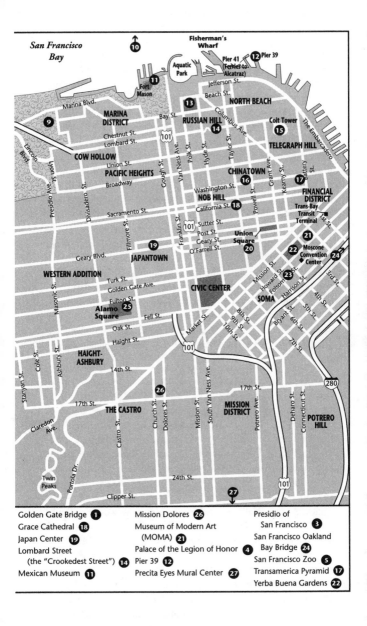

San Francisco Bay

Fisherman's Wharf

Pier 41 (Ferries to Alcatraz)

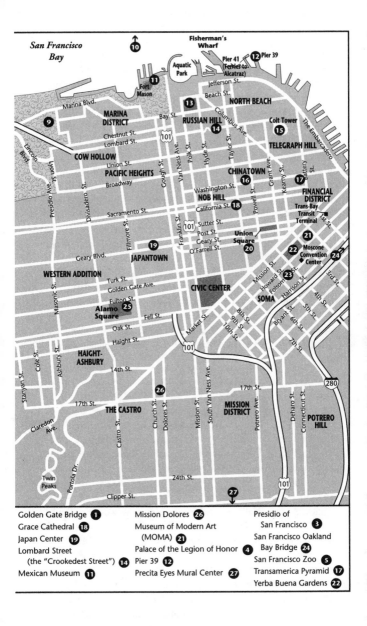

Pier 39 **12**

10

Aquatic Park

11

Fort Mason

Jefferson St.

Beach St.

13

NORTH BEACH

Marina Blvd.

MARINA DISTRICT

Bay St.

RUSSIAN HILL

Columbus Ave.

Colt Tower

15

Chestnut St.

Lombard St.

14

TELEGRAPH HILL

101

COW HOLLOW

Union St.

PACIFIC HEIGHTS

Broadway

9

Lincoln Blvd.

Presidio Ave.

Lyon St.

Divisadero St.

Fillmore St.

Van Ness Ave.

Gough St.

Polk St.

Hyde St.

Taylor St.

Grant Ave.

Kearny St.

Battery St.

CHINATOWN

16

Washington St.

NOB HILL

FINANCIAL DISTRICT

17

Trans-Bay Transit Terminal

Sacramento St.

California St.

18

Powell St.

101

Franklin St.

Sutter St.

Post St.

Geary St.

O'Farrell St.

Union Square

20

21

22

Moscone Convention Center

Geary Blvd.

19

JAPANTOWN

Mission St.

Howard St.

Folsom St.

Harrison St.

23

24

SOMA

WESTERN ADDITION

Turk St.

Golden Gate Ave.

Fulton St.

CIVIC CENTER

Masonic St.

Alamo Square 25

Fell St.

Oak St.

Haight St.

Market St.

8th St.

9th St.

10th St.

Bryant St.

3rd St.

4th St.

5th St.

6th St.

7th St.

Deharo St.

Connecticut St.

280

HAIGHT-ASHBURY

14th St.

Stanyan St.

Cole St.

Ashbury St.

Claredon Ave.

17th St.

THE CASTRO

26

Church St.

Dolores St.

Castro St.

Mission St.

South Van Ness Ave.

17th St.

MISSION DISTRICT

Potrero Ave.

POTRERO HILL

Twin Peaks

Portola Dr.

24th St.

101

27

Clipper St.

Golden Gate Bridge **1**

Grace Cathedral **18**

Japan Center **19**

Lombard Street (the "Crookedest Street") **14**

Mexican Museum **11**

Mission Dolores **26**

Museum of Modern Art (MOMA) **21**

Palace of the Legion of Honor **4**

Pier 39 **12**

Precita Eyes Mural Center **27**

Presidio of San Francisco **3**

San Francisco Oakland Bay Bridge **24**

San Francisco Zoo **5**

Transamerica Pyramid **17**

Yerba Buena Gardens **22**

including water, had to be shipped in. In 1963, after an apparent escape in which no bodies were recovered, the government closed the prison, and in 1972 it became part of the Golden Gate National Recreation Area. The wildlife that was driven away during the military and prison years has begun to return—the black-crested night heron and other seabirds are nesting here again—and a new trail has been built that passes through the island's nature areas. Tours, including an audio tour of the prison block and a slide show, are given by the park's rangers, who entertain their guests with interesting anecdotes.

It's a popular excursion and space is limited, so purchase tickets as far in advance as possible. The tour is operated by **Blue & Gold Fleet** (☎ **415/705-5555**) and can be charged to American Express, MasterCard, or Visa ($2 per ticket service charge on phone orders). Tickets may also be purchased in advance from the Blue & Gold ticket office on Pier 41.

Wear comfortable shoes and take a heavy sweater or windbreaker because even when the sun's out, it's cold. The National Parks Service also notes that there are a lot of steps to climb on the tour.

For those who want to get a closer look at Alcatraz without going ashore, several cruises offer short circumnavigations of the island (see "Self-Guided & Organized Tours," below, for complete information).

✪ **Cable Cars.** The Powell-Hyde and Powell-Mason lines begin at the base of Powell and Market sts.; the California St. line begins at the foot of Market St.

Although they may not be San Francisco's most practical means of transportation, cable cars are certainly the best loved. Designated official historic landmarks by the National Parks Service in 1964, they clank up and down the city's steep hills like mobile museum pieces, tirelessly hauling thousands of tourists each day to nowhere in particular.

San Francisco's cable cars were invented in 1869 by London-born engineer Andrew Hallidie, who got the idea by way of serendipity. As the story goes, Hallidie was watching a team of overworked horses haul a heavily laden carriage up a steep San Francisco slope. As he watched, one horse slipped and the car rolled back, dragging the other tired beasts with it. At that moment Hallidie resolved that he would invent a mechanical contraption to replace such horses, and just 4 years later, in 1873, the first cable car made its maiden run from the top of Clay Street. Promptly ridiculed as "Hallidie's Folly," the cars were slow to gain acceptance. One early onlooker voiced the general opinion by exclaiming, "I don't believe it—the damned thing works!"

Even today, many visitors have difficulty believing that these vehicles, which have no engines, actually work. The cars, each weighing about 6 tons, are hauled along by a steel cable, enclosed under the street in a center rail. You can't see the cable unless you peer straight down into the crack, but you'll hear its characteristic clickity-clanking sound whenever you're nearby. The cars move when the gripper (not the driver) pulls back a lever that closes a pincerlike "grip" on the cable. The speed of the car therefore is determined by the speed of the cable, which is a constant $9^1/2$ miles per hour—never more, never less.

The two types of cable cars in use hold, respectively, a maximum of 90 and 100 passengers, and the limits are rigidly enforced. The best views are had from the outer running boards, where you have to hold on tightly when taking curves. Everyone, it seems, prefers to ride on the running boards.

Often imitated but never duplicated, similar versions of Hallidie's cable cars have been used throughout the world, but all have been replaced by more efficient means of transportation. San Francisco planned to do so, too, but the proposal was met with so much opposition that the cable cars' perpetuation was actually written into the city charter in 1955. This mandate cannot be revoked without the approval of a majority of the city's voters—a distant and doubtful prospect.

San Francisco's three existing lines comprise the world's only surviving system of cable cars. For more information on riding them, see "Getting Around" in chapter 3, "Getting to Know San Francisco."

Coit Tower. Atop Telegraph Hill. ☎ **415/362-0808.** Admission (to the top of the tower) $3 adults, $2 seniors, $1 children 6–12. Daily 10am–6pm. Bus: 39 ("Coit").

In a city known for its great views and vantage points, Coit Tower is tops. Located atop Telegraph Hill, just east of North Beach, the round, stone tower offers panoramic views of the city and the bay.

Completed in 1933, the tower is the legacy of Lillie Hitchcock Coit, a wealthy eccentric who left San Francisco a $125,000 bequest "for the purpose of adding beauty to the city I have always loved" and also as a memorial to its volunteer firemen. She had been saved from a fire as a child and thereafter held the city's firefighters in particularly high esteem.

Inside the base of the tower are the impressive murals titled *Life in California, 1934,* which were completed under the WPA during the New Deal. They were completed by more than 25 artists, many of whom had studied under Mexican muralist Diego Rivera.

FISHERMAN'S WHARF & PIER 39

Few cities in America are as adept at wholesaling their historical sites as San Francisco, which has converted Fisherman's Wharf into one of the most popular tourist destinations in the world. Unless you come really early in the morning, you won't find any traces of the traditional waterfront life that once existed here; the only fishing going on around here is for tourists' dollars.

Originally called Meigg's Wharf, this bustling strip of waterfront got its present moniker from generations of fishers who used to base their boats here. Today, the bay has become so polluted with toxins that bright yellow placards warn against eating fish from these waters. A small fleet of fewer than 30 boats still operates from here, but basically Fisherman's Wharf has been converted into one long shopping mall stretching from Ghirardelli Square at the west end to Pier 39 at the east. Some people love it, others can't get far enough away from it, but most agree that Fisherman's Wharf, for better or for worse, has to be seen at least once in your life.

Ghirardelli Square, at 900 North Point, between Polk and Larkin streets (☎ 415/775-5500), dates from 1864 when it served as a factory making Civil War uniforms, but it's best known as the former chocolate-and-spice factory of Domingo Ghirardelli (say "Gear-a-deli"). The factory has been converted into a 10-level mall containing 50-plus stores and 20 dining establishments. Scheduled street performers play regularly in the West Plaza. The stores generally stay open from 10am to 9pm in the summer and until 6 or 7pm in the winter. Incidentally, the Ghirardelli Chocolate Company still makes chocolate, but it's located in a lower-rent district in the East Bay.

Pier 39, on the waterfront at Embarcadero and Beach Street (☎ 415/981-8030; shops are open daily from 10:30am to 8:30pm), is a 4¹/₂-acre, multilevel waterfront complex a few blocks east of Fisherman's Wharf. Constructed on an abandoned cargo pier, it is, ostensibly, a re-creation of a turn-of-the-century street scene, but don't expect a slice of old-time maritime life. This is the busiest mall of the lot and, according to the *London Observer,* the third most visited attraction in the world, behind Disney World and Disneyland—with more than 100 stores, 10 bay-view restaurants

Fisherman's Wharf & Vicinity

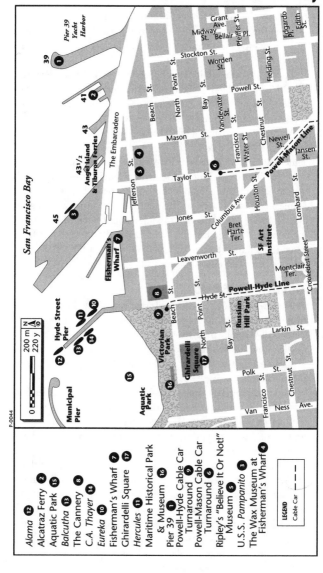

LEGEND
- - - Cable Car

Alama ⓬
Alcatraz Ferry ❷
Aquatic Park ⓯
Balcutha ⓭
The Cannery ❽
C.A. Thayer ⓮
Eureka ❿
Fisherman's Wharf ❼
Ghirardelli Square ⓱
Hercules ⓫
Maritime Historical Park & Museum ⓰
Pier 39 ❶
Powell-Hyde Cable Car Turnaround ❾
Powell-Mason Cable Car Turnaround ❻
Ripley's "Believe It Or Not!" Museum ❺
U.S.S. Pampanito ❸
The Wax Museum at Fisherman's Wharf ❹

119

(including the Bubba Gump Shrimp Co., an over-buttered spin-off from the *Forrest Gump* movie), a two-tiered Venetian carousel, and a new big-screen Cinemax Theater showing the *Secret of San Francisco.*

The latest major addition to Fisherman's Wharf is **Underwater World,** a $38-million, 707,000-gallon marine attraction filled with sharks, stingrays, and more, all witnessed via a moving footpath that transports visitors through clear acrylic tunnels.

Accommodating a total of 350 boats, two marinas flank the pier and house the Blue & Gold bay-sightseeing fleet. In recent years some 600 California sea lions have taken up residence on the adjacent floating docks. Until they abandon their new playground, which seems more and more unlikely, these playful, noisy creatures (some nights you can hear them all the way from Washington Square) create one of the best free attractions on the wharf. Ongoing docent-led programs are offered at Pier 39 on weekends from 11am to 5pm that teach visitors about the range, habitat, and adaptability of the California sea lion.

✪ GOLDEN GATE BRIDGE

1996 marked the 60th birthday of what is possibly the most beautiful, and certainly the most photographed, bridge in the world. Often half-veiled by the city's trademark rolling fog, San Francisco's Golden Gate Bridge spans tidal currents, ocean waves, and battering winds to connect the City by the Bay with the Redwood Empire to the north.

With its gracefully swung single span, spidery bracing cables, and sky-zooming twin towers, the bridge looks more like a work of abstract art than the practical engineering feat that it is, among the greatest of this century. Construction began in May 1937 and was completed at the then-colossal cost of $35 million.

The mile-long steel link, which reaches a height of 746 feet above the water, is an awesome bridge to cross. Traffic usually moves quickly, so crossing by car won't give you too much time to see the sights. If you drive ($3 toll, payable southbound) from the city, park in the lot at the foot of the bridge on the city side and make the crossing by foot. Back in your car, continue to Marin's Vista Point, at the bridge's northern end. Look back and you'll be rewarded with one of the greatest views of San Francisco.

Millions of pedestrians walk or bike across the bridge each year, gazing up at the tall red towers, out at the vistas of San Francisco and Marin County, and down into the stacks of oceangoing liners. You can walk out onto the span from either end, but be prepared—it's usually windy and cold, and the bridge vibrates. Still, walking even a short way is one of the best ways to experience the immense scale of the structure.

Bridge-bound **Golden Gate Transit buses** (☎ **415/923-2000**) depart every 30 to 60 minutes during the day for Marin County, starting from the Transbay Terminal at Mission and First streets and making convenient stops at Market and Seventh streets, at the Civic Center, and along Van Ness Avenue and Lombard Street.

Lombard Street. Between Hyde and Leavenworth sts.

Known as the "crookedest street in the world," the whimsically winding block of Lombard Street draws thousands of visitors each year (much to the chagrin of neighborhood residents, most of whom would prefer to block off the street to tourists). The angle of the street is so steep that the road has to snake back and forth to make a descent possible. The brick-lined street zigzags around the residences' bright flower gardens that explode with color during warmer months. This short stretch of Lombard Street is one way, downhill, and fun to drive. Take the curves slowly and in low gear, and expect a wait during the weekend. Save your film for the bottom, where, if you're lucky, you can find a parking space and take a few snapshots of the silly spectacle. You can also walk the block, either up or down, via staircases (without curves) on either side of the street.

Yerba Buena Gardens   Between Mission and Howard streets at Third Street, the Yerba Buena Center (☎ **415/978-2787**), which opened in 1993 adjacent to the Moscone Convention Center, is the city's new cultural facility, similar to New York's Lincoln Center. It stands on top of the northern extension of the underground Moscone Convention Center. The Center for the Arts presents music, theater, dance, and visual arts. It consists of two buildings, a 755-seat theater designed by James Stewart Polshek, and the Galleries and Arts Forum designed by Fumihiko Maki, which features three galleries and a space designed specially for dance. The complex also includes a 5-acre garden featuring several artworks. The most dramatic outdoor art piece is an emotional mixed-media memorial to Martin Luther King, Jr. Created by sculptor Houston Conwill, poet Estella Majozo, and architect Joseph de Pace, it features 12 glass panels, each inscribed with quotations from King, sheltered behind a 50-foot-high waterfall. The new children's addition, called Zeum, (☎ 415/777-2800), includes a cafe, interactive cultural center, a 1906 historic carousel, interactive play and learning garden, and movie theaters. Also in the Yerba Buena Center is a bowling alley, child-care center, an ice-skating rink, and an IMAX theater. As part of the plan to develop this area as the city's cultural hub, the California Historical Society opened at 678 Mission in late 1995 and the Mexican Museum will relocate in the area in 2000. For recorded information and tickets, call ☎ **415/978-ARTS.**

Take the muni metro to Powell or Montgomery, or the 30, 45, or 9x bus.

2   Museums

Ansel Adams Center for Photography. 250 Fourth St. ☎ **415/495-7000.** Admission $5 adults, $3 students, $2 seniors and children 13–17, free for children 12 and under. Tues–Sun 11am–5pm; until 8pm the 1st Thurs of each month. Muni Metro: Powell St. lines. Bus: 30, 45, or 9X.

This popular SoMa museum features five separate galleries for changing exhibitions of contemporary and historical photography. One area is dedicated solely to displaying the works and exploring the legacy of Ansel Adams.

Cable Car Barn Museum. Washington and Mason sts. ☎ **415/474-1887.** Free admission. Apr–Oct daily 10am–6pm; Nov–Mar daily 10am–5pm. Cable car: Both Powell St. lines stop by the museum.

If you've ever wondered how cable cars work, this nifty museum will explain (and demonstrate!) it all to you. Yes, this is a museum, but the Cable Car Barn is no stuffed shirt. It's the living powerhouse, repair shop, and storage place of the cable-car system and is in full operation. Built for the Ferries and Cliff House Railway in 1887, the building underwent an $18-million reconstruction to restore its original gaslight-era look, install an amazing spectators' gallery, and add a museum of San Francisco transit history.

The exposed machinery, which pulls the cables under San Francisco's streets, looks like a Rube Goldberg invention. Stand in the mezzanine gallery and become mesmerized by the massive groaning and vibrating winches as they thread the cable that hauls the cars through a huge figure eight and back into the system via slack-absorbing tension wheels. For a better view, move to the lower-level viewing room where you can see the massive pulleys and gears operating underground.

Also on display here is one of the first grip cars developed by Andrew S. Hallidie, operated for the first time on Clay Street on August 2, 1873. Other displays include an antique grip car and trailer that operated on Pacific Avenue until 1929, and dozens of exact-scale models of cars used on the various city lines. There's also a shop where you can buy a variety of cable-car gifts.

✪ **California Palace of the Legion of Honor.** In Lincoln Park (at 34th Ave. and Clement St.). ☎ **415/750-3600** or 415/863-3330 (for recorded information). Admission (including the Asian Art Museum and M. H. De Young Memorial Museum) $7 adults, $5 seniors 65 and over, $4 youths 12–17, free for children 11 and under (fees may be higher for special exhibitions); free the 1st Wed of each month when hours are 9:30am–8:45pm. Open Tues–Sun 9:30am–5pm; 1st Sat of the month until 8:45pm. Bus: 38 or 18.

Designed as a memorial to California's World War I casualties, the neoclassical structure is an exact replica of the Legion of Honor Palace in Paris, right down to the inscription "Honneur et Patrie" above the portal.

The Legion of Honor reopened in late 1995 after a 2-year, $34.6-million renovation and seismic upgrading that was stalled by the discovery of almost 300 turn-of-the-century coffins. The exterior's grassy expanses, cliff-side paths, and incredible view of the Golden Gate make this an absolute must-visit attraction before you even get in the door. But the inside is equally impressive. The museum's permanent collection covers 4,000 years of art and includes paintings, sculpture, and decorative arts from Europe, as well as international tapestries, prints, and drawings. The chronological display of more than 800 years of European art includes one of the world's finest collections of Rodin's sculptures.

Center for the Arts at Yerba Buena Gardens. 701 Mission St. ☎ **415/978-2700**; box office 415/978-ARTS. Admission $5 adults, $3 seniors and students; free every 1st Thurs of the month from 6–8pm. Tues–Sun 11am–6pm. Muni Metro: Powell or Montgomery. Bus: 30, 45, or 9X.

Cutting-edge computer art and multimedia shows are on view in the high-tech galleries. The initial exhibition, "The Art of *Star Wars,*" featured the special effects created by George Lucas for the film.

✪ **The Exploratorium.** 3601 Lyon St., in the Palace of Fine Arts (at Marina Blvd.). ☎ **415/563-7337** or 415/561-0360 (for recorded information). Admission $9 adults, $7 senior citizens and college students with ID, $5 children 6–17, $2.50 children 3–5, free for children under 3; free for everyone 1st Wed of each month. MC, V. Summer (Memorial Day–Labor Day) and holidays, Mon–Tues and Thurs–Sun 10am–6pm; Wed 10am–9:30pm. Rest of the year Tues and Thurs–Sun 10am–5pm; Wed 10am–9:30pm. Closed Thanksgiving Day, and Christmas Day. Free parking. Bus: 30 from Stockton St. to the Marina stop.

Scientific American magazine rates the Exploratorium as "the best science museum in the world"—pretty heady stuff for this exciting hands-on science fair that contains more than 650 permanent exhibits that explore everything from giant bubble blowing to Einstein's theory of relativity. It's like a mad scientist's penny arcade, an educational fun house, and an experimental laboratory all rolled into one. Touch a tornado, shape a glowing electrical current, finger-paint via computer, or take a sensory journey in total darkness in the Tactile Dome—you could spend all day here and still not see everything. Every exhibit at the Exploratorium is designed to be interactive, educational, safe, and most important, fun. And don't think this is just for kids; parents inevitably end up being the most reluctant to leave. On the way out, be sure to stop in the wonderful gift store, which is chock-full of affordable brain candy.

The museum is located in San Francisco's Marina District at the beautiful Palace of Fine Arts, the only building left standing from the Panama-Pacific Exposition of 1915, which celebrated the opening of the Panama Canal. The adjoining park and lagoon—the perfect place for an afternoon picnic—is home to ducks, swans, seagulls, and grouchy geese, so bring bread.

Mexican Museum. Bldg. D, Fort Mason, Marina Blvd. (at Laguna St.). ☎ 415/202-9700. Admission $3 adults, $2 children. Free 1st Wed of the month. Wed–Fri noon–5pm; Sat–Sun 11am–5pm. Bus: 76 or 28.

The first museum in the nation dedicated to the work of Mexican and other Latino artists, the Mexican Museum maintains an impressive collection of art covering pre-Hispanic, colonial, folk, Mexican fine art, and Chicano/Mexican-American art. Revolving art shows range from the art of New Mexican women to such subjects as Mexican surrealism. *Note:* The museum is expected to be relocated to the Yerba Buena Center at Third and Mission streets in 2000.

San Francisco Museum of Modern Art (MOMA). 151 Third St. (2 blocks south of Market St., across from Yerba Buena Gardens). ☎ 415/357-4000. Admission $8 adults, $5 senior citizens, $4 for students 14–with ID, free for children 12 and under; half price for everyone Thurs 6–9pm, and free for everyone the 1st Tues of each month. Labor Day–Memorial Day Thurs 11am–9pm; Fri–Tues 11am–6pm. Memorial Day–Labor Day Thurs 10am–9pm; Fri–Tues 10am–6pm. Closed Wed and major holidays. Muni Metro: J, K, L, or M to Montgomery Station. Bus: 15, 30, or 45.

Swiss architect Mario Botta, in association with Hellmuth, Obata, and Kassabaum, designed the $62-million museum, which opened in SoMa in January 1995. The building is the most welcomed new development in years and has made SoMa one of the more popular areas to visit for tourists and residents alike. The museum's collection consists of more than 15,000 works, including close to 5,000 paintings and sculptures by artists such as Henri Matisse, Jackson

Pollock, and Willem de Kooning. Other artists represented include Diego Rivera, Georgia O'Keeffe, Paul Klee, the Fauvists, and exceptional holdings of Richard Diebenkorn. MOMA was also one of the first to recognize photography as a major art form; its collection includes more than 9,000 photographs by such notables as Ansel Adams, Alfred Stieglitz, Edward Weston, and Henri Cartier-Bresson. Docent-led tours are offered daily. Times are posted at the museum's admission desk. Phone for details of upcoming events.

The Caffè Museo, located to the right of the museum entrance sets a new precedent for museum food with flavorful and fresh soups, sandwiches, and salads that are as respectable as those served in many local restaurants.

No matter what, don't miss the MuseumStore, which carries a wonderful array of architectural gifts, books, and trinkets. It's one of the best stores in town.

3 Neighborhoods Worth a Visit

To really get to know San Francisco, break out of the downtown and Fisherman's Wharf areas to explore the ethnically and culturally diverse neighborhoods. Walk the streets, browse the shops, grab a bite at a local restaurant—you'll find that San Francisco's beauty and charm is around every corner, not just at the popular tourist destinations.

Note: For information on Fisherman's Wharf, see "Famous San Francisco Sights" above. (For information on other San Francisco neighborhoods and districts that aren't discussed here, see the "Neighborhoods in Brief" section in chapter 3.)

NOB HILL

When the cable car was invented in 1873, this hill became the exclusive residential area of the city. The "Big Four" and the "Comstock Bonanza kings" built their mansions here, but they were all destroyed by the earthquake and fire in 1906. The only two surviving buildings were the Flood Mansion, which serves today as the Pacific Union Club, and the Fairmont Hotel, which was under construction when the earthquake struck. Today the burned-out sites of former mansions are occupied by the city's luxury hotels—the Mark Hopkins, the Stanford Court, the Fairmont, and the Huntington—as well as spectacular Grace Cathedral, which stands on the Crocker mansion site. It's worth a visit to Nob Hill if only to stroll around Huntington Park, attend a Sunday service at the cathedral, or ooh and aah your way around the Fairmont's spectacular lobby.

SOUTH OF MARKET (SOMA)

From Market Street to Townsend and the Embarcadero to Division Street, SoMa has become the city's newest cultural and multimedia center. The process started when alternative clubs began opening in the old warehouses in the area nearly a decade ago, followed by a wave of entrepreneurs seeking to start new businesses in what was once an extremely low-rent district compared to the neighboring Financial District. Today, gentrification and high rents are well underway, spurned by a building boom that started with the Moscone Convention Center and continues today with the new Center for the Arts at Yerba Buena Gardens and the San Francisco Museum of Modern Art, all of which continue to be supplemented by other institutions, businesses, and museums that are moving into the area daily. A substantial portion of nightlife also takes place in warehouse spaces throughout the district.

NORTH BEACH

In the late 1800s, an enormous influx of Italian immigrants into North Beach firmly established this aromatic area as San Francisco's "Little Italy." Today, dozens of Italian restaurants and coffeehouses continue to flourish in what is still the center of the city's Italian community. Walk down Columbus Avenue any given morning and you're bound to be bombarded with the wonderful aromas of roasting coffee and savory pasta sauces. Though there are some interesting shops and bookstores in the area, it's the dozens of eclectic little cafes, delis, bakeries, and coffee shops that give North Beach its Italian-bohemian character.

For a proper perspective of North Beach, sign up for a guided Javawalk with coffee-nut Elaine Sosa (see "Walking Tours" in this chapter).

✪ CHINATOWN

The first Chinese came to San Francisco in the early 1800s to work as servants. By 1851, there were 25,000 Chinese working in California, most of whom had settled in San Francisco's Chinatown. Fleeing famine and the Opium Wars, they had come seeking the promise of good fortune in the "Gold Mountain" of California, hoping to return with that prosperity to their families back in China. For the vast majority, the reality of life in California did not live up to the promise. First employed as workers in the gold mines during the gold rush, they were later used to build the railroads, working as little more than slaves and facing constant prejudice. Yet the community, segregated in the Chinatown ghetto, thrived. Growing prejudice led to the Chinese Exclusion Act of 1882, which halted all Chinese immigration for 10 years and limited it severely thereafter; the Chinese Exclusion Act was not repealed until 1943. The Chinese were also denied the opportunity to buy homes outside of the Chinatown ghetto until the 1950s.

Today San Francisco has the second largest community of Chinese in the United States (about 33% of the city's population is Chinese). More than 80,000 people live in Chinatown, but the majority of Chinese have moved out into newer areas like the Richmond and Sunset districts. Though frequented by tourists, the area continues to cater to the Chinese community who crowd the vegetable and herbal markets, restaurants, and shops. Tradition still runs deep here, too, and if you're lucky, through an open window you might hear women mixing mahjong tiles as they play the century-old game.

The gateway at Grant and Bush marks the entry to Chinatown. The **Chinese Historical Society of America,** at 650 Commercial St. (☎ **415/391-1188**), has a small but interesting collection relating to the Chinese in San Francisco, which can be viewed for free anytime Tuesday to Friday from 10am to 4pm. The heart of Chinatown is at Portsmouth Square where you'll find Chinese locals playing board games (often gambling) or just sitting quietly.

On Waverly Place, a street where the Chinese celebratory colors of red, yellow, and green are much in evidence, you'll find three temples, Jeng Sen at no. 146, Tien Hou at no. 125, and Norras at no. 109.

A block north of Grant, Stockton from 1000 to 1200 is the main shopping street of the community lined with grocers, fishmongers, tea sellers, herbalists, noodle parlors, and restaurants. Here, too, is the Kon Chow Temple at no. 855, above the Chinatown post office. Explore at your leisure.

JAPAN CENTER

Today more than 12,000 citizens of Japanese descent live in San Francisco, or *Soko,* as it is often called by the Japanese who first emigrated here. Initially, they settled in Chinatown and also South of Market along Stevenson and Jessie streets from Fourth to Seventh. After the earthquake in 1906, SoMa became a light industrial and warehouse area and the largest Japanese concentration took root in the Western Addition between Van Ness Avenue and Fillmore Street, the site of today's Japantown. By 1940 it covered 30 blocks.

In 1913 the Alien Land Law was passed, depriving Japanese Americans of the right to buy land. From 1924 to 1952 Japanese immigration was banned by the United States. During World War II, the U.S. government froze Japanese bank accounts, interned community leaders, and removed 112,000 Japanese Americans—two-thirds of them citizens—to camps in California, Utah, and Idaho. Japantown was emptied of Japanese, and their place was taken by war workers. Upon their release in 1945, the Japanese found their old neighborhood occupied. Most of them resettled in the Richmond and Sunset districts; some did return to Japantown but it had shrunk to a mere 6 or so blocks. Among the community's notable sights are the Buddhist Church of San Francisco at 1881 Pine St. at Octavia; the Konko Church of San Francisco at 1909 Bush at Laguna; the Sokoji-Soto Zen Buddhist Temple at 1691 Laguna St. at Sutter; and Nihonmachi Mall, 1700 block of Buchanan Street between Sutter and Post, which contains two steel fountains by Ruth Asawa; and the Japan Center.

Japan Center is an Asian-oriented shopping mall occupying 3 square blocks bounded by Post, Geary, Laguna, and Fillmore streets. At its center stands the five-tiered Peace Pagoda, designed by world-famous Japanese architect Yoshiro Taniguchi "to convey the friendship and goodwill of the Japanese to the people of the United States." Surrounding the pagoda, in a network of arcades, squares, and bridges, are dozens of shops and showrooms featuring everything from TVs and tansu chests to pearls, bonsai (dwarf trees), and kimonos. When it opened in 1968, the complex seemed as modern as a jumbo jet. Today, the concrete structure seems less impressive, but it still holds some interesting surprises. The **Kabuki Hot Spring,** at 1750 Geary Blvd. (☎ **415/922-6002**), is the center's most famous tenant, an authentic traditional Japanese bathhouse with deep ceramic communal tubs, as well as private baths. The Japan Center also houses numerous restaurants, teahouses, shops, and the luxurious 14-story Radisson Miyako Hotel.

There is often live entertainment on summer weekends, including Japanese music and dance performances, tea ceremonies, flower-arranging demonstrations, martial-arts presentations, and other cultural events. The Japan Center is open Monday to Friday from 10am to 10pm, Saturday and Sunday from 9am to 10pm. It can be reached by the no. 2, 3, or 4 bus (exit on Buchanan and Sutter streets) or nos. 22 or 38 (exit on the northeast corner of Geary Boulevard and Fillmore Street).

HAIGHT-ASHBURY

Few of San Francisco's neighborhoods are as varied or as famous as the Haight-Ashbury. Walk along Haight Street and you'll encounter everything from drug-dazed drifters begging for change to an armada of the city's most counterculture (read: cool) shops, clubs, and cafes. Yet turn anywhere off Haight, and instantly you're among the clean-cut, young urban professionals who are the only ones who can afford the steep rents in this hip 'hood. The result is an interesting mix of well-to-do and well-screw-you lifestyles rubbing shoulders with aging flower children, former Dead-heads, homeless people, and the throngs of tourists who try not to stare as they wander through this most human of zoos. Some find it depressing, others find it fascinating, but everyone agrees that it ain't what it was in the free-lovin' psychedelic Summer of Love. Is it still worth a visit? Absolutely, if only to enjoy a cone of Cherry Garcia at the now-famous Ben & Jerry's ice-cream shop on the corner of Haight and Ashbury streets, then wander and gawk at the exotic people of the area.

THE CASTRO

Castro Street, between Market and 18th, is the center of the city's gay community, as well as a lovely strolling neighborhood teeming with shops, restaurants, bars, and other institutions that cater to the area's colorful clientele. Among the landmarks are Harvey Milk Plaza, the Names Project quilt, and the Castro Theatre, a 1930s movie palace with a Wurlitzer. The gay community began to move here in the late 1960s and early 1970s from the earlier gay neighborhood called Polk Gulch, which still has a number of gay-oriented bars and stores. Castro is one of the most lively streets in the city, and the perfect place to shop for gifts and revel in how free-spirited this town is.

THE MISSION DISTRICT

Once inhabited almost entirely by Irish immigrants, the Mission District is now the center of the city's Latino community, an oblong area stretching roughly from 14th to 30th streets between Potrero Avenue in the east and Dolores on the west. In the outer areas many of the city's finest Victorians still stand, though many seem strangely out of place in the mostly lower-income neighborhoods. The heart of the community lies along 24th Street between Van Ness and Potrero, where dozens of excellent ethnic restaurants, bakeries, bars, and specialty stores attract people from all over the city. The Mission District at night isn't exactly the safest place to be, and walking around the area should be done with caution, but it's usually quite safe during the day and highly recommended.

For an even better insight into the community, go to the **Precita Eyes Mural Arts Center,** 348 Precita Ave., at Folsom Street (☎ 415/285-2287), and take one of the 1-hour-and-45-minute tours conducted on Saturday at 11am and 1:30pm, which cost $5 for adults, $4 for seniors, and $1 for under-18s. You'll see 85 murals in an 8-block walk. Every year they also hold a Mural Awareness Week (usually the 2nd week in May) when tours are given daily. Other signs of cultural life include a number of progressive theaters— Eureka, Theater Rhinoceros, and Theater Artaud, to name only a few.

At 16th and Dolores is the Mission San Francisco de Assisi (better known as Mission Dolores), which is the city's oldest surviving building (see "Churches & Religious Buildings," below) and the district's namesake.

4 Golden Gate Park

Everybody loves Golden Gate Park—people, dogs, birds, frogs, turtles, bison, trees, bushes, and flowers. Literally everything feels unified here in San Francisco's enormous arboreal front yard. But this great city landmark wasn't always a favorite place to convene. It was conceived in the 1860s and 1870s but took its current shape in the 1880s and 1890s thanks to the skill and effort of John McClaren, a Scot who arrived in 1887 and began the landscaping of the park. Totaling 1,017 acres, the park is a narrow strip that stretches from the Pacific coast inland. No one had thought about the challenge the sand dunes and wind would present to any landscape artist. McClaren developed a new strain of grass called "sea bent," which he had planted to hold the sandy soil along the Firth of Forth, and he used this to anchor the soil here too. He also built the two windmills that stand on the western edge of the park to pump water for irrigation. Every year the ocean eroded the western fringe of the park, and ultimately he solved this problem too. It took him 40 years to build a natural wall, putting out bundles of sticks which were then covered with sand by the tides. Under his brilliant eye, the park took shape.

Today's Golden Gate Park is a truly magical place. Spend one sunny day stretched out on the grass along JFK Drive, have a good

Golden Gate Park

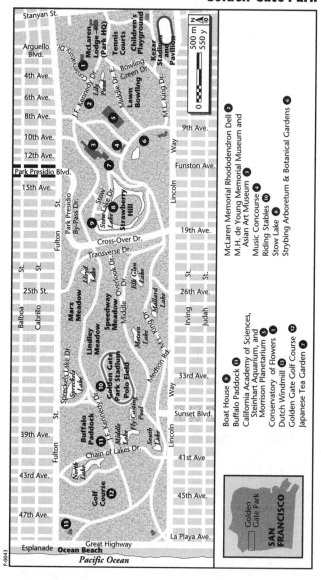

McLaren Memorial Rhododendron Dell **2**
M.H. de Young Memorial Museum and
Asian Art Museum **3**
Music Concourse **4**
Riding Stables **10**
Stow Lake **8**
Strybing Arboretum & Botanical Gardens **6**

Boat House **9**
Buffalo Paddock **11**
California Academy of Sciences,
Steinhart Aquarium, and
Morrison Planetarium **5**
Conservatory of Flowers **1**
Dutch Windmill **13**
Golden Gate Golf Course **12**
Japanese Tea Garden **7**

read in Shakespeare Garden, or stroll around Stow Lake and you too will understand the allure. It's an interactive botanical symphony, and everyone is invited to play in the orchestra.

The park is made up of hundreds of gardens and attractions attached by wooded paths and paved roads. While many stop-worthy sites are clearly visible, there are infinite hidden treasures, so pick up information if you want to find the more obscure, quaint spots. For information on the park, head first to the **McClaren Lodge and Park Headquarters,** which is open Monday to Friday (☎ 415/831-2700). Of the dozens of special gardens in the park, most recognized are the Rhododendron Dell, the Rose Garden, the Strybing Arboretum, and at the western edge of the park a spring-time array of thousands of tulips and daffodils around the Dutch windmill.

In addition to the highlights below, the park contains several rec-reational facilities: tennis courts, baseball, soccer and polo fields, golf course, riding stables, fly-casting pools, and boat rentals at the Straw-berry Hill boathouse. It is also the home of three major museums: the M. H. De Young Memorial Museum, the Asian Art Museum, and the California Academy of Sciences (see below). *Note:* There's talk of moving the De Young to an undetermined location, and the Asian Art Museum is moving to the old Main Library site in the Civic Center around 2001. If you plan to visit all the park's attrac-tions, consider buying the **Culture Pass,** which enables you to visit the three museums and the Japanese Tea Garden for $12. Passes are available at each site and at the Visitor Information Center. For fur-ther information call ☎ **415/391-2000.** Enter the park at Kezar Drive, an extension of Fell Street. Bus: 16AX, BX, 5, 6, 7, 66, or 71.

MUSEUMS INSIDE THE PARK

Asian Art Museum. In Golden Gate Park, near 10th Ave. and Fulton St. ☎ **415/379-8800;** 415/752-2635 for the hearing impaired. Admission (including the M. H. De Young Memorial Museum and California Palace of the Legion of Honor) $6 adults, $4 seniors 65 and over, $3 youths 12–17, free for children 11 and under (fees may be higher for special exhibitions); free admis-sion for everyone the 1st Wed (all day) of each month. Wed–Sun 10am–4:45pm; 1st Wed each month 10am–8:45pm. Bus: 5, 44, or 71.

Adjacent to the M. H. De Young Museum and the Japanese Tea Garden, this exhibition space, opened in 1966, can only display about 1,800 pieces from the museum's vast collection of 12,000. About half of the works on exhibit are in the ground-floor Chinese and Korean galleries and include world-class sculptures, paintings, bronzes, ceramics, jades, and decorative objects spanning 6,000 years of history. There is also a wide range of exhibits from more than 40 Asian countries—Pakistan, India, Tibet, Japan, Southeast Asia— including the world's oldest-known "dated" Chinese Buddha. The museum's free daily guided tours are highly informative and sincerely recommended. Call for times.

California Academy of Sciences. On the Music Concourse of Golden Gate Park. ☎ **415/750-7145** for recorded information. Admission (aquarium and Natural History Museum) $8.50 adults, $5.50 students 12–17 and seniors 65 and over, $2 children 4–11, free for children under 4; free for everyone the 1st Wed of every month. Planetarium shows $2.50 adults, $1.25 children under 18 and seniors 65 and over. Labor Day–Memorial Day daily 10am–5pm; Memorial Day–Labor Day daily 9am–6pm; 1st Wed of every month 10am–9pm. Muni Metro: N to Golden Gate Park. Bus: 5, 71, or 44.

Clustered around the Music Concourse in Golden Gate Park are three outstanding world-class museums and exhibitions that are guaranteed to entertain every member of the family. The **Steinhart Aquarium,** for example, is the most diverse aquarium in the world, housing some 14,000 specimens, including amphibians, reptiles, marine mammals, penguins, and much more, in 189 displays. A huge hit with the youngsters is the California tide pool and a "hands-on" area where children can touch starfish and sea urchins. The living coral reef is the largest display of its kind in the country and the only one in the West. In the Fish Roundabout, visitors are surrounded by fast-swimming schools of fish kept in a 100,000-gallon tank. Seals and dolphins are fed every 2 hours, beginning at 10:30am; the penguins are fed at 11:30am and 4pm.

The **Morrison Planetarium** presents sky shows as well as laser-light shows. Its sky shows offer guided tours through the universe projected onto a 65-foot domed ceiling. Approximately four major exhibits, with titles such as "Star Death: The Birth of Black Holes" and "The Universe Unveiled," are presented each year. Related cosmos exhibits are located in the adjacent Earth and Space Hall. Sky shows are featured at 2pm on weekdays and hourly every weekend and holiday (☎ 415/750-7141 for more information). **Laserium laser-light shows** are also presented in the planetarium Thursday through Sunday nights (☎ 415/750-7138 for more information).

The **Natural History Museum** includes several halls displaying classic dioramas of fauna in their habitats. The Wattis Hall of Human Cultures traces the evolution of different human cultures and how they adapted to their natural environment; the "Wild California" exhibition in Meyer Hall includes a 14,000-gallon aquarium and seabird rookery, life-size battling elephant seals, and two larger-than-life views of microscopic life forms; in McBean-Peterson Hall visitors can walk through an exhibit tracing the course of $3^{1}/_{2}$ billion years of evolution from the earliest life forms to the present day; in the Hohfeld Earth and Space Hall visitors can experience a simulation of two of San Francisco's biggest earthquakes, determine what their weight would be on other planets, see a real moon rock, and learn about the rotation of the planet at a replica of Foucault's Pendulum (the real one is in Paris).

OTHER HIGHLIGHTS

CONSERVATORY OF FLOWERS (1878)   Built for the 1894 Midwinter Exposition, this striking assemblage of glass architecture usually exhibits a rotating display of plants and shrubs at all times of the year. Unfortunately, recent years' rough weather has damaged the already-delicate structure and renovations aren't scheduled to be complete until 2004. Still, the exterior, which is modeled on the famous glass house at Kew Gardens in London, is indeed grand.

JAPANESE TEA GARDEN (1894)   McClaren hired the Hagiwara family to care for this garden developed for the 1894 Midwinter Exposition. It's a quiet place with cherry trees, shrubs, and bonsai crisscrossed by winding paths and high-arched bridges crossing over pools of water. Focal points and places for contemplation include the massive bronze Buddha that was cast in Japan in 1790 and donated by the Gump family, the Shinto wooden pagoda, and the Wishing Bridge, which reflected in the water looks as if it completes a circle. The garden is open daily October through February from 8:30am to 6pm (with the teahouse only open until 5:30pm), and March through September from 9am to 6:30pm. For **information** on admissions, call ☎ **415/752-4227.** For the **teahouse,** call ☎ **415/752-1171.**

STRYBING ARBORETUM & BOTANICAL GARDENS   Six thousand plant species grow here; among them some very ancient plants in a special "primitive garden," rare species, and a grove of California redwoods. Docent tours are given at 1pm daily during operating hours, which are Monday to Friday from 8am to 4:30pm and Saturday and Sunday from 10am to 5pm. For more information call ☎ **415/753-7089.**

✪ STRAWBERRY HILL/STOW LAKE   Rent a paddleboat, rowboat, or motorboat here and cruise around the circular lake as painters create still lifes and joggers pass along the grassy shoreline. Ducks waddle around waiting to be fed and turtles bathe on rocks and logs. Strawberry Hill, the 430-foot-high artificial island that lies at the center of Stow Lake, is a perfect picnic spot and boasts a bird's-eye view of San Francisco and the bay. It also has a waterfall and peace pagoda. To reach the **boathouse** call ☎ **415/752-0347.** Boat rentals are available daily from 9am to 4pm.

5 The Presidio & Golden Gate National Recreation Area

THE PRESIDIO

In October 1994, the Presidio was transferred from the U.S. Army to the National Park Service and became one of a handful of urban national parks that combines historical, architectural, and natural elements into one giant arboreal expanse. The 1,480-acre area incorporates a variety of terrain—coastal scrub, dunes, and prairie grasslands that shelter many rare plants and more than 150 species of birds, some of which nest here.

This military outpost has a 220-year history, stretching from its founding in September 1776 by the Spanish under José Joaquin Moraga to its closure in 1995. From 1822 to 1835 the property was in Mexican hands.

During the war with Mexico, American forces occupied the fort, and in 1848, when California became part of the Union, it was formally transferred to the United States. When San Francisco suddenly became an important urban area during the gold rush, the U.S. government installed battalions of soldiers, built Fort Point to protect the entry to the harbor, and expanded the post during the Civil War and later during the Indian Wars of the 1870s and 1880s. By the 1890s it was no longer a frontier post but a major base for American expansion into the Pacific. During the war with Spain in 1898, thousands of troops camped in tent cities awaiting shipment to the Philippines, and the sick and wounded were treated at the Army General Hospital. By 1905, 12 coastal defense batteries were built along the headlands. In 1914, troops under the command of Gen. John Pershing left here to pursue Pancho Villa and his men. The Presidio expanded during the 1920s when Crissy Army Airfield (the first airfield on the West Coast) was established, but the major action was seen during World War II after the attack on Pearl Harbor. Soldiers dug foxholes along nearby beaches, and the Presidio became the headquarters for the Western Defense Command. Some 1.6 million men shipped out from nearby Fort Mason to fight in the Pacific and many returned to the hospital, whose

Golden Gate National Recreation Area

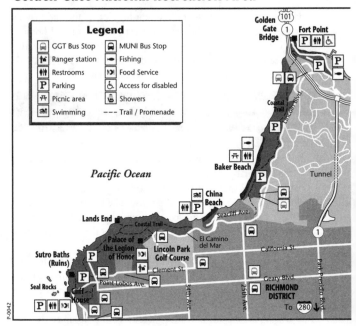

capacity peaked one year at 72,000 patients. In the 1950s, the Presidio served as the headquarters for the Sixth U.S. Army and a missile defense post, but its role has slowly been reduced. In 1972, it was included in new legislation establishing the Golden Gate National Recreation Area; in 1989, the Pentagon decided to close the post and transfer it to the National Park Service.

Today, the area features more than 510 historic buildings, a scenic golf course, a national cemetery, and a variety of terrain and natural habitats. The National Park Service offers a variety of walking and biking tours around the Presidio; reservations are suggested. The **Presidio Museum,** located at the corner of Lincoln Boulevard and Funston Avenue (open 10am to 4pm Wed to Sun), tells its story in dioramas, exhibitions, and photographs. For more information, call the **Visitor Information Center** at ☎ **415/561-4323.** Take the 82X, 28, or 76 bus.

San Francisco Zoo & Children's Zoo. Sloat Blvd. and 45th Ave. ☎ **415/ 753-7080.** Main zoo $7 adults, $3.50 seniors and youths 12–15, $1.50 for children 3–11, and free for children 2 and under if accompanied by an adult; children's zoo $1, free for children under 3 and free to everyone the 1st Wed

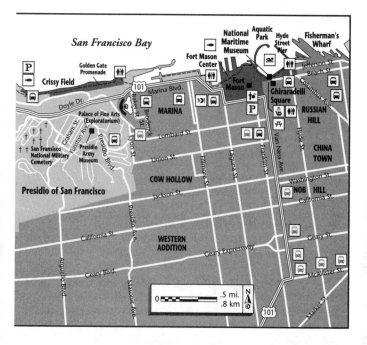

of each month. Carousel $2. Main zoo daily 10am–5pm. Children's zoo Mon–Fri 11am–4pm; Sat–Sun 10:30am–4:30pm. Muni Metro: L from downtown Market St. to the end of the line.

Located between the Pacific Ocean and Lake Merced, in the southwest corner of the city, the San Francisco Zoo is among America's highest-rated animal parks. Begun in 1889 with a grizzly bear named Monarch donated by the *San Francisco Examiner,* the zoo now sprawls over 65 acres and is growing. It attracts up to a million visitors each year. Most of the 1,000-plus inhabitants are contained in landscaped enclosures guarded by concealed moats. The innovative Primate Discovery Center is particularly noteworthy for its many rare and endangered species. Expansive outdoor atriums, sprawling meadows, and a midnight world for exotic nocturnal primates house such species as the owl-faced macaque, ruffed-tailed lemur, black-and-white colobus monkeys, patas monkeys, and emperor tamarins—pint-size primates distinguished by their long, majestic mustaches.

Other highlights include Koala Crossing, which is linked to the Australian WalkAbout exhibit that opened in 1995, housing kangaroos, emus, and wallaroos; Gorilla World, one of the world's largest exhibits of these gentle giants; and Penguin Island, home to a large breeding colony of Magellanic penguins. The new Feline Conservation Center is a wooded sanctuary and breeding facility for the zoo's endangered snow leopards, Persian leopards, and other jungle cats. Musk Ox Meadow is a $2^1/_2$-acre habitat for a herd of rare white-fronted musk oxen brought from Alaska. The Otter River exhibit features waterfalls, logs, and boulders for the North American otters to climb on. And the Lion House is home to rare Sumatran and Siberian tigers, Prince Charles (a rare white Bengal tiger), and the African lions (you can watch them being fed at 2pm Tues to Sun).

The Children's Zoo, adjacent to the main park, allows both kids and adults to get close to animals. The barnyard is alive with strokable domestic animals such as sheep, goats, ponies, and a llama. Also of interest is the Insect Zoo, which showcases a multitude of insect species, including the hissing cockroach and walking sticks.

A free, informal walking tour of the zoo is available on weekends at 11am. The Zebra Zephyr train tour takes visitors on a 30-minute "safari" daily (only on weekends in winter). The tour is $2.50 for adults, $1.50 for children 15 and under and seniors.

GOLDEN GATE NATIONAL RECREATIONAL AREA

The largest urban park in the world, the GGNRA makes New York's Central Park look like a putting green, covering three counties along 28 miles of stunning, condo-free shoreline. Run by the national parks service, the recreation area wraps around the northern and western edges of the city, and just about all of it is open to the public with no access fees. The muni bus system provides transportation to the more popular sites, including aquatic park, the cliff house, fort mason, and ocean beach. For more information, contact the National Park Service (☎ 415/556-0560). For more detailed information on particular sites, see the "staying active" section later in this chapter.

Here is a brief rundown of the salient features of the park's peninsula section, starting at the northern section and moving westward around the coastline:

Aquatic Park, adjacent to the Hyde Street Pier, has a small swimming beach, although it's not that appealing (and darn cold). Far more entertaining is a visit to the ship-shaped museum across the lawn that's part of the San Francisco Maritime National Historical Park.

Fort Mason Center occupies an area from Bay Street to the shoreline and consists of several buildings and piers that were used during World War II. Today they are occupied by a variety of museums, theaters, and organizations as well as by Greens vegetarian restaurant, which affords views of the Golden Gate Bridge (see chapter 5, "Dining," for more information). For information about Fort Mason events, call ☎ **415/441-5706.** The park headquarters is also at Fort Mason.

Farther west along the bay at the northern end of Laguna Street is Marina Green, a favorite local spot for kite-flying, jogging, and walking along the Promenade. The St. Francis Yacht Club is also located here.

From here begins the 3^1/$_2$-mile paved Golden Gate Promenade, San Francisco's best and most scenic biking, jogging, and walking path, which runs along the shore past Crissy Field (be sure to stop and watch the gonzo windsurfers) and ends at Fort Point under the Golden Gate Bridge.

Fort Point (☎ **415/556-1693**) was built in 1853 to protect the narrow entrance to the harbor. It was designed to house 500 soldiers manning 126 muzzle-loading cannons. By 1900, the fort's soldiers and obsolete guns had been removed, but the formidable brick edifice still remains. Fort Point is open Wednesday to Sunday from 10am to 5pm, and guided tours and cannon demonstrations are given at the site once or twice daily, depending on the time of year.

Lincoln Boulevard sweeps around the western edge of the bay to Baker Beach, where the waves roll ashore—a fine spot for sunbathing, walking, or fishing. Hikers can follow the Coastal Trail from Fort Point along this part of the coastline all the way to Lands End.

A short distance from Baker, China Beach is a small cove where swimming is permitted. Changing rooms, showers, a sundeck, and rest rooms are available.

A little farther around the coast appears Lands End looking out to Pyramid Rock. A lower and an upper trail provide a hiking opportunity amid windswept cypresses and pines on the cliffs above the Pacific.

Still farther along the coast lies Point Lobos, the Sutro Baths, and the Cliff House. The latter has been serving refreshments to visitors since 1863 and providing views of Seal Rocks, home to a colony of sea lions and many marine birds. There's an **information center** here (open daily from 10am to 5pm; ☎ **415/556-8642**) as well as the incredible Musée Mecanique, an authentic old-fashioned arcade with 150 coin-operated amusement machines. Only traces of the Sutro Baths remain today to the northeast of the Cliff House. This swimming facility was a major summer attraction that could accommodate up to 24,000 people before it burned down in 1966.

A little farther inland at the western end of California Street is Lincoln Park, which contains a golf course and the spectacular Palace of the Legion of Honor museum.

At the southern end of Ocean Beach, 4 miles down the coast, is another area of the park around Fort Funston where there's an easy loop trail across the cliffs (**visitor center:** ☎ **415/239-2366**). Here, too, you can watch the hang gliders taking advantage of the high cliffs and strong winds.

Farther south along route 280, Sweeney Ridge, which can only be reached by car, affords sweeping views of the coastline from the many trails that crisscross this 1,000 acres of land. It was from here that the expedition led by Don Gaspar de Portolá first saw San Francisco Bay in 1769. Sweeney Ridge is located in Pacifica and can be reached via Sneath Lane off Route 35 (Skyline Boulevard) in San Bruno.

The GGNRA also extends into Marin County, where it encompasses the Marin Headlands, Muir Woods National Monument, Muir Beach and Stinson Beach, and the Olema Valley behind the Point Reyes National Seashore.

6 Churches & Religious Buildings

Some of San Francisco's churches and religious buildings are worth checking out.

⭕ **Glide Memorial United Methodist Church.** 330 Ellis St. (west of Union Sq.). ☎ **415/771-6300.** Services held Sun at 9 and 11am. Muni Metro: Powell. Bus: 37.

There would be nothing special about this Tenderloin-area church if it weren't for its exhilarating pastor, Cecil Williams. Reverend Williams's enthusiastic and uplifting preaching and singing with homeless and poor people of the neighborhood has attracted nationwide fame. In 1994, during the pastor's 30th-anniversary celebration, singers Angela Bofill and Bobby McFerrin joined with comedian Robin Williams, author Maya Angelou, and talk-show queen Oprah Winfrey to honor him publicly. Williams's nondogmatic, fun Sunday services attract a diverse audience that crosses all socioeconomic boundaries. Go for an uplifting experience.

Grace Cathedral. California St. (between Taylor and Jones sts.). ☎ **415/ 749-6300.**

Although this Nob Hill cathedral, designed by architect Lewis P. Hobart, looks like it is made of stone, it is in fact constructed of reinforced concrete, beaten to achieve a stonelike effect. Construction began for this cathedral on the site of the Crocker mansion in 1928, but it was not completed until 1964. Among the more interesting features of the building are its stained-glass windows, particularly those by the French Loire studios, depicting such modern figures as Thurgood Marshall, Robert Frost, and Albert Einstein; the replicas of Ghiberti's bronze *Doors of Paradise* at the east end; the series of religious frescoes completed in the 1940s by Polish artist John de Rosen; and the 44-bell carillon.

✪ **Mission Dolores.** 16th St. (at Dolores St.). ☎ **415/621-8203.** Admission $2 adults, $1 children 5–12. May–Oct daily 9am–4:30pm; Nov–Apr daily 9am–4pm; Good Friday 10am–noon. Closed Thanksgiving Day and Christmas Day. Muni Metro: J to the corner of Church and 16th sts. Bus: 22.

San Francisco's oldest standing structure, the Mission San Francisco de Assisi (a.k.a. Mission Dolores) has withstood the test of time, as well as two major earthquakes, relatively intact. In 1776, at the behest of Franciscan Missionary Junípero Serra, Father Francisco Palou came to the Bay Area to found the sixth in a series of missions that dotted the California coastline. From these humble beginnings grew what was to become the city of San Francisco. The mission's small, simple chapel, built solidly by native Americans who were converted to Christianity, is a curious mixture of native construction methods and Spanish-colonial style. A statue of Father Serra stands in the mission garden, although the portrait looks somewhat more contemplative, and less energetic, than he must have been in real life. An audio tour is available, too, which lasts 45 minutes and costs $5 for adults, $4 for children, and is available during open hours.

7 Architectural Highlights

Alamo Square Historic District   San Francisco's collection of Victorian houses, known as "Painted Ladies," is one of the city's most famous assets. Most of the 14,000 extant structures date from the second half of the 19th century and are private residences. Spread throughout the city, many have been beautifully restored and ornately painted. The small area bordered by Divisadero Street on the west, Golden Gate Avenue on the north, Webster Street on the east, and Fell Street on the south—about 10 blocks west of the Civic

Center—has one of the city's greatest concentrations of these Painted Ladies. One of the most famous views of San Francisco— seen on postcards and posters all around the city—depicts sharp-edged Financial District skyscrapers behind a row of Victorians. This fantastic juxtaposition can be seen from Alamo Square, in the center of this historic district, at Fulton and Steiner streets.

CITY HALL & CIVIC CENTER Built in 1881 to a design by Brown and Bakewell, it is part of this "City Beautiful" complex done in the beaux arts style. The dome rises to a height of 308 feet on the exterior and is ornamented with occuli and topped by a lantern. The interior rotunda soars 112 feet and is finished in oak, marble, and limestone with a monumental marble staircase leading to the second floor, but you won't be able to see it; City Hall is currently closed for a complete renovation and isn't expected to reopen for a few years.

8 Especially for Kids

The following San Francisco attractions have major appeal to kids of all ages:

- Alcatraz Island (see p. 113)
- Cable cars (see p. 116)
- Cable Car Barn Museum (see p. 122)
- California Academy of Sciences, including Steinhart Aquarium (see p. 133)
- The Exploratorium (see p. 123)
- Golden Gate Bridge (see p. 120)
- Golden Gate Park (including the Children's Playground, Bison Paddock, and Japanese Tea Garden) (see below and p. 130)
- The San Francisco Zoo (see p. 136)

9 Self-Guided & Organized Tours

THE 49-MILE SCENIC DRIVE

The self-guided, 49-mile drive is one easy way to orient yourself and to grasp the beauty of San Francisco and its extraordinary location. Beginning in the city, it follows a rough circle around the bay and passes virtually all the best-known sights from Chinatown to the Golden Gate Bridge, Ocean Beach, Seal Rocks, Golden Gate Park, and Twin Peaks. Originally designed for the benefit of visitors to San Francisco's 1939 and 1940 Golden Gate International Exposition, the route is marked with blue-and-white seagull signs.

Although it makes an excellent half-day tour, this miniexcursion can easily take longer if you decide, for example, to stop to walk across the Golden Gate Bridge or to have tea in Golden Gate Park's Japanese Tea Garden.

The San Francisco **Visitor Information Center,** at Powell and Market streets (see "Visitor Information" in chapter 3), distributes free route maps. Since a few of the Scenic Drive marker signs are missing, the map will come in handy. Try to avoid the downtown area during the weekday rush hours from 7 to 9am and 4 to 6pm.

BOAT TOURS

One of the best ways to look at San Francisco is from a boat bobbing on the bay. There are several cruises to choose from, many of which start from Fisherman's Wharf. There is now only one major company.

Blue & Gold Fleet, at Pier 39, Fisherman's Wharf (☎ **415/ 773-1188**), tours the bay year-round in a sleek, 400-passenger sightseeing boat, complete with food and beverage facilities. The fully narrated, $1^1/_4$-hour cruise passes beneath the Golden Gate and Bay bridges, and comes within yards of Alcatraz Island. Frequent daily departures from Pier 39's West Marina begin at 10am during summer and 11am in winter. Tickets cost $16 for adults, $12 for juniors 5 to 17 and seniors over 62, $8 for children 5 to 11, and children under 5 sail free.

BUS TOURS

Gray Line, with offices in the Transbay Terminal, First and Mission streets, Pier 39, and Union Square (☎ **800/826-0202** or 415/ 558-9400), is San Francisco's largest bus-tour operator. They offer several itineraries on a daily basis. There is a free pickup and return service between centrally located hotels and departure locations. Reservations are required for most tours, which are available in several foreign languages including French, German, Spanish, Italian, Japanese, and Korean.

WALKING TOURS

Javawalk is a 2-hour walking tour by self-described "coffeehouse lizard" Elaine Sosa. As the name suggests, it's loosely a coffee walking tour through North Beach, but there's a lot more going on than drinking cups of brew. Javawalk also serves up a good share of historical and architectural trivia, offering something for everyone. The best part of the tour, however, may be the camaraderie that

Kids' Favorites at Fisherman's Wharf

The following sights are all clustered on or near Fisherman's Wharf. To reach this area by cable car, take the Mason line to the last stop and walk to the wharf; by bus, take no. 30, 32, or 42. If you're arriving by car, park on adjacent streets or on the wharf between Taylor and Jones streets.

The Haunted Gold Mine, 113 Jefferson St. (☎ 415/ 202-0400), under the same ownership as the Wax Museum, is a fun house complete with mazes, a hall of mirrors, spatial-disorientation tricks, wind tunnels, and animated ghouls. Even very young children will probably not find it too scary, and it's good old-fashioned carnival fun. Admission is $11.95 for adults, $9.95 for children ages 13 to 17, $8.95 for seniors, $5.95 for children ages 6 to 12, and free for children under 6. Summer hours are Sunday to Thursday from 9am to 11pm, and Friday and Saturday from 9am to midnight; winter hours are Sunday to Thursday from 9am to 10pm, and Friday and Saturday from 9am to 11pm.

The popular battle-scarred World War II fleet submarine **USS Pampanito,** Pier 45, Fisherman's Wharf (☎ 415/775-1943), saw plenty of action in the Pacific. It has been completely restored, and you can crawl around inside. An audio tour is included with

develops among the tour-goers. Sosa keeps the tour interactive and fun, and it's obvious that she knows a profusion of tales and trivia about the history of coffee and its North Beach roots. It's a guaranteed good time, particularly if you're addicted to caffeine. Javawalk is offered Tuesday to Saturday at 10am. The price is $20 per person, with kids 12 and under at half price. For information and reservations ☎ 415/673-WALK (9255).

San Francisco's Chinatown is always fascinating, but for many visitors with limited time it's hard to know where to search out the "nontouristy" shops, restaurants, and historical spots in this microcosm of Chinese culture. **Wok Wiz Chinatown Walking Tours & Cooking Center** (654 Commercial St. between Kearny and Montgomery streets; ☎ 800/281-9255 or 415/981-8989), founded 13 years ago by author, TV personality, cooking instructor, and restaurant critic Shirley Fong-Torres, is the answer. The Wok Wiz tours take you into nooks and crannies not usually seen by tourists. Most admission, which runs $5 for adults, $3 for children 13 to 17, and free for seniors and children under 12; there is also a family pass for $15 (two adults, up to four kids). The *Pampanito* is open daily May through October from 9am to 8pm; November through April it is open daily from 9am to 6pm (until 8pm Fri and Sat nights).

Ripley's Believe It or Not! Museum, 175 Jefferson St. (☎ 415/771-6188; www.ripleysf.com), has been drawing curious spectators through its doors for 30 years. Inside, you'll experience the extraordinary world of improbabilities: a one-third scale match-stick cable car, a shrunken human torso once owned by Ernest Hemingway, a dinosaur made from car bumpers, a walk through a kaleidoscope tunnel, and video displays and illusions. Robert LeRoy Ripley's infamous arsenal may lead you to ponder whether truth is in fact stranger than fiction. Admission is $8.50 for adults, $7 for seniors over 60, $5.50 for children 5 to 12, and free for children under 5. From June 15 through Labor Day it is open Sunday to Thursday from 9am to 11pm, until midnight on Friday and Saturday; the rest of the year it is open Sunday to Thursday from 10am to 10pm, until midnight on Friday and Saturday. Call for special hours on major holidays.

of her guides are Chinese, speak fluent Cantonese or Mandarin, and are intimately acquainted with all of Chinatown's alleys and small enterprises, as well as Chinatown's history, folklore, culture, and food.

Tours are conducted daily from 10am to 1:30pm and include dim sum (Chinese lunch). There's also a less expensive tour that does not include lunch. It's an easy walk, fun and fascinating, and you're bound to make new friends. Groups are generally held to a maximum of 12, and reservations are essential. Prices (including lunch) are $37 for adults, $35 for seniors 60 and older, and $30 for children under 12.

10 Staying Active

Half the fun in San Francisco takes place outdoors. If you're not in the mood to trek it, there are plenty of other things to do that will allow you to enjoy the surroundings.

ACTIVITIES

BICYCLING   Two city-designated bike routes are maintained by the Parks and Recreations department. One winds $7^1/_2$ miles through Golden Gate Park to Lake Merced; the other traverses the city, starting in the south, and follows a route over the Golden Gate Bridge. These routes are not dedicated to bicyclists, and caution must be exercised to avoid crashing into pedestrians. Helmets are recommended for adults, and required by law for kids under 18. A bike map is available from the San Francisco Visitor Information Center, at Powell and Market streets (see "Visitor Information" in chapter 3), and from bicycle shops all around town.

Ocean Beach has a public walk- and bikeway that stretches along 5 waterfront blocks of the Great Highway between Noriega and Santiago streets. It's an easy ride from Cliff House or Golden Gate Park.

Park Cyclery, at 1749 Waller St. (☎ **415/751-7368**), is a shop in the Haight that rent bikes. Located next to Golden Gate Park, the cyclery rents mountain bikes exclusively, along with helmets. The charge is $5 per hour, $25 per day, and it's open Friday to Wednesday from 10am to 6pm.

BOATING   At the **Golden Gate Park Boat House** (☎ **415/ 752-0347**) on Stow Lake, the park's largest body of water, you can rent a rowboat or pedal boat by the hour and steer over to Strawberry Hill, a large, round island in the middle of the lake, for lunch. There's usually a line on weekends. The boat house is open daily, June through September from 9am to 5pm, and the rest of the year daily from 9am to 4pm.

Cass Marina, 1702 Bridgeway, in Sausalito (☎ **800/472-4595** or 415/332-6789), rents sailboats measuring 22 to 101 feet. Sail under the Golden Gate Bridge on your own or with a licensed skipper. In addition, large sailing yachts leave from San Francisco and Sausalito on a regularly scheduled basis. Call for schedules, prices, and availability of sailboats or check them out on the Web at **cassmarina.com.** The marina is open daily from 9am to sunset.

CITY STAIR-CLIMBING   Many U.S. health clubs now have stair-climbing machines and step classes, but in San Francisco, you need only to go outside. The following city stair climbs will provide you not only with a good workout, but with great sightseeing too.

Filbert Street Steps, between Sansome Street and Telegraph Hill, are a particular challenge. Scaling the sheer eastern face of Telegraph

Hill, this 377-step climb wends its way through verdant flower gardens and charming 19th-century cottages. Napier Lane, a narrow wooden plank walkway, leads to Montgomery Street. Turn right, and follow the path to the end of the cul-de-sac where another stairway continues to Telegraph's panoramic summit.

The **Lyon Street Steps**, between Green Street and Broadway, were built in 1916. This historic stairway street contains four steep sets of stairs totaling 288 steps in all. Begin at Green Street and climb all the way up, past manicured hedges and flower gardens, to an iron gate that opens into the Presidio. A block east, on **Baker Street**, another set of 369 steps descends to Green Street.

GOLF   San Francisco has a few beautiful golf courses. At press time, one of the most lavish, the **Presidio Golf Course** (☎ 415/ 561-4664), had just opened up to the public for the first time (greens fees $35 Mon to Thurs, $45 Fri, and $55 Sat–Sun.) There are also two decent municipal golf courses in town if you're itching to put on your golf shoes and swing some clubs.

Golden Gate Park Course. 47th Ave. and Fulton St. ☎ **415/751-8987.** Greens fees $10 per person Mon–Fri; $13 Sat–Sun. Daily 6am–dusk.

This small 9-hole course covers 1,357 yards and is par 27. All holes are par 3, tightly set, and well trapped with small greens. The course is a little weathered in spots, but it's a casual, fun, and inexpensive place to tee off local-style.

Lincoln Park Golf Course. 34th Ave. and Clement St. ☎ **415/221-9911.** Greens fees $23 per person Mon–Fri; $27 Sat–Sun. Daily 6:30am–dusk.

San Francisco's prettiest municipal course has terrific views and fairways lined with Monterey cypress trees. Its 18 holes encompass 5,081 yards, for a par 68, and the 17th hole has a glistening ocean view. This is the oldest course in the city and one of the oldest in the West.

Mission Bay Golf Center. Sixth St. at Channel St. (from downtown San Francisco, take Fourth St. south to Channel St. and turn right). ☎ **415/431-7888.** Bucket of balls $7. Mon 11:30am–11pm; Tues–Sun 7am–11pm. Last bucket sold at 10pm.

San Francisco's most popular driving range, the Mission Bay Golf Center is an impeccably maintained 7-acre facility that consists of a double-decker steel and concrete arc containing 66 covered practice bays. The grass landing area extends 300 yards, has nine target greens, and is lit for evening use. There's also a putting green, as well as a chipping and bunker practice area.

SKATING (Conventional & In-Line)   Although people skate in Golden Gate Park all week long, Sunday is best, when John F. Kennedy Drive between Kezar Drive and Transverse Road is closed to automobiles. A smooth "skate pad" is located on your right, just past the Conservatory. **Skates on Haight,** at 1818 Haight St. (☎ 415/752-8376), is the best place to rent either in-line or conventional skates, and is located only 1 block from the park. Protective wrist guards and knee pads are included free. The cost is $8 per hour for in-line or "conventional" skates, $28 for all-day use. Major credit card and ID deposit are required. The shop is open Monday to Friday from 10am to 6:30pm, and Saturday and Sunday from 10am to 6pm.

TENNIS   More than 100 courts throughout the city are maintained by the **San Francisco Recreation and Parks Department** (☎ 415/753-7001). All are available free, on a first-come, first-served basis. The exceptions are the 21 courts in Golden Gate Park; a $4-to-$6 fee is charged for their use, and courts must be reserved in advance for weekend play. Call the number above on Wednesday between 7 and 9pm, or on Thursday and Friday from 9am to 5pm. For weekend reservations call ☎ 415/753-7101.

WALKING & HIKING   The **Golden Gate National Recreation Area** offers plenty of opportunities for walking and hiking. One pleasant walk, or bike ride for that matter, is along the Golden Gate Promenade, from Aquatic Park to the Golden Gate Bridge. The 3¹/₂-mile paved trail leads along the northern edge of the Presidio, out to Fort Point. You can also hike along the Coastal Trail all the way from near Fort Point to the Cliff House. The park service maintains several other trails in the city. For more information or to pick up a map of the Golden Gate National Recreation Area, stop by the park service headquarters at Fort Mason at the north end of Laguna Street (☎ 415/556-0560).

Though most drive to this spectacular vantage point, a more rejuvenating way to experience Twin Peaks is to walk up from the back roads of U.C. Medical Center (off Parnassus) or from either of the two roads that lead to the top (off Woodside or Clarendon avenues). Early morning is the best time to trek, when the city is quiet, the air is crisp, and the sightseers haven't crowded the parking lot. Keep an eye out for cars, since there's no real hiking trail, and be sure to walk beyond the lot and up to the highest vantage point.

11 Spectator Sports

The Bay Area's sports scene includes several major professional franchises, including football, baseball, and basketball. Check the local newspapers' sports sections for daily listings of local events.

Baseball is represented by the **San Francisco Giants,** who play at 3Com/Candlestick Park, Giants Drive and Gilman Avenue (☎ **415/467-8000**), from April through October. Tickets are usually available up until game time, but seats can be dreadfully far from the action. You can get tickets through **BASS Ticketmaster** (☎ **510/762-2277**). Special express bus service is available from Market Street on game days; call **Muni** (☎ **415/673-6864**) for pickup points and schedule information. Bring a coat—this 60,000-seat stadium is known for its chilly winds.

The Bay Area's other team is the 1989 world-champion **Oakland Athletics,** who play at the Oakland Coliseum Complex, at the Hegenberger Road exit from I-880, in Oakland (☎ **510/430-8020**). The stadium holds 50,000 spectators and is serviced by BART's Coliseum station. Tickets are available from the Box Office or by phone through **BASS Ticketmaster** (☎ **510/762-2277**).

Pro basketball is represented by the **Golden State Warriors,** who play at the Oakland Coliseum Complex, at the Hegenberger Road exit from I-880, in Oakland (☎ **510/986-2200**). The NBA Warriors play basketball in the 15,025-seat Oakland Coliseum Arena. The season runs from November through April, and most games are played at 7:30pm. Tickets are available at the arena, and by phone through BASS Ticketmaster (☎ **510/762-2277**).

As of 1995, the Bay Area once again plays home to two professional football teams. The **San Francisco 49ers** play at 3Com/Candlestick Park (Giants Drive and Gilman Avenue) (☎ **415/468-2249**). Games are played on Sundays from August through December; kickoff is usually at 1pm. Tickets sell out early in the season, but are available at higher prices through ticket agents beforehand and from scalpers at the gate. Ask your concierge or visit **City Box Office,** 153 Kearny St., Suite 302 (☎ **415/392-4400**). Special express bus service is available from Market Street on game days; call **Muni** (☎ **415/673-6864**) for pickup and schedule information.

Also back in the Bay Area are the 49ers' archenemy, the **Oakland Raiders.** Their home turf is the Oakland Alameda County Coliseum, off the 880 Freeway (Nimitz) (☎ **800/949-2626** for ticket information).

Shopping

Like its population, San Francisco's shopping is worldly and intimate. Every persuasion, style, era, and fetish is represented here, not in a big, tacky shopping mall, but rather in hundreds of quaint and dramatically different boutiques scattered throughout the city. Whether it's Chanel or Chinese herbal medicine you're looking for, San Francisco's got it. Just pick a shopping neighborhood and break out your credit cards—you're sure to end up with at least a few take-home treasures.

1 The Shopping Scene

MAJOR SHOPPING AREAS

San Francisco has many shopping areas, but the following places are where you'll find most of the action:

Union Square and Environs   San Francisco's most congested and popular shopping mecca is centered around Union Square and enclosed by Bush, Taylor, Market, and Montgomery streets. Most of the big department stores and many high-end specialty shops are in this area. Be sure to venture to Grant Avenue, Post and Sutter streets, and Maiden Lane.

Union Street   Union Street, from Fillmore to Van Ness, caters to the upper-middle-class crowd. This area is a great place to stroll, window-shop the plethora of boutiques, cafes, and restaurants, and watch the beautiful people parade by. Serviced by bus lines 22, 41, 42, and 45.

Fillmore Street   Some of the best shopping in town is packed into 5 blocks of Fillmore Street in Pacific Heights. From Jackson to Sutter streets, Fillmore is the perfect place to grab a bite and peruse the high-priced boutiques, craft shops, and incredible houseware stores. Don't miss Zinc Details and Fillamento. Serviced by bus lines 1, 2, 3, 4, 12, 22, and 24.

Haight Street   Green hair, spiked hair, no hair, or mohair—even the hippies look conservative next to Haight Street's dramatic fashion freaks. The shopping in the 6 blocks of upper Haight Street, between Central Avenue and Stanyan Street, reflects its clientele and offers everything from incense and European and American street styles to furniture and antique clothing. Bus lines 7, 66, 71, and 73 run the length of Haight Street. The Muni metro N line stops at Waller Street and at Cole Street.

SoMa   Though this area isn't suitable for strolling, you'll find almost all the discount shopping in warehouse spaces South of Market. You can pick up a discount-shopping guide at most major hotels. Many bus lines pass through this area.

Hayes Valley   It may not be the prettiest area in town (with some of the shadier housing projects a few blocks away), but while most neighborhoods cater to more conservative or trendy shoppers, lower Hayes Street, between Octavia and Gough, celebrates anything vintage, artistic, or downright funky. Though still in its developmental stage, it's definitely the most interesting new shopping area in town, with furniture and glass stores, thrift shops, trendy shoe stores, and men's and women's clothiers. There are also lots of great antique shops south on Octavia and on nearby Market Street. Bus lines include 16AX, 16BX, and 21.

Fisherman's Wharf & Environs   The tourist-oriented malls run along Jefferson Street and include hundreds of shops, restaurants, and attractions including Ghirardelli Square, Pier 39, and the Cannery.

2 Shopping A to Z

BOOKS

In addition to the independents below, you'll find **Borders Books & Music** at 400 Post St. (☎ **415/399-1633**) and a **Barnes & Noble** at 2550 Taylor St. (☎ **415/292-6762**).

The Booksmith. 1644 Haight St. (between Clayton and Cole sts.). ☎ **800/ 493-7323** or 415/863-8688. http://www.booksmith.com. E-mail: read@booksmith.com.

Haight Street's best selection of new books is housed in this large, well-maintained shop. It carries all the top titles, along with works from smaller presses, and more than 1,000 different magazines. Open Monday to Saturday from 10am to 9pm and Sunday from 10am to 6pm.

○ City Lights Booksellers & Publishers. 261 Columbus Ave. (at Broadway). ☎ **415/362-8193.**

Brooding literary types browse this famous bookstore owned by Lawrence Ferlinghetti, the renowned beat-generation poet. The three-level bookshop prides itself on a comprehensive collection of art, poetry, and political paperbacks, as well as mainstream books.

✪ **A Clean, Well-Lighted Place for Books.** 601 Van Ness Ave. (between Turk St. and Golden Gate Ave.). ☎ **415/441-6670.**

Voted best bookstore by the *San Francisco Bay Guardian,* this independent has good new fiction and nonfiction sections and also specializes in music, art, mystery, and cookbooks. The store is very well known for its schedule of author readings and events. For a calendar of events, call the store or check their Web site at **http://www.bookstore.com**. Open Sunday to Thursday from 10am to 11pm, and Friday and Saturday from 10am to midnight.

CHINA, SILVER & GLASS
The Enchanted Crystal. 1895 Union St. (at Laguna St.). ☎ **415/885-1335.**

This shop has an extensive collection of fine crystal, art glass, jewelry, and one-of-a-kind decorative art, including one of the largest crystal balls in the world (from Madagascar). Open Monday to Saturday from 10am to 6pm and Sunday from noon to 5pm.

✪ **Gump's.** 135 Post St. (between Kearny St. and Grant Ave.). ☎ **415/982-1616.**

Founded over a century ago, Gump's offers gifts and treasures ranging from Asian antiquities to contemporary art glass and exquisite jade and pearl jewelry. Many items are made specifically for the store. Gump's also has one of the most revered window displays each holiday season. Open Monday to Saturday from 10am to 6pm.

DEPARTMENT STORES
Macy's. Corner of Stockton and O'Farrell sts., Union Sq. ☎ **415/397-3333.**

The seven-story Macy's West features contemporary fashions for women and juniors, including jewelry, fragrances, cosmetics, and accessories. The third floor offers a "hospitality suite" where visitors can leave their coats and packages, grab a cup of coffee, or find out more about the city from the concierge. The top floors contain home furnishings, while the Cellar sells kitchenware and gourmet foods. You'll even find a Boudin Cafe (great sandwiches!) and Wolfgang Puck Cafe on the premises. Across the street, Macy's East has five floors of men's and children's fashions, as well as the recently added largest Men's Polo by Ralph Lauren shop in the country and the Fresh Choice cafe. Macy's most recent acquisition, the old Emporium building at 835 Market (between Fourth and Fifth streets), is now temporarily Macy's Home Store. Macy's is open Monday to Saturday from 10am to 8pm and Sunday from 11am to 7pm.

Neiman Marcus. 150 Stockton St., Union Sq. ☎ **415/362-3900.**

Some call this unit of the Texas-based chain "Needless Mark-up." But if you've got the cash, the men's and women's clothes, precious gems, and conservative formal wear here are some of the most glamorous in town. The Rotunda Restaurant, on the top floor, is a beautiful, relaxing place for lunch and afternoon tea. Open Monday, Thursday, and Friday from 10am to 6pm, Tuesday, Wednesday, and Saturday from 10am to 7pm, and Sunday from noon to 6pm.

Nordstrom. 865 Market St. (in the San Francisco Shopping Centre). ☎ **415/243-8500.**

Renowned for its personalized service, this is the largest member of the Seattle-based fashion department-store chain. Nordstrom occupies the top five floors of the San Francisco Shopping Centre and is that mall's primary anchor. Equally devoted to women's and men's fashions, the store has one of the best shoe selections in the city, and thousands of suits in stock. The Nordstrom Café, on the fourth floor, has a panoramic view and is an ideal place for an inexpensive lunch or light snack. The fifth floor is occupied by Nordstrom Spa, the perfect place to relax after a hectic day of bargain-hunting. Open Monday to Saturday from 9:30am to 9pm and Sunday from 10am to 7pm.

DISCOUNT SHOPPING

There are many factory-outlet stores in San Francisco, selling overstocked and discontinued fashions at bargain prices. All of the following shops are located south of Market Street, in the city's warehouse district (SoMa).

Esprit Outlet Store. 499 Illinois St. (at 16th St.). ☎ **415/957-2550.**

All the Esprit collections and Susie Tompkins merchandise are available here at 30% or more off regular prices. In addition to clothes, the store sells accessories, shoes, and assorted other items. Open Monday to Friday from 10am to 8pm, Saturday from 10am to 7pm, and Sunday from 11am to 5pm.

✪ **Jeremys.** 2 South Park. (between Bryant and Brannan sts. at Second St.). ☎ **415/882-4929.**

This SoMa boutique offers top designer fashions from shoes to suits at rock-bottom prices. There are no cheap knockoffs here, just good men's and women's clothes and accessories. Jeremy's also has its own stylish clothing line. Open Monday to Saturday 11am to 7pm and Sunday noon to 6pm.

FASHIONS

Grand. 1435 Grant Ave. (between Green and Union sts.). ☎ **415/951-0131.**

Invited to an underground club and forgot your funky rave attire?
Grand's North Beach shop features the latest in fashion-forward
street wear by local designers. Garb comes both baggy and tight; the
style is club, and the price is right. Open daily from noon to 7pm.

Gucci America. 200 Stockton St. (between Geary and Post sts.). ☎ **415/
392-2808.**

Donning Gucci's golden Gs is not a cheap endeavor. But if you've
got the cash, you'll find all the latest lines of shoes, leather goods,
scarves, and pricey accessories, such as a $7,000 handmade croco-
dile bag. Open Monday to Saturday 10am to 6pm and on Sunday
noon to 5pm.

✪ **Wilkes Bashford.** 375 Sutter St. (at Stockton). ☎ **415/986-4380.**

Wilkes Bashford is one of the most expensive and well-known clothing stores in the city. In its 31 years in business, the boutique has
garnered a reputation for stocking only the finest clothes in the
world (which can often be seen on Mayor Willie Brown, who does
his suit shopping here). Most fashions come from Italy and France
and include women's designer sportswear and couture and men's
Kiton and Brioni suits (at $3,000 and up, they're considered the
most expensive suits in the world). Open Monday to Wednesday
and Friday and Saturday from 10am to 6pm, Thursday from 10am
to 8pm. Closed Sunday.

MEN'S FASHIONS

Brooks Brothers. 201 Post St. (at Grant Ave.). ☎ **415/397-4500.**

In San Francisco, this bulwark of tradition is located 1 block east of
Union Square. Brooks Brothers introduced the button-down collar
and single-handedly changed the standard of the well-dressed busi-
nessman. The multilevel shop also sells traditional casual wear,
including sportswear, sweaters, and shirts. Open Monday to Friday
from 9:30am to 7pm, Saturday from 9:30am to 6pm, and Sunday
from 11am to 6pm.

Cable Car Clothiers. 441 Sutter St. (between Grant Ave. and Kearny St.).
☎ **415/397-4740.**

Dapper men head to this beautiful landmark building for traditional
attire, such as three-button suits with natural shoulders, Aquascutum
coats, McGeorge sweaters, and Atkinson ties. Open Monday to Saturday from 9:30am to 5:30pm.

MAC. 5 Claude Lane (off Sutter St. between Grant Ave. and Kearny St.).
☎ **415/837-0615.**

The more-classic-than-corporate man shops here for imported tailored suits in new and intriguing fabrics. Lines include London's Katherine Hamnett, Belgium's SO, Italy's Alberto Biani, New York's John Bartlett, and one of our personal favorites, San Francisco's Lat Naylor. Open Monday to Saturday from 11am to 6pm and Sunday from noon to 5pm. Their women's store is located at 1543 Grant Ave. (between Filbert and Union streets; ☎ **415/837-1604**).

WOMEN'S FASHIONS

Bella Donna. 539 Hayes St. (between Laguna and Octavia sts.). ☎ **415/861-7182.**

Another blessing to the small but growing Hayes Valley alternative shopping mecca is this expensive but quality boutique offering luxurious women's clothing, such as hand-knit sweaters, silky slip dresses, and fashionable knit hats. There's also a wonderful (albeit expensive) collection of vases and other household trinkets, as well as a small selection of remainder fabrics. Upstairs, the wedding and bridal section focuses on the vintage look. Open Tuesday through Saturday from 11am to 7pm and Sunday from 11am to 5pm; bridals by appointment.

The Chanel Boutique. 155 Maiden Lane (between Stockton St. and Grant Ave.). ☎ **415/981-1550.**

Ever fashionable and expensive, Chanel is appropriately located on Maiden Lane, the quaint downtown side street where the most exclusive stores and spas cluster. You'll find what you'd expect from Chanel: clothing, accessories, scents, cosmetics, and jewelry. Open Monday to Saturday from 10am to 6pm and Sunday from 11am to 5pm.

Métier. 355 Sutter St. (between Grant and Stockton sts.). ☎ **415/989-5395.**

The classic, sophisticated, and expensive creations for women found here include European ready-to-wear lines and designers Peter Cohen, Georgina Von Etzdorf, Alberto Biani, and local Lat Naylor, as well as a distinguished collection of antique-style, high-end jewelry from LA's Kathie Waterman. Open Monday to Saturday from 10am to 6pm. Closed Sunday.

Solo Fashion. 1599 Haight St. (at Clayton St.). ☎ **415/621-0342.**

While strolling upper Haight, stop in here for a good selection of upbeat, contemporary, English-style street wear, along with a collection of dresses designed exclusively for this shop. Open daily from 11am to 7pm.

FOOD

✪ **Joseph Schmidt Confections.** 3489 16th St. (at Sanchez St.). ☎ **415/ 861-8682.**

Chocolate takes the shape of exquisite sculptural masterpieces—such as long-stemmed tulips and heart-shaped boxes—that are so beautiful, you'll be hesitant to bite the head off your adorable chocolate panda bear. But once you do, you'll know why this is the most popular chocolatier in town. Prices are also remarkably reasonable. Open Monday to Saturday from 10am to 6:30pm.

✪ **Ten Ren Tea Company.** 949 Grant Ave. (between Washington and Jackson sts.). ☎ **415/362-0656.**

At the Ten Ren Tea Company you will be offered a steaming cup of roselle tea, made of black tea and hibiscus. In addition to a selection of almost 50 traditional and herbal teas, the company stocks related paraphernalia, such as pots, cups, and infusers. If you can't make up your mind, take home a mail-order form. Open daily from 9am to 9pm.

GIFTS

Cost Plus Imports. 2552 Taylor St. (between North Point and Bay sts.). ☎ **415/928-6200.**

At the Fisherman's Wharf cable-car turntable, Cost Plus is a vast warehouse crammed to the rafters with Chinese baskets, Indian camel bells, Malaysian batik scarves, and innumerable other items from Algeria to Zanzibar. More than 20,000 items from 40 nations are purchased directly from their country of origin and packed into this well-priced warehouse. They also have a decent wine shop. Open daily from 9am to 9pm.

✪ **Dandelion.** 55 Potrero Ave. (at Alameda St.). ☎ **415/436-9500.**

Many locals were dismayed when, after almost 20 years in business, Dandelion closed its doors on California Street a few years back. But owners Steve, Del, and Carl weren't finished for good. Their new location is larger and even more packed with the most wonderful collection of gifts, collectibles, and furnishings. There's something for every taste and budget here, ranging from an excellent collection of teapots, decorative dishes, and gourmet foods, to silver, books, cards, and picture frames. Don't miss the Zen-like second floor, with its variety of peaceful furnishings in Indian, Japanese, and Western styles. Open Tuesday through Saturday from 10am to 6pm; closed Sunday and Monday.

Good Vibrations. 1210 Valencia St. (at 23rd St.). ☎ **800/BUY-VIBE** for mail order, or 415/974-8980.

A laypersons' sex-toy, book, and video emporium, Good Vibrations is specifically designed (but not exclusively) for women. Unlike most sex shops, it's not a back-alley business, but rather a straightforward shop with healthy and open attitudes about human sexuality. They also have a vibrator museum. Open daily from 11am to 7pm. A second location is in Berkeley at 2504 San Pablo Ave.

Quantity Postcards. 1441 Grant St. (at Green St.). ☎ **415/986-8866.**

You'll find the perfect postcard for literally everyone you know here, as well as some depictions of old San Francisco, movie stars, and Day-Glo posters featuring concert-poster artist Frank Kozik. Prices range from 35¢ to $2 per card, and even if you don't need any cards, you'll enjoy browsing the eclectic collection of mailables. Open daily from 11am to 11pm.

✪ **SFMOMA MuseumStore.** 151 Third St. (2 blocks south of Market St., across from Yerba Buena Gardens). ☎ **415/357-4035.**

With an array of artistic cards, books, jewelry, housewares, knickknacks, and creative tokens of San Francisco, it's virtually impossible not to find something you'll consider a must-have. Aside from being one of the locals' favorite shops, it also offers far more tasteful mementos than most Fisherman's Wharf options. Open Friday to Wednesday from 10:30am to 6:30pm and Thursday from 10:30am to 9:30pm.

HOUSEWARES

✪ **Biordi Art Imports.** 412 Columbus Ave. (at Vallejo St.). ☎ **415/392-8096.**

Whether it's your intention to decorate your dinner table, color up your kitchen, or liven the living room, Biordi's Italian Majolica pottery is the most exquisite and unique way to do it. The owner has been importing these hand-painted collectibles for 50 years, and every piece is a show-stopper. Call for a catalog if you like. They'll ship anywhere. Open Monday to Saturday from 9:30am to 6pm. Closed Sunday.

✪ **Fillamento.** 2185 Fillmore St. (at Sacramento St.). ☎ **415/931-2224.**

The best housewares store in the city, Fillamento's three floors are always packed with shoppers searching for the most classic, artistic, and refined housewares. Whether you're looking to set a good table or revamp your bedroom, you'll find it all here. Open daily from 10am to 6pm.

The Wok Shop. 718 Grant Ave. (at Clay St.). ☎ **888/780-7171** for mail order, or 415/989-3797.

This shop has every conceivable implement for Chinese cooking, including woks, brushes, cleavers, circular chopping blocks, dishes, oyster knives, bamboo steamers, strainers—you name it. The shop also sells a wide range of kitchen utensils, baskets, handmade linens from China, and aprons. Open Sunday to Friday from 10am to 6pm and Saturday from 10am to 9pm.

✪ **Zinc Details.** 1905 Fillmore St. (between Bush and Pine sts.). ☎ **415/776-2100.**

One of our favorite stores in the city, Zinc Details has received accolades from everyone from Elle Decor Japan to Metropolitan Home for its amazing collection of locally handcrafted glass vases, pendant lights, ceramics, and furniture. Each piece is a true work of art created specifically for the store (except vintage items) and these pieces are in such high demand that the store's wholesale accounts include Barney's New York and The Guggenheim Museum Store. Open daily from 11am to 7pm.

JEWELRY

Jerusalem Shoppe. 313 Noe St. (at Market St.). ☎ **415/626-7906.**

Known for its extensive collection of silver and gold gemstone jewelry by more than 300 local and international artists, this shop also displays other unique treasures, from clothing and accessories to imported antique Indian quilts. Open Monday to Friday from 11am to 10pm and Sunday from 10:30am to 9pm.

Tiffany & Co. 350 Post St. (at Powell St.). ☎ **415/781-7000.**

Even if you don't have lots of cash to buy an exquisite bauble that comes in Tiffany's famous light-blue box, enjoy this renowned store à la Audrey Hepburn in *Breakfast at Tiffany's*. The designer collection features Paloma Picasso, Jean Schlumberger, and Elsa Peretti in both silver and 18-karat gold, and there's an extensive gift collection in sterling, china, and crystal. Open Monday to Saturday from 10am to 6pm.

Union Street Goldsmith. 1909 Union St. (at Laguna St.). ☎ **415/776-8048.**

A showcase for Bay Area goldsmiths, this exquisite shop sells custom-designed jewelry in all karats. Many pieces emphasize colored stones

in their settings. Open Monday to Saturday from 11am to 5:45pm
and Sunday from noon to 4:45pm.

MARKETS/PRODUCE
✪ **Farmers Market.** Embarcadero, in front of the Ferry Building. ☎ **510/
528-6987.**

Every Tuesday and Saturday from 8:30am to 1:30pm, northern
California fruit, vegetable, bread, and dairy vendors join local res-
taurateurs in selling fresh, delicious edibles. There's no better way
to enjoy a bright San Francisco morning than strolling this gourmet
street market and snacking your way through breakfast. You can also
pick up locally made vinegars and oils—they make wonderful gifts.

RECORDS & CD'S
Recycled Records. 1377 Haight St. (between Central and Masonic sts.).
☎ **415/626-4075.**

Easily one of the best used-record stores in the city, this loud shop
in the Haight has a good selection of promotional CDs and cases of
used "classic" rock LPs. Sheet music, tour programs, and old *TV
Guides* are sold. Open Monday to Saturday from 10am to 10pm and
Sunday from 11am to 7pm.

Streetlight Records. 3979 24th St. (between Noe and Sanchez sts.).
☎ **415/282-3550.**

Overstuffed with used music in all three formats, this place is best
known for its records and excellent CD collection. Rock music is
cheap here, and a money-back guarantee guards against defects. Their
second location is at 2350 Market St., between Castro and Noe streets
(☎ **415/282-8000**); call for open hours. Open Monday to Saturday
from 10am to 10pm and on Sunday from 10:30am to 8:30pm.

Virgin Megastore. 2 Stockton (at Market St.). ☎ **415/397-4525.**

With thousands of CDs, including an impressive collection of
imports, videos, laser discs, a multimedia department, a cafe, and
related books, any music-lover could blow his/her entire vacation
fund in this enormous Union Square store. Open Monday to Thursday from 9am to 10pm, Friday and Saturday from 9am to midnight,
and Sunday from 10am to 10pm.

SHOES
Birkenstock Natural Footwear. 1815 Polk St. (between Washington and
Jackson sts.). ☎ **415/776-5225.**

This relaxed store is known for its California-style, form-fitting san-
dals. Other orthopedically correct shoes are also available, including

Finn Comforts and traditional Danish clogs by Dansko. Open daily from 10:30am to 6pm.

Bulo. 437A Hayes St. (at Gough St.). ☎ **415/864-3244.**

If you have a fetish for foot fashions, you must check out Bulo, which carries nothing but imported Italian men's and women's shoes. The selection is small but styles run the gamut, from casual to dressy, reserved to wildly funky. Since new shipments come in every 3 to 4 weeks, their selection is ever-changing, eternally hip, and unfortunately, ever-expensive, with many pairs going for close to $200. Open Monday to Saturday from 11:30am to 6:30pm and Sunday from noon to 6pm.

TOYS

The Disney Store. 400 Post St. (at Powell St.). ☎ **415/391-6866.**

Capitalizing on the world's love for The Mouse and his friends, this store offers everything Disney-oriented you could possibly want— from clothes and toys to high-end commissioned art from the Disney gallery. Those looking for a simple token can fork over $3 for a plastic character, while more serious collectors can throw down $9,000 for a Yamagata Disney lithograph. Open in winter Monday to Friday from 10am to 7pm, Saturday from 10am to 6pm, and Sunday from 11am to 5pm. Hours are extended during the summer and holiday season; call for details. Another location is at Pier 39 (☎ **415/391-4119**).

FAO Schwarz. 48 Stockton St. (at O'Farrell St.). ☎ **415/394-8700.**

The world's greatest—and most overpriced—toy store for both children and adults is filled with every imaginable plaything, from hand-carved, custom-painted carousel rocking horses, dolls, and stuffed animals, to gas-powered cars, train sets, and hobby supplies. At the entrance is a singing 22-foot clock tower with 1,000 different moving parts. Open Monday to Friday from 10am to 6pm and on Sunday from 11am to 5pm.

VINTAGE CLOTHING

Aardvark's. 1501 Haight St. (at Ashbury St.). ☎ **415/621-3141.**

One of San Francisco's largest secondhand clothing dealers, Aardvark's has seemingly endless racks of shirts, pants, dresses, skirts, and hats from the last 30 years. Open daily from 11am to 7pm.

Buffalo Exchange. 1555 Haight St. (between Clayton and Ashbury sts.). ☎ **415/431-7733.**

This large storefront on upper Haight Street is crammed with racks of antique and new fashions from the 1960s, 1970s, and 1990s. It stocks everything from suits and dresses to neckties, hats, handbags, and jewelry. Buffalo Exchange anticipates some of the hottest new street fashions. Open Monday to Saturday from 11am to 7pm and Sunday from noon to 6pm. A second shop is located at 1800 Polk St. (at Washington Street; ☎ **415/346-5741**).

○ **Good Byes.** 3463 Sacramento St. (between Laurel and Walnut sts.). ☎ **415/346-6388.**

One of our favorite new- and used-clothes stores in San Francisco, Good Byes carries only high-quality clothing and accessories, including an exceptional selection of men's fashions at unbelievably low prices (for example, $350 preowned shoes for $35). Women's wear is in a separate boutique across the street. Open Monday to Wednesday, Friday, and Saturday from 10am to 6pm; Thursday from 10am to 8pm; and Sunday from 11am to 5pm.

La Rosa. 1711 Haight St. (at Cole). ☎ **415/668-3744.**

On a street packed with vintage-clothing shops, this is one of the more upscale options, featuring a selection of high-quality, dry-cleaned secondhand goods. Formal suits and dresses are its specialty, but you'll also find sport coats, slacks, and shoes. You may also want to visit its more moderately priced sister store, Held Over, on Haight near Ashbury. Open daily from 11am to 7pm.

WINE

○ **Wine Club San Francisco.** 953 Harrison St. (between Fifth and Sixth sts.). ☎ **415/512-9086.**

The Wine Club is a discount warehouse that offers bargain prices on more than 1,200 domestic and foreign wines. Bottles cost between $4 and $1,100. Open Monday to Saturday from 9am to 7pm and Sunday from 11am to 6pm.

San Francisco After Dark

*F*or a city with fewer than a million inhabitants, San Francisco's overall artistic enterprise is nothing short of phenomenal. The city's opera is justifiably world renowned, the ballet is well respected, and the theaters are high in both quantity and quality. Dozens of piano bars and top-notch lounges are augmented by one of the best dance-club cultures this side of New York, and skyscraper lounges offer some of the most dazzling city views in the world. In short, there's always something going on in the city, so get off your fanny and get out there.

For up-to-date nightlife information, turn to the *San Francisco Weekly* and the *San Francisco Bay Guardian,* both of which contain comprehensive current listings. They are available free at bars and restaurants, and from street-corner boxes all around the city. *Where,* a free tourist monthly, also has information on programs and performance times; it's available in most of the city's finer hotels. The Sunday edition of the *San Francisco Examiner* and *Chronicle* also features a "Datebook" section, printed on pink paper, with information and listings on the week's upcoming events.

TICKETS

Tix Bay Area (☎ 415/433-7827) sells half-price tickets to theater, dance, and music performances on the day of the show only; tickets for Sunday and Monday events, if available, are sold on Saturday. They also sell advance, full-price tickets for most performance halls, sporting events, concerts, and clubs. A service charge, ranging from $1 to $3, is levied on each ticket. Only cash or traveler's checks are accepted for half-price tickets; Visa and MasterCard are accepted for full-price tickets. Tix is located on Stockton Street, between Post and Geary streets on the east side of Union Square (opposite Maiden Lane). It's open Tuesday to Thursday from 11am to 6pm, and Friday and Saturday from 11am to 7pm.

Tickets to most theater and dance events can also be obtained through **City Box Office,** 153 Kearny St., Suite 402 (☎ 415/392-4400). American Express, MasterCard, and Visa are accepted.

BASS Ticketmaster (☎ 510/762-2277) sells computer-generated tickets to concerts, sporting events, plays, and special events. Downtown BASS Ticketmaster ticketing offices include Tix Bay Area (see above) and at Warehouse stores throughout the city. The most convenient location is at 30 Powell St.

1 The Performing Arts

Special concerts and performances are staged in San Francisco year-round. **San Francisco Performances,** 500 Sutter St., Suite 710 (☎ 415/398-6449), has been bringing acclaimed artists to the Bay Area for more than 15 years. Shows run the gamut from classical chamber music to dance and jazz. Performances are in several venues, including the city's Performing Arts Center, Herbst Theater, and the Center for the Performing Arts at Yerba Buena Center. The season lasts from late September through May. Tickets cost $12 to $55, and are available through **City Box Office** (☎ 415/392-4400). There is also a 6pm Thursday after-work concert series at the EC Cabaret, 3 Embarcadero Center, in fall and winter; $6 admission at the door (☎ 415/398-6449 for information).

CLASSICAL MUSIC

In addition to two world-class groups, described below, visitors might also be interested in the **San Francisco Contemporary Music Players** (☎ 415/252-6235), whose concerts are held at the Center for the Arts at Yerba Buena Gardens; they play modern chamber works by international artists. Tickets, available by phone (☎ 415/978-ARTS), cost $14 for adults, $10 for seniors, and $6 for students.

Philharmonia Baroque Orchestra. Performing in the Herbst Theater, 401 Van Ness Ave. ☎ **415/392-4400** (box office). Tickets $29–$39.

Acclaimed by the *New York Times* as "the country's leading early music orchestra," Philharmonia Baroque performs in San Francisco and all around the Bay Area. The season lasts from September through April. The company's administrative offices can be reached at ☎ 415/391-5252.

San Francisco Symphony. Performing at Davies Symphony Hall, 201 Van Ness Ave. (at Grove St.). ☎ **415/864-6000** (box office). Tickets $11–$73.

Founded in 1911, the internationally respected San Francisco Symphony has long been an important part of this city's cultural life under such legendary conductors as Pierre Monteux and Seiji Ozawa. In 1995, Michael Tilson Thomas took over from Herbert

Blomstedt and has already led the orchestra to new heights and crafted an exciting repertoire of classical and modern music. The season runs from September through June. Summer symphony activities include a Composer Festival and a Summer Pops series.

OPERA

In addition to San Francisco's major opera company, you might also check out the amusing **Pocket Opera,** 44 Page St., Suite 404A (☎ 415/575-1100). From mid-January to mid-June, this comic company stages farcical performances in English of well-known operas accompanied by a chamber orchestra. The staging is intimate and informal, without lavish costumes and sets. The cast ranges from 3 to 16 players, and is supported by a similar-size orchestra. The rich repertoire includes such works as *Don Giovanni* and *The Barber of Seville.* Performances are on Saturday or Sunday. Call for complete information and show times. Tickets cost $10 (students) to $25.

San Francisco Opera. Performing at newly refurbished War Memorial Opera House, 301 Van Ness Ave. (at Grove St.). ☎ **415/864-3330** (box office). Tickets $10–$140.

The San Francisco Opera was the United States's first municipal opera, and is one of the city's cultural icons. Brilliantly balanced casts may feature celebrated stars like Frederica Von Stade and Placido Domingo, along with promising newcomers and the regular members, in productions that range from traditional to avant-garde. All productions have English supertitles. The opera season starts in September and lasts just 14 weeks. Performances are held most evenings, except Monday, with matinees on Sundays. Tickets go on sale as early as June, and the best seats sell out quickly. Unless Pavarotti or Domingo is in town, some less-coveted seats are usually available until curtain time.

THEATER

American Conservatory Theater (A.C.T.). Performing at the Geary Theater, 415 Geary St. (at Mason St.). ☎ **415/749-2228.** Tickets $14–$51.

American Conservatory Theater (A.C.T.) made its debut in 1967 and quickly established itself as the city's premier resident theater group. The troupe is so venerated that A.C.T. has been compared to the superb British National Theatre, the Berliner Ensemble, and the Comédie Française. The A.C.T. season runs from October through June and features both classical and experimental works.

A.C.T. recently returned to its home, the fabulous **Geary Theater** (1910), a national historic landmark, after the theater sustained severe damage in the 1989 earthquake and was closed for renovations. Now it's fully refurbished and modernized to such an extent that it is regarded as one of America's finest performance spaces.

Lorraine Hansberry Theatre. Performing at 620 Sutter St. ☎ **415/ 474-8800.**

San Francisco's top African-American theater group performs in a 300-seat theater off the lobby of the Sheehan Hotel, near Mason Street. Special adaptations from literature are performed along with contemporary dramas, classics, and world premieres. Tickets range from $15 to $25. Phone for dates and programs.

The Magic Theatre. Performing at Bldg. D, Fort Mason Center, Marina Blvd. (at Buchanan St.). ☎ **415/441-8822.** Tickets $15–$26. Discounts for students and seniors.

The highly acclaimed Magic Theatre continues to be a major West Coast company dedicated to presenting the works of new playwrights; over the years it has nurtured the talents of such luminaries as Sam Shepard and Jon Robin Baitz. Shepard's Pulitzer prize–winning play *Buried Child* premiered here. More recent productions have included works by Athol Fugard, Claire Chafee, and Nilo Cruz. The season usually runs from September through July; performances are offered Wednesday to Sunday.

DANCE

In addition to the local companies, top traveling troupes like the Joffrey Ballet and the American Ballet Theatre make regular appearances. Primary modern dance spaces include the **Theatre Artaud,** 450 Florida St., at 17th Street (☎ 415/621-7797); the **Cowell Theater,** at Fort Mason Center, Marina Boulevard, at Buchanan Street (☎ 415/441-3400); **Dancer's Group/Footwork,** 3221 22nd St., at Mission Street (☎ 415/824-5044; Web site: http:// www.dancenet.org); and the **New Performance Gallery,** 3153 17th St., at Shotwell in the Mission District (☎ 415/863-9834). Check the local papers for schedules or contact the theater box offices directly.

San Francisco Ballet. Performances at War Memorial Opera House, 301 Van Ness Ave. (at Grove St.). ☎ **415/865-2000.** Tickets and information. Tickets $7–$100.

Founded in 1933, the San Francisco Ballet is the oldest professional ballet company in the United States and is regarded as one of the country's finest, performing an eclectic repertoire of full-length, neoclassical, and contemporary ballets. Even the *New York Times* proclaimed, "The San Francisco Ballet under Helgi Tomasson's leadership is one of the spectacular success stories of the arts in America." The 1998/1999 Repertory Season runs from February through June. All performances are accompanied by the San Francisco Ballet Orchestra.

2   Comedy & Cabaret

Bay Area Theatresports (BATS). Bayfront Theater at the Fort Mason Center, Bldg. B, 3rd floor. ☎ **415/474-8935.** Tickets $5–$15.

Combining improvisation with competition, Bay Area Theatresports (BATS) operates an improvisational tournament, in which four-actor teams compete against each other, taking on improvisational challenges from the audience. Judges then flash scorecards good-naturedly, or honk a horn for scenes that just aren't working. Shows are staged on Monday only. Phone for reservations.

Beach Blanket Babylon. At Club Fugazi, 678 Green St./Beach Blanket Babylon Blvd. (between Powell St. and Columbus Ave.). ☎ **415/421-4222.** Tickets $20–$50.

Now a San Francisco tradition, Beach Blanket Babylon evolved from Steve Silver's Rent-a-Freak service—a group of party-givers extraordinaire who hired themselves out as a "cast of characters" to entertain, complete with fabulous costumes and sets, props, and gags. After their act caught on, it was moved into the Savoy-Tivoli, a North Beach bar. By 1974, the audience had grown too large for the facility, and Beach Blanket has been at the 400-seat Club Fugazi ever since.

The show is a comedic musical send-up that is best known for its outrageous costumes and oversized headdresses. It's been playing almost 22 years now, and still almost every performance sells out. The show is updated often enough that locals still attend. Those under 21 are welcome at Sunday matinees at 3pm when no alcohol is served; photo ID is required for evening performances. It's wise to write for tickets *at least* a month in advance for weekend-performance tickets, or obtain them through Tix (see above). *Note:* When you purchase tickets, they will be within a specific section depending upon price; however, seating is still first-come/first-seated within that section. Performances are given on Wednesday and Thursday at 8pm, on Friday and Saturday at 7 and 10pm, and on Sunday at 3 and 7pm.

Cobb's Comedy Club. 2801 Beach St. (between Leavenworth and Hyde sts.).
☎ **415/928-4320.** Cover $5 Mon–Wed, $10–$13 Fri–Sat, $10 Thurs and Sun
(plus a 2-beverage minimum nightly). Validated parking.

Located in the Cannery at Fisherman's Wharf, Cobb's features such
national headliners as George Wallace, Emo Philips, and Jake
Johannsen. There is comedy every night, including a 15-comedian
All-Pro Monday showcase (a 3-hr. marathon). Cobb's is open to
those 18 and over, and occasionally to kids ages 16 and 17 if they
are accompanied by a parent or legal guardian (call ahead first).
Shows are Monday to Wednesday at 8pm, Thursday and Sunday at
9pm, and Friday and Saturday at 8 and 10pm.

Finocchio's. 506 Broadway (at Kearny St.). ☎ **415/982-9388.** Cover $14.50
(2-drink minimum).

For more than 50 years this family-run cabaret club has showcased
the best female impersonators in a funny, kitschy show. Three different revues are presented nightly (usually Thurs to Sat at 8:30, 10,
and 11:30pm), and a single cover is good for the entire evening.
Parking is available next door at the Flying Dutchman.

Punch Line. 444 Battery St., plaza level (between Washington and Clay sts.).
☎ **415/397-4337** or 415/397-7573 (for recorded information). Cover $5 Sun,
$8–$15 Tues–Sat (plus a 2-drink minimum nightly).

Adjacent to the Embarcadero One office building, this is the largest comedy nightclub in the city. Three-person shows with top
national and local talent are featured Tuesday to Saturday. Showcase
night is Sunday, when 15 to 20 rising stars take the mike. There's
an all-star showcase or a special event on Monday nights. Buy tickets in advance (if you don't want to wait in line) from **BASS**
outlets (☎ **510/762-2277**). Shows are Tuesday to Thursday and
Sunday at 9pm, and on Friday and Saturday at 9 and 11pm.

3 The Club & Music Scene

The greatest legacy from the 1960s is the city's continued tradition
of live entertainment and music, which explains the great variety of
clubs and music scenes available in a city of this size. The hippest
dance places are located South of Market Street (SoMa), in former
warehouses, while most popular cafe culture is still centered in
North Beach.

Note: The club and music scene is always changing, often
outdating recommendations before the ink can dry on a page. Most
of the venues below are promoted as different clubs on various

nights of the week, each with its own look, sound, and style. Discount passes and club announcements are often available at hip clothing stores and other shops along upper Haight Street.

Drink prices at most bars, clubs, and cafes range from about $3.50 to $6, unless otherwise noted.

DIAL-A-SCENE   The local newspapers won't direct you to the city's underground club scene, nor will they advise you which of the dozens of clubs are truly hot. To get dialed in, do what the locals do—turn to the **Be-At Line** (☎ 415/626-4087) for its daily recorded update on the town's most hoppin' hip-hop, acid-jazz, and house clubs. The scene is reported by one of its coolest residents, Mayor Brown's street-suave son, Michael. For the grooviest message and inside scoop on the feel-good, underground party scene, tune in to the **Bug Out Line** (☎ 415/437-6905). **Housewares Rave** (☎ 415/281-0125) highlights the heavy techno scene. The **Spot Line** (☎ 415/346-7768) will tell you where to find their DJ spinning R&B and acid jazz. The far more commercial **Club Line** (☎ 415/979-8686) offers up-to-date schedules for the city's larger dance venues.

ROCK & BLUES CLUBS

In addition to the following listings, see "Dance Clubs," below, for (usually) live, danceable rock.

Blues. 2125 Lombard St. (at Fillmore St.). ☎ **415/771-BLUE.** Cover $3–$6.

This small, dark blues bar is packed most nights with an eclectic ethnic mix of locals. The bands are usually pretty good and easy to dance to. Owner Max Young claims it's "the only real dark, dingy blues club in the city." Gotta love that.

The Fillmore. 1805 Geary Blvd. (at Fillmore St.). ☎ **415/346-6000.** Tickets $9–$25.

Reopened after years of neglect, The Fillmore, made famous by promoter Bill Graham in the 1960s, is once again attracting big names. Check the local listings in magazines, or call the theater for information on upcoming events.

The Saloon. 1232 Grant Ave. (at Vallejo St.). ☎ **415/989-7666.** Cover $4–$5 Fri–Sat.

An authentic gold rush survivor, this North Beach dive is the oldest extant bar in the city. Popular with both bikers and daytime pinstripers, there's live blues nightly.

Slim's. 333 11th St. (at Folsom St.). ☎ **415/522-0333.** Cover free to $20 (plus a 2-drink minimum when seated at table).

Co-owned by musician Boz Scaggs, who sometimes takes the stage under the name "Presidio Slim." This glitzy restaurant/bar seats 300, serves California cuisine, and specializes in excellent American music—homegrown rock, jazz, blues, and alternative music—almost nightly. Menu items range from $3 to $8.50.

JAZZ & LATIN CLUBS

✪ **Cafe du Nord.** 2170 Market St. (at Sanchez St.) ☎ **415/861-5016.** Nominal cover varies.

Although it's been around since 1907, this basement-cum-jazz-supper club has finally been recognized as a respectable jazz venue. With a younger generation now appreciating the music, the place is often packed from the 40-foot mahogany bar to the back room with a pool table. Du Nord is even putting out its own compilation CDs now, which are definitely worth purchasing.

Jazz at Pearl's. 256 Columbus Ave. (at Broadway). ☎ **415/291-8255.** No cover, but there is a 2-drink minimum. Valet parking $3.

This is one of the best venues for jazz in the city. Ribs and chicken are served with the sounds, too, with prices ranging from $4 to $8.95. The live jams last until 2am nightly.

Up & Down Club. 1151 Folsom St. (between Seventh and Eighth sts.). ☎ **415/626-2388.** Cover varies.

One of the original homes for SoMa's now-familiar new-jazz scene, the Up & Down jazz supper club attracts a trendy crowd to both its restaurant and dance floor. Dinner's at 8pm (reservations required), the music starts at 9:30pm, and dancing begins at 10pm.

DANCE CLUBS

While a lot of clubs around town allow dancing, at the followings clubs dancing is the number-one priority—these are the places to go if all you want to do is shake your groove thang.

Club Ten 15. 1015 Folsom St. (at Sixth St.). ☎ **415/431-1200.** Cover $5–$10.

Get decked out and plan for a late-nighter if you're headed to this enormous party warehouse. Three levels and dance floors offer a variety of dancing venues, complete with a 20- and 30-something gyrating mass who live for the DJs' pounding house, disco, and acid-jazz music. Each night is a different club that attracts its own crowd that ranges from yuppie to hip-hop. As this book goes to press, **Nikita** (☎ 415/267-0568) is held on Friday from 10pm to 6am, featuring different sounds: 1970s disco, progressive house, techno, trip-hop, and acid jazz. Saturday is **Release,** a combo of hip-hop and disco, deep house, and acid jazz (☎ 415/281-0823 for schedules). Other nights are hot, too, so call ☎ 415/431-1200 for a complete schedule of events.

Nickie's Bar-be-cue. 460 Haight St. (between Fillmore and Webster sts.). ☎ **415/621-6508.** Cover $3–$5.

Don't show up here for dinner. The only hot thing you'll find here is the small, crowded dance floor. But don't let that stop you from checking it out—Nickie's is a sure thing. Every time we come here, the old-school disco hits are in full-force, casually dressed happy dancers lose all inhibitions, and the crowd is mixed with all types of friendly San Franciscans. This place is perpetually hot, so dress accordingly. And you can always cool down with a pint from the wine-and-beer bar. Keep in mind, lower Haight is on the periphery of some shady housing projects, so don't make your rental car look tempting, and stay alert as you walk through the area.

Paradise Lounge. 1501 Folsom St. (at 11th St.). ☎ **415/861-6906.** Cover $3–$15.

Labyrinthine Paradise features three dance floors simultaneously vibrating to different beats. Smaller, auxiliary spaces include a pool room with a half-dozen tables. Poetry readings are also given.

Sound Factory. 525 Harrison St. (at First St.). ☎ **415/243-9646.** Cover $10 Fri, $15 Sat.

Herb Caen dubbed this disco theme park the "mother of all discos." The maze of rooms and nonstop barrage of house, funk, lounge vibes, and club classics attracts swarms of young urbanites looking to rave it up until sometimes as late as 6am. Management tries to eliminate the riffraff by enforcing a dress code (no sneakers, hooded sweatshirts, or sports caps).

SUPPER CLUBS

If you can eat dinner, listen to live music, and dance (or at least wiggle in your chair) in the same room, it's a supper club—that's our criteria.

Coconut Grove Supper Club. 1415 Van Ness Ave. (between Bush and Pine sts.) ☎ **415/776-1616.** Cover $5 Tues–Thurs, $8 Fri–Sat.

Reopened in 1996 after being shunned for outrageous prices, the new—and far less expensive—Coconut Grove Supper Club is doing a brisk business serving a California/tropical/Cajun menu and live music to a mostly young, hip audience. Dancing and chocolate martinis are the main attraction. The dress code is lax, but vintage is definitely the main attire.

Harry Denton's Starlight Room. Atop the Sir Francis Drake Hotel, 450 Powell St., 21st floor. ☎ **415/395-8595.** Cover $5 Wed–Thurs after 7pm, $10 Fri–Sat after 8pm.

Come dressed to the nines or in casual attire to this old-fashioned cocktail-lounge-cum-nightclub where tourists and locals sip cocktails at sunset and boogie down to live swing and big-band tunes after dark. The room is classic 1930s San Francisco, with red-velvet banquettes, chandeliers, and fabulous views. But what really attracts flocks of all ages is a night of Harry Denton–style fun, which usually includes plenty of drinking and unrestrained dancing. The full bar stocks a decent collection of single-malt scotches and champagnes, and you can snack from the pricey Starlight appetizer menu. Like Harry's SoMa dance club, early evening is more relaxed, but come the weekend, this place gets loose.

Julie's Supper Club. 1123 Folsom St. (at Seventh St.). ☎ **415/861-0707.** No cover.

Julie's is a longtime standby for cocktailing and late dining. Divided into two rooms, the vibe is very 1950s cartoon, with a space-aged "Jetsons" appeal. Good-looking singles prowl, cocktails in hand, as live music plays by the front door. The food is hit-and-miss, but the atmosphere is definitely a casual and playful winner with a little interesting history; this building is one location where the Symbionese Liberation Army held Patty Hearst hostage back in the 1970s. Menu items range from $7.50 to $16. A smaller, more stylish sister of the Supper Club is **Julie Ring's Heart and Soul,** located in the Russian Hill district at 1695 Polk St. at Clay (☎ **415/673-7100**).

RETRO CLUBS

Well, daddyo, I hope you didn't throw out those old duds of yours, because America's halcyon days are back in fashion. So don your fedora and patent leather shoes, cause you don't mean a thing if you can't swing.

Bruno's. 2389 Mission St. (at 20th St.). ☎ **415/550-7455.** Cover $3 to $7 after 9:30pm.

Before its recognition as a destination restaurant, Mission District hipsters were already keen on this retro hot spot. There's live music nightly in the back lounge, and the long, 1950s-style full bar is almost always crowded with a mixture of wanna-bes, the cool, and the curious. Appetizers and desserts are served until 1am.

Club Deluxe. 1511 Haight St. (at Ashbury St.). ☎ **415/552-6949.** Cover $4.

Before the recent 1940s trend hit the city, Deluxe and its fedora-wearing clientele had been celebrating the bygone era for years. Fortunately, even with all the retro-hype, the vibe here hasn't changed. Expect an eclectic mix of throw-backs and generic San Franciscans in the intimate, smoky bar and adjoining lounge, and live jazz or blues most nights. Although many regulars dress the part, there's no attitude here, so come as you like.

Hi-Ball Lounge. 473 Broadway (between Kearny and Montgomery). ☎ **415/397-9464.** Cover $3–$7.

Retro-jazz is in full swing in the city, and one of the most popular places to hear it—and dance to it—is at this North Beach joint. Harking back to Broadway at its best, the vibe is full-on 1940s/1950s, from the red banquettes and stage curtains, to the small, dark, and smoky room. Live bands perform nightly to a young, swingin' crowd. There's also a swing-dance class 1 night a week.

4 The Bar Scene

Albion. 3139 16th St. (between Valencia and Guerrero sts.). ☎ **415/552-8558.**

This Mission District club is a grit-and-leather in-crowd place packed with artistic types and various SoMa hipsters. Live music plays Sunday between 5 and 8pm and ranges from ragtime and blues to jazz and swing.

Backflip. 601 Eddy St. (at Larkin St.). ☎ **415/771-FLIP.**

Adjoining the rock 'n' roll Phoenix Hotel, this shimmering aqua-blue cocktail lounge—designed to induce the illusion that you're carousing in the deep end—serves tapas and Caribbean-style appetizers to a mostly young, fashionable crowd, so please don't order a Cosmopolitan. Since this is a new hot spot in town, the scene continues to change. On Thursday the crowd seems to be young and gay/alternative; weekends, wanna-be-cool yuppies tend to pack the place. Regardless, if you're headed here, you can expect the unexpected, kick back with a martini, and enjoy the city's finest eye candy.

✪ **Bottom of the Hill.** 1233 17th St. (at Missouri St.). ☎ **415/621-4455.** Cover $3–$7.

Voted one of the best places to hear live rock in the city by the *San Francisco Bay Guardian,* this popular neighborhood club attracts an eclectic crowd ranging from rockers to real-estate salespeople. The main attraction is live music every night of the week, but it also offers pretty good burgers and kebabs, outdoor seating on the back patio, and an awesome $4 all-you-can-eat barbecue on Sunday from 4 to 7pm. There's also happy hour Monday to Friday from 4 to 7pm.

Li Po Cocktail Lounge. 916 Grant Ave. (between Washington and Jackson sts.). ☎ **415/982-0072.**

A divey Chinese bar, Li Po is made special by a clutter of dusty Asian furnishings and mementos that include an unbelievably huge rice-paper lantern hanging from the ceiling, and a glittery golden shrine to Buddha behind the bar.

Perry's. 1944 Union St. (at Laguna St.). ☎ **415/922-9022.**

If you read *Tales of the City,* you already know that this bar and restaurant has a colorful history as a pickup place for Pacific Heights and Marina singles. Though the times are not as wild, locals still come to casually check out the happenings at the dark mahogany bar. A separate dining room offers breakfast, lunch, dinner, and brunch at candlelit tables. It's a good place for hamburgers, simple fish dishes, and pasta. Menu items range from $5 to $20.

The Red Room. 825 Sutter St. (at Jones St.). ☎ **415/346-7666.**

At one time the hottest cocktail lounge in town (though it's cooled off a bit), this ultramodern, Big Apple–style bar and lounge reflects no other spectrum but ruby red. Really, you gotta see this one.

Spec's. 12 Saroyan Place (off Columbus Ave.). ☎ **415/421-4112.**

Spec's incognito locale on Saroyan Place, a tiny alley at 250 Columbus Ave., makes it less of a walk-in bar and more of a lively locals' hangout. Its funky decor—maritime flags that hang from the ceiling, exposed brick walls lined with posters, photos, and various oddities—gives it character that intrigues every visitor. A "museum," displayed under glass, contains memorabilia and items brought back by seamen who drop in between sails, and the clientele is funky enough to keep you preoccupied while you drink a beer.

Toronado. 547 Haight St. (at Fillmore St.). ☎ **415/863-2276.**

Lower Haight isn't exactly a charming street, but there's plenty of nightlife there catering to an artistic/grungy/skateboarding 20-something crowd. While Toronado definitely draws in the young 'uns, its 40-plus microbrews on tap and 60 bottled beers also entice a more eclectic clientele who come in search of beer heaven. The brooding atmosphere matches the surroundings: an aluminum bar, a few tall tables, dark lighting, and a back room packed with tables and chairs. A DJ picks up the pace on Friday and Saturday nights.

Vesuvio. 255 Columbus Ave. (at Broadway). ☎ **415/362-3370.**

Situated along Jack Kerouac Alley across from the famed City Lights Bookstore is this renowned literary beatnik hangout that's not just riding its historic coattails. The atmosphere is way cool, as are the people who frequent it. Bring a chess board, borrow a game here, or write in a notebook, but whatever you do, make sure you look brooding and intense. Popular with neighborhood writers, artists, songsters, and wanna-bes, Vesuvio is crowded with self-proclaimed philosophers, and everyone else ranging from longshoremen and cab drivers to businesspeople. The convivial space is two stories of cocktail tables, complemented by a changing exhibition of local art and an ongoing slide show. In addition to drinks, Vesuvio features an espresso machine. No credit cards are accepted.

BREW PUBS

GordonBiersch Brewery. 2 Harrison St. (on the Embarcadero). ☎ **415/243-8246.**

GordonBiersch Brewery is San Francisco's largest brew-restaurant, serving decent food and tasty brew. There are always several beers to choose from, ranging from light to dark. Menu items range from $3.50 to $17.50.

San Francisco Brewing Company. 155 Columbus Ave. (at Pacific St.). ☎ **415/434-3344.** www.sfbrewing.com.

Surprisingly low-key for an ale house, this cozy brew pub serves its brew along with burgers, fries, and the like. The bar is one of the city's few remaining old saloons, aglow with stained-glass windows, tile floors, skylit ceiling beveled glass, a mahogany bar, and a massive overhead fan running the full length of the bar—a bizarre contraption crafted from brass and palm fronds. The handmade copper brew kettle is visible from the street. There's music most evenings. Darts, chess, backgammon, cards, and dice are all available. Menu items range from $3.25 to $16. The happy-hour special, a dollar per 10-ounce microbrew beer (or $1.75 a pint), runs daily from 4 to 6pm and midnight to 1am.

Thirsty Bear Brewing Company. 661 Howard St. (1 block east of the Moscone Center). ☎ **415/974-0905.**

Seven superb, handcrafted varieties of brew, ranging from a fruit-flavored Strawberry Ale to a steak-in-a-cup stout, are always on tap at this stylish high-ceilinged brick edifice. Excellent Spanish food, too (see chapter 5, "Dining"). Pool tables and dart boards are upstairs, and live music (jazz, flamenco, blues, alternative, and classical) can be heard most nights.

20 Tank Brewery. 316 11th St. (at Folsom St.). ☎ **415/255-9455.**

Right in the heart of SoMa's popular strip, this huge, come-as-you-are bar is known for serving good beer at fair prices. Pizzas, sandwiches, chilies, and assorted appetizers are also available. Menu items range from $1.95 to $12.95. Pub games include darts, shuffleboard, and dice.

COCKTAILS WITH A VIEW

The Carnelian Room. 555 California St., in the Bank of America Building (between Kearny and Montgomery sts.). ☎ **415/433-7500.**

Located on the 52nd floor of the Bank of America Building, the Carnelian Room offers uninterrupted views of San Francisco. From a window-front table you feel as if you can reach out, pluck up the TransAmerica Pyramid, and stir your martini with it. In addition to cocktails, "Discovery Dinners" are offered for $35 per person. Jackets and ties are required for men. *Note:* The Carnelian Room has the most extensive wine list in the city—1,275 selections to be exact.

Cityscape. Atop Hilton Tower I, 333 O'Farrell St. (at Mason St.), 46th floor. ☎ **415/923-5002.**

When you sit under the glass roof and sip a drink here, it's as if you're sitting out under the stars and enjoying views of the bay. There's nightly dancing to a DJ's picks from 10pm. The mirrored columns and floor-to-ceiling draperies help create an elegant and romantic ambiance.

Crown Room. In the Fairmont Hotel, 950 Mason St., 24th floor. ☎ **415/772-5131.**

Of all the bars listed here, the Crown Room is definitely the plushest. Reached by an external glass elevator, the panoramic view from the top will encourage you to linger. In addition to drinks (steep at $7 to $9), dinner buffets are served for $34.

Equinox. In the Hyatt Regency Hotel, 5 Embarcadero Center. ☎ **415/788-1234.**

The sales "hook" of the Hyatt's rooftop, Equinox is a revolving floor that gives each table a 360° panoramic view of the city every 45 minutes. In addition to cocktails, dinner is served daily.

Harry Denton's Starlight Room. Atop the Sir Francis Drake Hotel, 450 Powell St., 21st floor. ☎ **415/395-8595.**

See "Supper Clubs," earlier in this chapter, for a full review.

Top of the Mark. In the Mark Hopkins Intercontinental, 1 Nob Hill (California and Mason sts.). ☎ **415/616-6916.**

This is one of the most famous cocktail lounges in the world. During World War II, it was considered de rigueur for Pacific-bound servicemen to toast their good-bye to the States here. The spectacular glass-walled room features an unparalleled view. Live entertainment is offered at 8:30 nightly, but there is a $6 to $10 cover charge these nights, too. There's afternoon tea service from 3 to 5pm Monday to Saturday, and Sunday brunch, which is served from 10am to 2pm, costs $35 without champagne, $45 with. Drinks are also pricey, ranging from $6 to $8.

PIANO BARS

San Francisco is lucky to have several lively piano bars. As in other cities, these specialized lounges are perfectly suited to the grand hotels in which they are usually located.

Nob Hill Terrace. In the Mark Hopkins Intercontinental, 1 Nob Hill (California and Mason sts.). ☎ **415/392-3434.**

Drinks ($5 to $8) are served nightly in a delightfully intimate, skylit room with hand-painted murals. It's located just off the lobby.

The Piazza Lounge. In the Parc Fifty-Five Hotel, 55 Cyril Magnin St. (Market and North Fifth sts.). ☎ **415/392-8000.**

Sink into a handsome velvet chair, gaze out into the three-story atrium, and relax to a mix of old and new melodies played on an ebony grand piano.

The Redwood Room. In the Clift Hotel, 495 Geary St. ☎ **415/775-4700.**

A true art-deco beauty, this ground-floor lounge is one of San Francisco's most comfortable and nostalgic piano bars. Its gorgeous redwood interior was completely built from a single 2,000-year-old tree. It's further enhanced by the large, brilliantly colored Gustav Klimt murals. Drinks go for $6 to $9.

SPORTS BARS

Bayside Sports Bar and Grill. 1787 Union St. (at Octavia St.). ☎ **415/673-1565.**

This is easily one of the largest sports bars in the city, equipped with a state-of-the-art superlarge-screen television, 29 smaller ones, 19 beers on tap, and two pool tables. The crowd is mainly Marina yuppies (lots of baseball caps, sweatshirts, and Lycra shorts), which is made bearable by the fast, friendly food service (mostly burgers, sandwiches, and such) and the myriad of sports channels. Happy hour is Monday to Friday from 4 to 6pm.

Green's Sports Bar. 2239 Polk St. (at Green St.). ☎ 415/775-4287.

If you think San Francisco sports fans aren't as enthusiastic as those on the East Coast, we dare you to try to get a seat (or even get in) at Green's Sports Bar during a 49ers game. Green's is a classic old sports bar, with lots of polished dark woods and windows that open out onto Polk Street, but it's loaded with modern appliances, including a large-screen television, 10 smaller ones, 18 beers on tap, and a pool table. They don't serve food here, but you can bring in grub for the game. A late-night happy hour runs Sunday to Wednesday from 10pm to 2am.

WINE BARS

Eos. 101 Carl St. (at Cole St.). ☎ 415/566-3063.

If you're downtown, London Wine Bar. If you're around the Civic Center, Hayes and Vine. For anything west of these two, your top choice is Eos, a fairly new and highly successful restaurant and wine bar in Cole Valley (near the Haight). Around the corner from the restaurant is this chic, lively wine bar filled mostly with a young Cole Valley clientele who dabble among the 400 vintages from around the world.

Hayes and Vine. 377 Hayes St. (at Gough St.). ☎ 415/626-5301.

Choose among 350 wines from around the world at this unpretentious wine bar staffed by true cognoscenti of fine wine (which is a good thing, since you'll probably have never heard of 90% of these wines). Be sure to ask about taking a "flight," where you can try several different wines for a fixed price. Cheese, breads, and desserts are also served.

London Wine Bar. 415 Sansome St. (between Sacramento and Clay sts.). ☎ 415/788-4811.

This British-style wine bar and store is a popular after-work hangout among Financial District suits. It's more of place to drink and chat than to admire fine wines. Usually two to three dozen wines are open at any given time, mostly from California. It's a great venue for sampling local Napa Valley wines before you buy.

5 Gay & Lesbian Bars & Clubs

As with straight establishments, gay and lesbian bars and clubs target varied clienteles. Whether you're into leather or Lycra, business or bondage, there's gay nightlife here just for you. Listed below are some of the city's more established, mainstream gay hangouts.

✪ **The Café.** 2367 Market St. (at Castro St.). ☎ **415/861-3846.**

When this place first got jumping, it was the only predominantly lesbian dance club on Saturday nights in the city. But once the guys found out how much fun the girls were having, they joined the party. Today it's still a very happening mixed gay and lesbian scene with two bars, a steamy, free-spirited dance floor, and a small patio.

The EndUp. 401 Sixth St. (at Harrison St.). ☎ **415/357-0827.** Cover varies.

It's a different nightclub every night of the week, but regardless of who's throwing the party, the place is always jumping with the DJ's blasting tunes. There are two pool tables, a flaming fireplace, outdoor patio, and a mob of gyrating souls on the dance floor. Some nights are straight, so call for gay nights.

Metro. 3600 16th St. (at Market St.). ☎ **415/703-9750.** No cover.

With modern art on the walls and much use of terra-cotta, the Metro provides the gay community with high-energy dance music and the best view of the Castro District from its large balcony. The bar seems to attract people of all ages who enjoy the friendly bartenders and the highly charged, cruising atmosphere. There's also a Chinese restaurant on the premises if you get hungry.

The Stud. 399 Ninth St. (at Harrison St.). ☎ **415/863-6623.** Cover $2–$6 weekends.

The Stud has been around for 30 years, is one of the most successful gay establishments in town, and is mellow enough for straights as well as gays. The interior has an antique-shop look and a miniature train circling over the bar and dance floor. Music here is a balanced mix of old and new, and nights vary from cabaret and oldies to disco. Call in advance for the evening's venue. Drink prices range from $1.25 to $5.75.

Twin Peaks Tavern. 401 Castro St. (at 17th and Market sts.). ☎ **415/864-9470.** No cover.

Right at the intersection of Castro, 17th, and Market streets is one of the Castro's most famous gay hangouts, which caters to an older crowd and is considered the first gay bar in America. Because of its relatively small size and desirable location, the place becomes fairly crowded and convivial by 8pm, earlier than many neighboring bars.

6   Film

The **San Francisco International Film Festival,** held in March of each year, is one of America's oldest film festivals. Tickets are relatively inexpensive. Entries include new films by beginning and established directors. For a schedule or information, call ☎ **415/ 931-FILM.** Tickets can be charged by phone through **BASS Ticketmaster** (☎ **510/762-2277**).

Even if you're not here in time for the festival, don't despair. The classic, independent, and mainstream cinemas in San Francisco are every bit as good as the city's other cultural offerings.

REPERTORY CINEMAS

Castro Theatre. 429 Castro St. (near Market St.). ☎ **415/621-6120.**

Built in 1922, the beautiful Castro Theatre is known for its screenings of classic cinema and for its Wurlitzer organ, which is played before each show. There's a different feature here almost nightly, and more often than not it's a double feature. Bargain matinees are usually offered on Wednesday, Saturday, Sunday, and holidays. Phone for schedules, prices, and show times.

Red Vic. 1727 Haight St. (between Cole and Shrader sts.). ☎ **415/668-3994.**

The worker-owned Red Vic movie collective recently moved from the Victorian building that gave it its name. The theater specializes in independent releases and contemporary cultish hits. Prices are $6 for adults, $3 for seniors and kids 12 and under. Phone for schedules and show times.

Roxie. 3117 16th St. (at Valencia St.). ☎ **415/863-1087.**

The Roxie consistently screens the best new alternative films anywhere. The low-budget contemporary features shown here are largely devoid of Hollywood candy coating; many are West Coast premieres. Films change weekly, sometimes sooner. Phone for schedules, prices, and show times.

Index

See also separate Accommodations and Restaurant indexes, below.
Page numbers in italic refer to maps.